Sustainable Resource Management

SUSTAINABLE RESOURCE MANAGEMENT

K.K. Singh
Alka Tomar
Vinod Phogat
Suman Phogat

Prints Publications Pvt Ltd
New Delhi

Published by

Prints Publications Pvt Ltd
Viraj Tower-2, 4259/3, Ansari Road,
Darya Ganj, New Delhi-110002
Tel. : +91-11-45355555
Fax: +91-11-23275542
E-mail : contact@printspublications.com
Website : www.printspublications.com

First Edition : 2022 (Hardbound)

ISBN: 978-93-936745-7-9

Price: ₹ 1495/-

Published and Printed by Mr. Pranav Gupta (Managing Director) on behalf of Prints Publications Pvt Ltd, New Delhi.

CONTENTS

FOREWORD

With the technological revolution there was rapid industrialization without restriction and only economic development was supposed to be the parameters of human prosperity, peace and happiness. Unfortunately, some of the very development activities have caused colossal destruction to the global human ecosystem. Air and water pollution, soil degradation, extinction of wildlife species, global warming, depletion of forest wealth, exhaustion of mineral oil/ores and many other forms of environmental degradation have raised doubts about the wisdom of the pattern of development which is being pursued now-a-days. In addition to these, newer problems like encroachment of anthropogenic activities on the limited land available, appearance of non-degradable synthetics, accumulation of toxic wastes, leaching from landfills and mines pose challenges for rational managements of natural resources. Thus, escalating rate of erosion of natural resources is of great concern because the idea of sustainable development and conservation has been bypassed in major developmental planning and implementation.

Of all natural resources, water is most severely threatened by pollution. According to several estimates, 60% of the discharged pollutants (sewage, industrial wastes, fertilizers, pesticides and landfills and mines leachates) reenter the water supplies. Contaminated water kills around 2.2 million people every year. Approximately 40% of world population now faces chronic shortage of fresh water for daily needs. Hence, water pollution control measures are on high priority in many countries and among numerous pollution control agencies. Land degradation is also a principal constraint in meeting the food demands of rising population. Since 1990, two-thirds of the world's farmlands suffer from soil degradation. Over-exploitation of natural resources has further aggravated the situation. At the threshold of the 21st century, a grim scenario is looming large with burgeoning population starved of natural resources and chocked by pollution. To combat the deleterious effects of intensive farming and rapid industrialization, particularly with regards to adverse environmental effects, requires the development and implementation of technologies and policies that will result in sustainable management of natural resources.

The Paris NGO Conference advocated a different way of development, one where ecological and social concerns for all humanity and future generations have given priority. Besides, the question of consumption patterns is becoming a subject of research and public interest in environment and the widespread belief that current rates of resource exploitation are unsustainable. Thus, the challenge of environment versus development is very clear. The choice is upon man, either to turn the direction of development into more sensible and traditional channels or to continue reckless exploitation of the earth's resources and leave a legacy of dissolution and death for our children and the generations to come.

The problems of pollution and reckless degradation of natural resources cannot be solved without proper understanding of their causes and effects. Simultaneously, it is necessary to build up professional capabilities to develop and frame policies, measures and programmes for environmental management. Unless concerted efforts are made to save the biosphere from catastrophic collapse, tomorrow will be too late. Thus, abatement of pollution and conservation of ecosystem is therefore imperative for attaining the goal of sustainable development. In the light of the above facts, the title of the book **'Sustainable Resource**

Management' is very pertinent. The book provides holistic overview of the topical environmental issues the human being has been facing today.

I appreciate the efforts made by Dr. K.K.Singh, Mrs. Alka Tomar, Dr. V.Phogat and Dr. Suman Phogat for compiling and editing the chapters of this book meticulously. Lastly, I would like to congratulate the authors, editors and publisher for bringing out this book.

Dr. Komal Singh, IAS
Divisional Commissioner
Gwalior (MP)

PREFACE

Air, water, soil and forests constitute the natural resources of a country. For centuries man has exploited these resources of the planet Earth recklessly and destroyed them what nature took millions of years to achieve. It is a grim and dark harvest of poisoned air, polluted water and soil, suffering children and vanishing beauties of lakes, forests and rivers, along with all the varied species of flora and fauna. Stupendous increases in population, industrialization, rapid urbanization and intensive farming have caused tremendous damage resulting in environmental imbalances and degradation on a global scale. The changes in the environment have endangered the very survival of humankind on this planet Earth.

Preservation of the environment is therefore, essential for the very existence of the human beings. Thus, sustainable management of natural resources has emerged as an issue of major international concern. In India too, environmental protection and the conservation of natural resources has been a national priority in the wake of 1972 Stockholm Conference on Human and Environment. The world commission on Environment and Development in its report published in 1987 have stressed the importance of ensuring that today's economic progress is not at the cost of tomorrow's development prospects. The growing interest in the concept of sustainability was given added stimulus at the United Nations Conference on Environment and Development (UNCED), held in Rio de Janeiro in June, 1992. Agenda 21, a major action plan developed at UNCED, focused attention on the need to make development more economically and environmentally sustainable and socially acceptable. It is, therefore, essential to make the masses aware of the changes in the quality of our environment and strategies to prevent the situation from worsening further. Proper monitoring would also help in focusing on the seriousness of the problem of environmental pollution and generate real concern among policy makers.

The contents of this reference book aims to provide a general framework to ensure sustainable management of natural resources for the well being of society through proper strategies of environmental protection, conservation and management.

Chapter 1 explains various fundamental aspects of conservation of biodiversity. Chapter 2 deals with resource conservation through land treatment of municipal waste water. Chapter 3 is devoted to bioremediation to restore the health of aquaculture pond ecosystem. Chapter 4 describes probiotics in food. Chapter 5 gives a detail account of microbial phytase in combating phosphorous pollution. Chapter 6 is focused on phytoplankton and zooplankton distributions in a stressed environment. Chapter 7 deals with mitigation of water pollution through flora and fauna. In chapter 8, water pollution and its management is discussed. Chapter 9 deals with role of microorganisms in relation to management of water pollution. Chapter 10 deals with control techniques for organic vapour emissions.

The present book is the outcome of the contributions of the various renowned scientists/academicians. We are indebted to a number of institutes and universities of India and abroad who helped us immensely by their respective contributions. It is hoped that this book will be of immense value to students, teachers, researchers of various disciplines, policy makers and planners having concern for the conservation and sustainable management of natural resources. Last but not the least, we are very grateful to Mr. Pranav Gupta, Managing Director of Prints Publications Pvt Ltd, New Delhi, for his kind cooperation and support for this book.

Editors

LIST OF CONTRIBUTORS

A. Kumar, Scientist, Air Pollution Control Division, NEERI, Nehru Marg, Nagpur-440020.

A.G. Devi Prasad, Post Graduate Dept. of Environmental Sciences, University of Mysore, Manasagangothri, Mysore-570006, Karnataka

A.S. Juwarkar, Environmental Biotechnology Division, NEERI, Nehru Marg, Nagpur-440020

A. Venkateswara Rao, Manager, Technical Services, Aquaculture Products Division, Neospark Drugs and Chemicals Pvt. Ltd., 241 B.L.Bagh, Panjagutta, Hyderabad-500082 (AP)

Aleya Lotfi, Laboratoire de Biologie Environnementale, Universite de Franche-Comte, 1 Place Leclere, 25030 Besancon Cedex (France)

Alka Tomar, Dy.Director & Head, Centre for Media Studies, Saket, New Delhi.

Anjana Chowdhary, Research Scholar, Dept. of Botany, Govt. Dungar College, Bikaner (Raj.)

Asha A. Juwarkar, Environmental Biotechnology Division, National Environmental Engineering Research Institute (NEERI), Nehru Marg, Nagpur-440020

Ashok K. Choudhary, Research Scholar, Dept. of Soil Science, S.K.N. College, Jobner (Raj.)

Bijender Singh, Dept. of Microbiology, University of Delhi, South Campus, New Delhi-110021

G. Kalaichelvan, Fermentation Lab, Tamil Nadu Agricultural University, Coimbatore-641003, (TN)

Gayatri Verma, Principal, S.M. Degree College, Palidogra, Sonkh, Mathura, (U.P.)

K.K. Singh, Research Officer, Project Directorate (Res.), Agriculture and Soil Survey, Krishi Bhawan, Bikaner (Raj.).

K.R. Arun Kumar, Fermentation Lab, Tamil Nadu Agricultural University, Coimbatore-641003, (TN)

K. Ramaswamy, Fermentation Lab, Tamil Nadu Agricultural University, Coimbatore-641003, (TN)

Khattabi Hichan, Laboratoire de Biologie Environnementale, Universite de Franche-Comte, 1 Place Leclere, 25030 Besancon Cedex (France)

Kirti V. Dubey, Environmental Biotechnology Division, NEERI, Nehru Marg, Nagpur-440020

Krishna G. Bhattacharya, Dept. of Chemistry, Gauhati University, Guwahati-781014, Assam.

Mahadevi Singh, Teacher, Sophia Sr. Secondary School, Bikaner (Raj.)-334002.

Mudry Jacques, Laboratoire de Geosciences, Universite de Franche-Comte, 16, route de Gray, 25030, Besancon Cedex (France)

N.R. Rajendra Prasad, Post Graduate Dept. of Environmental Sciences, University of Mysore, Manasagangothri, Mysore-570006, Karnataka

N. Ramalingam, Fermentation Lab, Tamil Nadu Agricultural University, Coimbatore-641003, (TN)

P.R. Thawale, Environmental Biotechnology Division, National Environmental Engineering Research Institute (NEERI), Nehru Marg, Nagpur-440020

Padma S. Rao, Environmental Biotechnology Division, National Environmental Engineering Research Institute (NEERI), Nehru Marg, Nagpur-440020

Parvinder Kaur, Dept. of Microbiology, University of Delhi, South Campus, New Delhi-110021

Ramesh Chandra Parida, Prof., Dept. of Chemistry, College of Basic Science and Humanities, Orissa University of Agriculture and Technology, Bhubaneswar-751003 (Orissa)

S.K. Singh, Environmental Biotechnology Division, National Environmental Engineering Research Institute (NEERI), Nehru Marg, Nagpur-440020

S. Karthikeyan, Fermentation Lab, Tamil Nadu Agricultural University, Coimbatore-641003, (TN)

Suman Phogat, Lecturer, C.R. College of Education, Hisar (Har.)

Sushmita Sen Gupta, Dept. of Chemistry, Gauhati University, Guwahati-781014, Assam.

T. Satyanarayana, Dept. of Microbiology, University of Delhi, South Campus, New Delhi-110021

U. Sivakumar, Fermentation Lab, Tamil Nadu Agricultural University, Coimbatore-641003, (TN)

V. Phogat, Department of Soil Science, CCS Haryana Agricultural University, Hisar (Haryana)

V.S. Saxena, Ex-Additional Secretary, Environment, Rajasthan, A-2, Van Vihar, Tonk Road, Jaipur-302018 (Raj.)

Vinod Singh, Lecturer, Department of Geography, Govt. Dungar College, Bikaner (Raj.)

CHAPTER 1

CONSERVATION OF BIODIVERSITY : AN OVERVIEW

Anjana Chowdhary[1], Vinod Singh[2] and Alka Tomar[3]

[1]Department of Botany, Government Dungar College, Bikaner, Rajasthan-334002

[2]Department of Geography, Government Dungar College, Bikaner, Rajasthan-334002

[3]CMS Environment, Research House, Saket, New Delhi-110017

ABSTRACT

This chapter deals with biodiversity and its loss due to various anthropogenic factors like deforestation, pollution, faulty agricultural practices and habitat alteration. Impact and significance of biodiversity in human life has been underscored. Various methods of biodiversity conservation as well as role of common citizen, women and indigenous people in this regard have been discussed in detail.

Key Words : Biodiversity, Conservation

Introduction

Biodiversity was defined by IUCN and UNEP in 1992 as the variability among living organisms from all sources including, *inter alia*, terrestrial, marine and other aquatic systems and the ecological complex of which they are part. This includes the biodiversity within the species (genetic), among the species and at the ecosystem level. India, because of its tropical geographical location and diverse topography, has rich and varied fauna and flora. It is estimated that more than 45,000 plant species and 81,000 animal species are found in India. It is one of the 12 mega biodiversity countries of the world. Areas of mega diversity are such habitats where maximum biodiversity occurs. Zhukovsky counted twelve such mega diversity areas in 1968 which included China, Indo China – Indonesia, Australia – New Zealand, Indian sub-continent, Central Asia, Western Asia, Mediterranean coast, Africa, Europe – Siberia, Central America, Bolivia – Peru – Chile and North America. Norman Myers, first of all, gave the concept of *hot spot* in 1988, which is a habitat exceptionally rich in species, especially those local, rare species which are not found elsewhere in the world. Mittermeier *et al.,* (2000) reported 25 hot spots in a revised list which cover about 2% area of the world. Included in these are 15 tropical forests, five Mediterranean type and five main or completely islands. Of these, nine were designated as *leading* and eight as the *hottest* hot spots (Fig.1). These *hot spots* were demarcated in order to determine preference for *In-situ* conservation. Following criteria were used to determine *hot spots* :- (i) Predominantly endemic species which are not found anywhere else, and (ii) A high degree of threat of habitat destruction. About 60-70% of the global

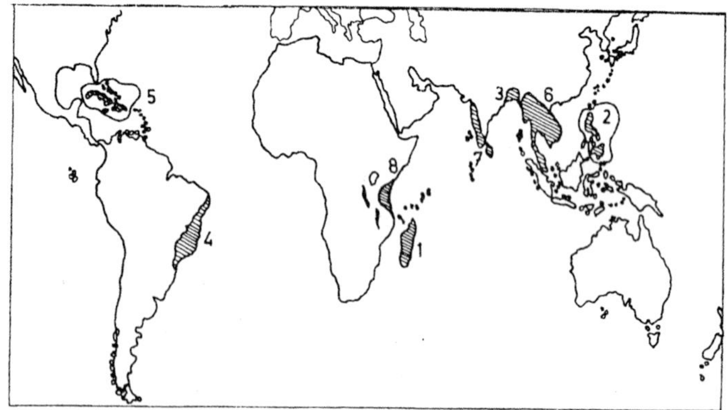

Fig. 1 : Hottest spots of biodiversity (after Myers)

biodiversity is found in such mega diversity and *hot spot* countries (Tyagi *et al.*, 2005).

1. Madagascar
2. Philippines
3. Sunderland (Sundarban, India)
4. Brazil Atlantic Forests
5. Caribbean
6. Indo-Burma
7. Western Ghats-Sri Lanka
8. Coastal Forests of Tanzania-Kenya

A wide range of physiographic and climatic conditions in India have resulted in a diversity of ecological habitats like forests, grasslands, wetlands, coastal and marine ecosystem and desert ecosystem, which harbour and sustain immense biodiversity. With hardly 2 percent forest area of the world and over 17 per cent of world's livestock population, India holds more than 60 percent of tiger population, above 60 percent of the Asiatic Element population and more than 70 percent of the India Rhino population of the world (Oberai, *2000*). Biodiversity in India is threatened because of deforestation, shifting cultivation, industrialization and unplanned management and, therefore, there is a need to conserve biodiversity.

Biodiversity and its Impact on Human Life

Every human civilization on earth has been rooted in the biodiversity of nature. The domestication of wild crops made the first farming possible. Genetic resources taken from the wild still sustain modern societies, providing food, fodder, medicines and industrial raw material.

Biodiversity - the vast array of species of plants, animals and micro-organisms created by nature is the 'foundation of human life' on earth. They have provided the basic necessities of our social, cultural, economic and biological life. Human life on earth would be simply impossible if there were no micro-organisms, no wild plant, animal and insect species. How much do we realize about those thousands of wild worms, insects, birds and bats that work day and night in the soil in the farmlands and in the forest to provide food and fodder to us. Human life depends upon their survival which is linked in a complex chain of food web. If the chain becomes 'weak' (by extinction of species) at any point it will be translated all along the chain. If the chain continues to become weaker at several points as it is becoming today due to large scale extinction of species, the chain of life on earth would finally break and disintegrate.

Ironically human life on earth depends only upon few narrow spectrum of those species of plant life which provide our entire food, fodder, fuel, fertilizer, furniture (timber) and medicinal needs. We have not yet explored those millions of species which nature have created. A number of them are getting extinct even before we come to know about them. Modern human society have retained only few varieties of high yielding (HYVs) crops which one grown in modern agriculture.

The future of mankind is dependent upon just three species of crops - wheat, rice and maize which provide half of the world's food supply. Such overwhelming dependence on few crops with narrow genetic diversity can be dangerous for the civilization. There is probably no more serious environmental threat to mankind than the continued decay of the genetic variability of crop plants. The loss of tropical forest causes the extinction of increasing number of species and reduction in the genetic diversity of others. Preserving the 'gene pools' found in tropical forest is vitally important. Future of our agriculture vitally depends upon the gene pool of the wild relatives of modern crop plants which are found in the tropical forests. With only 8 crops supplying 85 per cent of the world's food, new types of crops could be essential for human survival on earth.

All other environmental threats to the human civilization can be overcome through technology but for the loss of biodiversity. Species once lost from the face of the earth can not be brought back. Extinction is forever. Biodiversity erosion is affecting not only our ecological system but also social and economic systems. The destruction of biodiversity undermines the basic operation of the ecosystem. The loss of ecosystem function provided freely by the natural forests and vegetation entails real and social costs.

With major changes in the earth's climate already on the way due to 'green-house effect' and 'global warming' accompanied by depletion of stratospheric ozone layer, preserving the earth's biodiversity of plants particularly crop plants holds the key to human survival. The justification lies in the need for maintaining genetic variability for plant breeding. The maximum genetic diversity is going to provide the raw material with which the human society would adapt to change.

Biodiversity in wild and domesticated forms is the source of most of human needs - food, fuel, fodder, fertilizer, fiber, timber and medicine; clothing and housing; much of the cultural diversity and most of the intellectual and spiritual inspirations. Many species have been fundamental to stabilization of climate, protection of watersheds, protection of soil and to the protection of nurseries and breeding grounds. Undoubtedly, it is the very basis of human existence on earth. One can not imagine the situation in which the fungus *Penicillium* or the *Cinchona* tree were to become exitinct before mankind discovered 'pencillin' and 'quinine' respectively from them. Both drugs saved millions of lives during world war II and after (Mayers, *1986).*

Loss of Biodiversity

The Nature Conservancy and the National Heritage Network, USA concluded that almost one-third (31.9%) species are vulnerable, imperiled or already extinct. Mussels, crayfish, fishes and amphibians-all species dependent on fresh water habitats are most at risk. Flowering plants are also of great concern, with 1/3 of their numbers in trouble worldwide, the loss of biodiversity is even more disturbing. At least 484 animals species and 654 plants species have become extinct since 1600. The "Global Biodiversity Assessment", commissioned by UNEP to provide information for the Convention on Biological Diversity estimates that some 5,400 known species of animals and 26,000 plant species are in danger of becoming extinct.

Biodiversity is the richest in the tropics - a richness that is almost unimaginable. Biologist E. Q. Wilson identified 43 species of ants on a single tree in a Peruvian rain forest, a level of diversity equal to the entire ant fauna of the British Isles. Other scientists found 300 species of trees in a single 2.5 acre (1 ha) plot and as many as 10,000 species of insects on a single tree in Peru. Assuring the existence of 2 million species in the tropical forests (a conservative estimate) and a clearance rate of 1.8% per year for those forests, Wilson calculated that tropical deforestation is responsible for the loss of 4,000 species a year.

Thus, loss of biodiversity is another major environmental crisis. The growing population and mismanagement of forest habitats, especially flora and fauna cause gradual loss and destruction of forest ecosystem. India is the 12th plant-rich country in the world, rich in diversity and biological resources of the world's 2,50,000 plant species, India has 45,000 species and 4,900 flowering plants. A report has indicated that of India's total 2,00,000 living species, many forest and plant species are fast disappearing as their survival resources are destroyed (Bedi and Pattnaik, 1999).

(a) Deforestation and Biodiversity

The phenomenon of deforestation may be explained in terms of loss of forests, i.e., loss of plant growth which may be due to a number of causes which bring about an imbalance in the ecosystem as a whole. Globally, forests are vanishing at a rate of about 17 million ha per year and in India, the satellite imagery reveals that the country is losing on an average 1.3 to 1.5 million ha of forests per year. It is a well known fact that forests form the primary nutritional base of a country and that they are global genetic store-houses and controllers of the hydrological cycle. They check the climatic deterioration as well . Deforestation globally symbolizes the situation of over exploitation of natural resources. Unfortunately the old Thai saying - 'Experience is a comb which nature gives to man after he is bald' holds true in this case of earth fast becoming bald (devoid of forests).

The causes of deforestation include cutting of trees to obtain timber, fuelwood, fodder and grazing, extraction of resin, construction of roads and human-settlements, snowfall and avalanches, acquiring land for cultivation, and climatic changes due to pollutions etc. The effects of deforestation may be observed as loss of biodiversity, adverse effects on natural phenomenon like rainfall, atmospheric quality, floods, land slides, earth quakes and other natural disasters, soil erosion, desertification and scarcity of timber, fuelwood, fodder, forest products like resin, various foods, drugs, oils, waxes and fibre etc. and raw materials for industries. Another effect of deforestation can be seen in loss of tribal people and their culture globally (Singh and Aggarwal, 1998).

The loss of biodiversity has resulted in extinction of many plant and animal species all over the world. The Botanical Survey of India (1980) and the Zoological Survey of India (1981) estimated 45000 plant species and 75000 animals species in our country out of which 79 species of mammals, 44 of birds, 15 of reptiles, 3 of amphibians and nearly 1500 plant species were found to be on the verge of extinction.

(b) Threat to Aquatic Biodiversity

Three types of human threats to aquatic biodiversity are *(i)* resource misuse, *(ii)* pollution and *(iii)* exotic species. Resource misuse ranges from building dams to live stock grazing.

Some impacts of damming and diverting waters include loss of stream habitat, blockage of fish runs, and loss of downstream nutrients. Long-term effects are, however, not known. Dams destroy riverine habitat and obstruct movement of aquatic organisms (Table 1), severely affecting biodiversity both directly and immediately, and also more subtly due to long-term secondary, tertiary or cumulative effects.

Table 1 : Impacts of dams and diversions on biodiversity

Dam Activity	Primary Effect	Secondary and Tertiary Effect
Flooding of backwaters	Destruction of riverine and riparian habitat; creation of barrier for movement along and across riverine and riparian corridor.	Loss of species, loss of riverine and riparian connectivity; depressed species population, extirpation, extinction.

Contd.

River obstruction	Interception of downstream flow of nutrients and silt	Decreased nutrient supply to downstream habitats; biotic impoverishment of downstream communities
Regulation of water flow	Decrease in peak flows (flood control; hydroelectric dams)	Decrease in natural disturbance cycles and in flushing flows; degradation of downstream habitat; biotic impoverishment of downstream communities
	Irregular flow (hydroelectric power)	Abnormal fluctuation in downstream habitat; depressed populations; extirpation; extinction.
	Decrease in winter flows (irrigation)	Decrease in available habitat in winter; depressed populations; extirpation extinction.
	Warming of water.	Degradation of downstream aquatic habitat; depressed populations; extirpation; extinction.
Water diversion	Decrease in downstream water flows.	Decrease in available habitat downstream; depressed population; extirpation; extinction.
	Diversion of water to farmlands	Loss of wildlands to agriculture; decreased available habitat; depressed populations.
	Water to river with increased salinity.	Increased salinization of degraded habitat; depressed populations

Source : Noss and Cooperrider (1994).

Diversion of water creates some problems in the system from which it is diverted, and also causes damage in its new path in course of time. Diversion of water for irrigation can lead to salinization and water logging of soils. Because most existing farmlands have already been converted from their natural vegetation, their value for conserving biodiversity today is quite low. As their fertility can be destroyed by water logging and salinization, the demand for fresh fertile lands will put additional pressure on remaining natural areas. Also, salinity problem are most confined to farmlands. Salinity problems can be party relieved by flushing the accumulated salts out of the soils (Noss and Cooperrider, 1994).

(c) Pollution

Another major factor causing loss of biodiversity is pollution, which can directly kill many kinds of plants and animals, seriously reducing their populations. For example, pollutants from the Mississippi River have created a 7,700 square-mile "dead zone" in the Gulf of Mexico where oxygen completely disappears from depth below 20 meters every summer. Shrimp, fish, crabs and other commercially valuable sea life are either killed or forced to migrate away from the huge area along the Mississippi and Louisiana coastline. Every oil spill kills sea birds and, often, sea mammals. In January 2000, a massive cyanide spill into the Tisza River (a tributary of the Danube) from a Romanian gold mine wiped out life in the river for 250 miles downriver and immediately put 15,000 fishermen out of work. Recent declines in populations of frogs, turtles, alligators and fish have been tentatively traced to the widespread presence of chemicals known as endocrine disrupters - commonly used chlorine compounds and plastics, as well as some pesticides. Because of their molecular structure, these compounds may mimic the effects of some hormones and thus disrupt the normal course of embryological development or sexual activity of animals.

Pollution destroys or alters habitats, with consequences just as severe as those caused by deliberate conversions. Acid deposition and air pollution cause forests to die; sediments and nutrients kill species in lakes, rivers and bays; DDT devastates wild-bird populations; and the depletion of the ozone layer increases the impact of ultraviolet light on wild species. The list is endless. Some scientists project that global warming from the green house effect may be the greatest catastrophe to hit natural biota in 65 million years (The fossil record reveals that a massive extinction of plants and animals occurred at that time, probably caused by a major asteroid hitting Earth). Scientists speculate that the rate of climatic warming will far outpace the ability of most species of plants to migrate morthward, thus trapping them in inhospitable climates. Every species that dies out will doubtlessly take others with it. If forest trees are unable to migrate, neither can the rest of the wildlife that depend on them for food and habitat.

Most of the global pollution problems can be traced to the industrialized world, where energy-generating and other technologies continue to pour pollutants into the air and water at increasing rates. For this reason, it is important not to point the finger of blame, primarily at the developing world, where population growth is such a problem. Global climate change and pollution from toxic substances are the legacy of the already developed nations (Wright and Nebel, 2004).

(d) Faulty Agricultural Practices

Various farming operations improperly carried out lead to adverse effects such as loss of top soil through water and wind erosion. Soil erosion by water in the form of rill and sheet erosion is a serious problem in the red and lateritic soils of south and eastern India where about 40 tonnes ha^{-1} of top soil is lost annually. Out of 70 million ha of black soils of central India, 6.7 million ha are already unproductive due to the development of gullies, ravines and torrents. Shifting cultivation practiced largely in the North-Eastern India has caused serious land degradation over 4.4 million ha of land. It has led to extinction of some unique flora and fauna of the region.

On the other hand, salinization and alkalinization of soil takes place due to improper management of irrigation water. An area of 6 million ha of land is affected by water logging and another 7 million ha is salinised due to faulty irregation practices. Water logging due to inadequate drainage, depletion of ground water due to excessive extraction, pollution of surface and ground water with pesticides and fertilizer residues, loss of biological diversity and erosion of germplasm resources through removal of natural fauna and flora are the adverse effects of faulty farming practices.

(e) Physical Alterations of Habitats

Although multiple causes are usually the rule of losses of biodiversity, one of the greatest sources of loss is the physical alteration of habitats through the processes of conversion, fragmentation and simplification. Habitat destruction has already been responsible for 36% of known extinctions.

Conversion

Natural areas are converted to farms, housing subdivisions, shopping malls, marinas and industrial centers. When, for example, a forest is cleared, it is not just the trees that are destroyed, every other plant and animal that occupies the destroyed ecosystem, either permanently or temporarily (e.g. migrating birds), also suffers. The idea that this wild life simply will move "next door" and continue to live in an undisturbed section is erroneous. Any loss of natural habitat can result in only one thing : a proportional reduction in all populations that require that habitat. Thus the decline in songbird populations cited earlier has been traced to a combination of the loss of winter forest habitat in Central and South America and the increasing fragmentation of summer forest habitat in North America.

Fragmentation

Natural landscapes generally have large patches of habitat that are well connected to other, similar patches. Human-dominated landscapes, however, consist of a mosaic of different land uses, resulting in small, often geometrically configured patches that frequently contrast highly with neighboring patches. For the continued survival of any natural population, the number of individuals must never fall below a critical number, and that requires a certain minimum area. This minimum area must be large enough to compensate for years of adverse weather. That is, more area will be required during a dry year then during a normal year. If development reduces the habitat to a point where it cannot support the critical number during an adverse year, the entire population will perish. Similarly, development (such as a highway) that fragments a territory and prevents migration between the two fragments will cause a population to perish if neither area can adequately support the critical number. Also, reducing the size of a habitat creates a greater proportion of edges, a situation that favours some species, but may be detrimental to others. For example, the Kirtland's warbler is an endangered species that is highly dependent on large patches of second-growth jack pines. The species is endangered because its habitat has been greatlyy fragmented, creating edges that favour the brown-headed cowbird, a nest parasite that can invade the forest and lay its eggs in the nest of the rare warbler.

Simplification

Human use of habitats often simplifies them. We might, for example, remove fallen logs and dead trees from woodlands for firewood, thus diminishing an important microhabitat on which several species depend. When a forest is managed for the production of a few or one species of tree, tree diversity of a cluster of plant and animal species gets dependent on the less favoured trees. Streams are sometimes "Channelized" - their beds are cleared of fallen trees and rifles and sometimes the stream is straightened out by dredging. Such alterations inevitably bring on a loss of diversity of fish and invertebrates that live in the stream.

(f) Population Factor

Past losses in biodiversity can be attributed to the expansion of the human population over the globe. Continuing human population growth will bring on continued alteration of natural ecosystems and the inevitable loss of more wild species. The losses will be greatest where biodiversity is greatest and human population growth is highest - in the developing world. Africa and Asia have lost almost two-thirds of their original natural habitat. People's desire for a better way of life, the desperate poverty of rural populations and the global market for timber and other natural resources are powerful forces that will continue to draw dawn biological wealth on these continents.

In East Africa, where human population growth has been explosive for several decades, the conversion of Savanna and woodlands to cultivation or intensive grazing by goats and cattle has driven most of the African elephant population into the existing wild life reserves, causing a great reduction in their numbers. The other large African mammals have experienced similar reduction, as the needs of the rural populations inevitably conflict with those of the large wild animals of East Africa. Similar losses in large mammals populations (wolves, bison, elk, bear, cougar etc.) occurred as North America was gradually transformed into a great agricultural and industrial continent.

One key to holding down the loss in biodiverstiy lies in bringing human population growth down. If the human population increases to 10 billion, as some demographers believe that it will, the consequences for the natural world are frightening.

(g) Over Use

It should be obvious that killing whales, fish, or trees faster than they can reproduce will lead to the ultimate extinction of the species. In spite of that, over use is another major assault against wild species, responsible for 23% of recent extinctions. Over use is driven by a combination of economic greed, ignorance and desperation. The plight of birds in Europe is a good example. It is said, with some justification, that a line can be drawn across the continent north of which people watch birds and south of which they eat them. Some 700,000 "protected" birds are shot in Greece each year, Malta accounts for about 3 million a year and Italy holds a shameful record of an astronomical 50 million birds killed and eaten each year ! Most of these are small song birds.

Another prominent form of over use is the trafficking in wild life and products derived from wild species. Much of this "trade" is illegal world wide, it is estimated to be at least $ 10 billion a year. It flourishes because some consumers are willing to pay exorbitant prices for such things as furniture made from tropical hard woods like teak, exotic pets, furs from wild animals, traditional medicines from animal parts, and innumerable other "luxuries", including polar-bear rugs, baskets made from elephant and rhinoceros feet, ivory handled knives and reptile skin shoes and handbags. For example some Indonesian and South American parrots sell for upto $ 10,000 in the United States, a panda-skin rug can bring in $ 25,000, and the gallbladder of the North American black bear, which is valued as folk medicine in Korea, can fetch as much as $ 2,000. Such prices create a powerful economic incentive to exploit the species involved.

The long-term prospect of extinction does not curtail the activities of exploiters because the prospect of a huge immediate profit out weighs it. Even when the species is protected, the economic incentive is such that poaching and black-market trade continue. Tiger and rhinoceros populations in the world have declined drastically in the last two decades (a 90% decline for rhinos) and are on the brink of extinction. Driving this decline is the widespread, but unfounded, belief in far Eastern countries that parts from these animals have medicinal or aphrodisiac properties. The World Wide Fund reported that some 66 Sumatran tigers were killed recently, representing 20% of the Sumatran tiger population.

Conservation of Biodiversity

Conservation is a long term process which ensures availability of a resource in future. The conservation of natural and biological diversity in plants is both a matter of insurance and investment, necessary to sustain and improve production of agricultural and related enterprises to keep open future options, as a buffer against hazardous environmental changes, as the new material for much scientific and industrial innovation, and a matter of morals.

There are three basic objectives of conservation of biological diversity (Priyanka, 2000) :

1. To maintain essential ecological process and life support system.
2. Preservation of genetic diversity, and
3. To ensure that any utilization of species ecosystem is sustainable.

(a) Protection of Water Resources

It is impossible to achieve sustainable development unless the world's water resources are carefully preserved. In this context, the following features are note worthy : (i) Less than 1 part in 100,000 of the earth's water is available for human use. (ii) Polluted water affects the health of some 1.2 billion people and contributes to the death of some 1.5 million children under 5 years every year. (iii) The availability and quality of fresh water are closely linked to environmental changes, especially urbanization and deforestation.

Freshwater resources are likely to be further depleted by the rapid growth of population, especially in developing countries. Any plan for sustainable development should ensure that current decisions on water resources do not jeopardize the interests of future generations. This implies not only preserving the present resources of fresh water, but also careful planning to avoid future stress. Two methods are used to evaluate development alternatives. They are based on matrices or simulation models. Matrix mathods are designed to consider all possible interactions and impacts and then decide on their relative importance in terms of specified criteria (WMO, 1993). Simulation models are also used to assess the impact of a specified plan for water management. Certain conflicts of interest also arise in hydrology between sustainability and development. The following facts are relevant in this context :

(i) About 80% of the world's arable lands is rainfed. Its productivity can be increased by better retention of soil moisture and the use of drought resistant varieties of crops. Fish production in individual catchments is also useful.

(ii) The potential for irrigation should be fully utilized by avoiding misuse of land.

(iii) Water resources for irrigation come mainly from surface water resources, water reservoirs and tube-wells. These sources should not be degraded by salinization. Wastage of irrigation water should be minimized. In many areas, more water than is necessary is used for growing a crop. In rainfed agriculture, steps should be taken to prevant water-logging and excessive salinity by proper drainage.

(b) Conservation of Biodiversity in IGNP Area

The *Indira Gandhi Canal Project* in the Thar desert of India is a unique human endeavour to transform the vast arid tracts lying unproductive into a land of plenty and prosperity. As we are aware, when we consider biodiversity, we should consider it from three levels, *i.e.* ecosystem diversity, species diversity and genetic diversity. The rainfall pattern is completely skewed over this tract-less rains (average 100 mm/yr) in western part of Jaisalmer district whereas relatively more rains (average 250 mm/yr) in Hanumangarh district. Numbers of rainy days are also few in the west and it increases as one moves to eastern part. With the varying aridity indices the area can at least be categorized as hyper - arid and arid. Topographically also two kinds of landforms are common-undulating dunes and interdunal plains, except low hills and rocky plateau of Malani series of hills in Jaisalmer districts. Aeolian depositions result into formation of dunes and its dynamics. Thorny tree species like *Acacia senegal* (Kumtha) or *Prosopis cineraria* (Khejri) are found as climax vegetation in dunal areas/habitats. However, tree densities in hyper arid areas are comparatively less in arid ecosystem. Sewan grass *(Lassirus sindicus)* is a perennial grass found in low rainfall areas and blooms luxuriously in rainy season. Nutritional status and palatability of this grass species is very high and relished by local cattle (Singh and Kapoor, 2001).

In these two ecosystems, vegetations found are categorized as Tropical Thorn Forests. On grass land ecosystem, due to overgrazing unpalatable and less nutritive species like *Throsia purpurea, Crotolaria burhia and Aristida funiculate* flourish on such sites. Large amount of top feed from plants like *Zizyphus nummularia, Prosopis cineraria and Calligonum polygonoides, Capparis decidua and Salvadora oleoides* are exploited for domesticated animals. Pastoral birds like Painted Partridge, Grey Partridge, Sand grouse, Imperial Sand grouse, Common quail, Great Indian Bustard, Babbler, Dove, Bulbul and Parakeet are common to grass lands. Since in summers grasses dry up, these birds turn carnivorous partly. Different gerbils and rats from rodent communities are major consumers of ground herbage. Among large animals of grass lands common are Blue bull, black buck, chinkara, hare and their usual predators like desert fox, jackal etc. Locusts and grasshoppers are common arthropods. Sanela is a common reptile in tough soils. In dunal habitats, shrubby vegetation like Phog, Bui, Sinia, Jharberi and runners like tumba are found as good soil binders. Khejri, Kakera, Pharas etc. are tree species common on dunes. On rocky out crops *Euphorbia* (Thor), Kumtha Kakera are seen with bushes of Aonl *(Cassia auriculata)*. In saline pockets species like Kair, Ber, Lana *(Haloxylon selecornium)*, Sajji *(Suaeda spp.)* are found. Black buck, chinkara etc., relish leaves of these halophytes using them as natural salt licks.

Today, some scientists feel that $1/5^{th}$ of all plant species on land face extinction in the ensuing 20 years. According to the Indian Sub-Continent Plant Specialist Group and IUCN, more than 1500 species in the Indian sub-continent are on the verge of extinction. Some of these species also exhibit a certain degree of endemism and specific to the areas. As in wildness, some domestic breeds of cow, goat, sheep and camel are endemic to this area like Rathi and Tharparkar breeds of cows. Similarly in agri-ecosystem there were hardy varieties of coarse crop, pulses and cereals which used to grow with very little of water and comparatively drought resistant species.

With advent of irrigated agriculture, the erosion of biodiversity has started and existing ecosystems with their constituents are under threats. Since plain areas have come under irrigated command, grasslands are mainly affected. Intensive irrigated managements are replacing extensive dryland farming techniques. With this traditional ploughing with bullocks or camels are being carried out with tractor driven disc-plough. As a result, deep rooted shrubs are damaged, which earlier used to be very good soil binders. Old standing trees of Khejdi are being indiscriminately felled due to mechanised farming. Similarly, xerophytic vegetations of this region are gradually in the process of being wiped out with availability of more moisture in soils. Age-old grasslands are being sacrificed for cultivation. Similarly, due to rising water table soil moisture has increased in areas in proximity to canal command lands. It is, therefore, rightly apprehended that the Sewan grass that is endemic to this area will be totally eliminated because this unique grass, which can thrive in a very low rainfall of 100 mm, can not tolerate more soil moisture or water logging conditions. With the disappearance of Sewan pastures, all pastoral animals and birds will be affected. However, in agri-ecosystem number of new crop species are introduced due to economic reasons, but most of these species are alien to arid ecology. Similarly, due to initiation of an ambitious afforestation programme in IGNP area, lot of new tree species of exotic nature have comeup. Since large water bodies have been created over the terrain, hydrophytes are now seen. Avifauna of this region has increased manifolds. Large number of resident and migratory water birds are found in wetland ecosystems. Aquatic animals in the categories of fishes, amphibians and reptiles are visible now. Due to availability of food, water and shelter, populations of mammalion animals also show an increasing trend. Black buck, Chinkara, Blue Bull, wild bear, desert fox, desert cat, jackal, porcupine, hare have increased in number. In the areas which have come under inundation, animals like gerbils, rats, mice and sanda are threatened and pushed back to elevated plains (Mishra and Singh, 2002).

In order to protect and preserve these biological wealth not only for the use of present generation as well as for the posterity, both short and long term strategies are to be adopted as follows (Anonymous, 2002) :

Ex-situ and In-situ Conservation

Setting up National Parks, sanctuaries and closed areas may help carry out *In-situ* conservation. At present, an area of 3162 km^2 of Jaisalmer and Barmer districts is notified as Desert National Park by the State Government under the provision of sanctuary. There are a number of scattered areas in IGNP area, where the communities protect all kinds of their flora and fauna out of socio-religious sentiments. These are locally called as *Orans*, meaning sacred groves. These orans are repository of biodiversity. Hence these orans need to be inventoried and protected. There are 16 number of Ghaggar depressions in stage-I area of IGNP and few depressions for channellising the excess water in both stage-I & II. These are almost permanent water bodies. These water bodies attract large number of migratory birds and are of great tourist attraction. Hence, by giving them the status of closed areas, they can be commercially exploited for eco-tourism purposes. On the other hand, large stretches of grass lands need to be restored and should be kept free from allotment for cultivation purposes.

For *Ex-situ* conservation, biological parks or Gene Pool gardens are to be established for captive breeding of all kinds of endemic flora and fauna. Due to present ecological change, mutational changes are bound to come in all kinds of flora and fauna, particularly of endemic species. Therefore, research backup should be ensured for identifying strains and carry out clonal propagation/breeding of target species to preserve the present genetic traits in them.

Education and Awareness Drive

An intensive awareness drive is to be launched for farmers, general public, government departments, army and other armed force personnel, BSF and other paramilitary forces about importance of biodiversity conservation and their linkages with the spirit of sustainable development. Farmers should be told about judicious water management and planting of tree saplings on their farmlands. In educational institutions, students should be given education in nature conservation and relevant rules and regulations to protect biodiversity. Adequate publicity should be made and messages should be displayed at strategic points to remind people about significance of nature conservation. Popular mass communication media like folklores or folksongs should be extensively used to educate the common mass.

Community Participation

Biodiversity conservation cannot be achieved without active participation of the local commuinities. Water users committees, Forest Protection Committees etc. are ideal forums through which biodiversity can be preserved. Communities should be informed about the serious consequences of the loss of biodiversity and made to realize it as a community resource.

Enactment of Stringent Laws and Rules

Government should enact laws and rules preventing the people from overuse of water. Grassland and hard-pan areas should be preserved by issuing notification. Land use of *Orans* should not be changed under any circumstances. Cutting and removing of *Phog* for firewood purposes from all kinds of Public and Community lands should be prohibited. Relevant rules need to be framed under the provision of Environmental Protection Act, Forest Conservation Act, Wildlife Protection Act as well as proposed Biodiversity Protection Act convering IPR etc. to preserve biodiversity of this region. No further construction of canal systems and other infrastructural activities in IGNP should be taken up without a thorough study of Environment Impact Assessment.

(c) Wild Life Conservation in Protected Areas

About 5 percent of the world's land surface is now covered by nature reserves and protected for biodiversity conservation on earth. Over the last 100 years forest reserves have been created to protect wild lives. Yellowstone Park in USA was first to be created in 1872 as a National Park for biodiversity conservation. The Manu Biosphere Reserve in the South-eastern region of Peru and at the farthest tip of the Amazon river is a place of pristine beauty existing much as it did 10,000 years ago. It is the last refuge of some rare and endangered plants and animals such as playful "giant otters", and tiny, one-pound "squirrel monkeys". Manu is home to about 200 species of mammals, over 1000 species of birds and 1200 species of butterflies. In earlier days, the primitive human societies protected forest patches called 'Sacred Groves' which sheltered rich biological diversity. They are still found in several parts of the world.

In the modern times, protection became more scientific. With the formation of the world conservation union (IUCN) emphasis started to be laid on protection of endangered species threatened with extinction and those that are 'endemic' *i.e.* confined to particular regions of earth. Brazil put its highest priority in protecting 30 areas to cover endemic species of birds, plants and lizards. IUCN classified world protected area into 8 categories - from large undisturbed reserves, usually close to the public, to areas that provide sustainable production of timber, game and other natural resources for human use. By the beginning of 1992, there were 8000 of them covering 8.5 million km^2 on earth. They range in size from small coral islands of 1,200 hectares to the vast Greenland National Park covering 70 million hectare. The 4th World Congress on National Parks and protected areas held in Venezuela in 1992 called to double the world's protected areas. Some 100 particularly valuable areas are internationally recognized by UNESCO as **World Heritage Sites.**

Some key world heritage sites for biodiversity conservation are

1. Wood Buffalo National Park, Canada.
2. Redwood National Park, USA.

3. Yellowstone National Park, USA.
4. Grand Canyon National Park, USA.
5. Manu National Park, Peru.
6. Iguacu National Park, Brazil.
7. Iguazu National Park, Argentina.
8. Sinharaja Forest Reserve, Sri Lanka.
9. Thungyal - Jual Kha Khaeng Wild life Sanctuaries, Thailand.
10. Ujong Kulon National Park, Indonesia.
11. Komodo National Park, Indonesia.
12. Great Barrier Reef, Australia.
13. Tasmanian Wilderness, Australia.
14. Mount Taishan, China.
15. Mount Athos, Greece .
16. Niokolo-Koba National Park, Senegal.
17. St. Kilda Island, UK.
18. Mount Cook National Park, New Zealand.
19. Nanda Devi National Park, India.
20. Keoladeo National Park, India.
21. Manas Wild Life Sanctuary, India.
22. Kaziranga National Park, India.
23. Sunderbans National Park, India.
24. Chitwan National Park, Nepal.
25. Kathmandu Valley, Nepal.
26. Sagarmatha National Park, Nepal.

(d) Biodiversity Conservation by Indigenous People of World

The documentation of local people's knowledge of the biodiversity began thousands of years ago as Greek, Egyptian, Chinese, Indian and native American scholars recorded folk ways of classifying and using plants and animals. Indigenous communities have generally preserved their tradition, art, culture and agriculture.

The rainforest Indians, such as the Kuna of Panama and the Kenyah of Central Kalimantan in Indonesia have managed their forest ecosystems in pristine state since centuries.

The Kenyah Indians of Indonesia have lived in dense tropical forests for centuries by making clearing on secondary forest of 8 to 20 years old vegetation. The original primary forest is never cut down. Once its garden soil begins to wear out, the Kenyah leave the land fallow for about 20 years and move on to another secondary forest while the primary forests rich in biological diversity are left intact.

The Manu Biosphere Reserve in the Amazon protect four indigenous cultures including the Michiguenga who have proctected their ancient customs in peaceful coexistence with rain forest, the Michiguenga possess a remarkable understanding of their environment, using the abundant plant biodiversity as food, fodder, fuel, fertilizer and medicines without disturbing the local ecosystem and the nature's delicate balance.

The seafaring people of South Sulawesi, an indigenous community of Indonesia called Buginese, Makassarese and Mandarses have helped in the conservation of "Mango Germplasm" and the diversity found in them (Wirawan, 1994). The indigenous communities living around the Amazonian Jau National Park in Brazil have preserved rare species of turtles. The Tuareg pastoralist indigenous community of Gourma in Northern Mali of the Sahel belt in West Africa consume wild cereals like *Cenchrus biflorus*. This grass grows in sandy soils and dunes in arid and semi-arid zones of West Africa for more than 3500 years.

Among the Lua community of northern Thailand, about 120 types of crops are grown; the fallow swiddens continue to be productive for grazing and collecting, with over 300 species utilized. The Hanunoo of the Philippines may plant 15-species of crops at one time or another in the same Swidden. Among the Tsenbaga Mareng of Papua New Guinea, each field contains some 15 to 20 major crops, plus dozens of minor crops spread seemingly at random through the field.

Under traditional systems of shifting cultivation in South-East Asia wild life flourishes very well with elephants, wild cattle, deer and wild pigs all feeding in the abandoned field; tigers, leopards and other predators are, in turn, attracted by the herbivores. The older fields contain a high proportion of fruit trees which are attractive to primates, squirrels and hornbills and variety of other animals (McNeely, 1994).

The invaluable role of indigenous people in the conservation of the plant genetic resources is now beginning to be recognized. However, the economic benefits from the utilization of the materials seldom accrue to them . Those who have conserved biodiversity tend to remain poor, while those who have converted such genetic resources into commercial products through biological technology are rich (Swaminathan, 1994).

Chemical investigations of 300 wild medicinal plants preserved by indigenous people shows unknown compounds with promising biological activity. In 1990's the National Cancer Institute (*NCI*) of US recognized that the leaf extract '*Michellamine B*' from the plant *Ancistrocladus korupensis* obtained from indigenous people of Cameroon forest in South Affrica had the capacity to inhibit *HIV AIDS* virus. Before a contract was renegotiated with the Cameroon Government, the NCI had already taken out a "patent" on the isolated compound *Michellamine B*. The Cameroon case provides a window into the problems faced by the indigenous people of the poor tropical countries. Another plant called *Homolanthus Nutans* from the Samoa island in South Pacific has been serenade by the NCI for anti - AIDS drugs. The plant which was used by the local indigenous people as a tonic and for the treatment of yellow fever has yielded a compound named "Prostatin" which prevents HIV-I virus replication. These discoveries also give evidence of link between biodiversity conservation and local indigenous knowledge of the ethnic people.

There is a delicate interrelationship between the biological diversity and the cultural diversity of the inhabitants. Disruption of forest ecosystem is resulting in degeneration of this culture and loss of knowledge.

The present information and development age, which has tended to disrupt the continuity in the traditional life style of the indigenous people, must also be covered under "Intellectuals Property Right". While the knowledge itself may not be patentable, the products of that knowledge, namely "folk varieties", "land races" and genetic diversity at the "intra-specific" level provide the basic raw material for modern plant breeding and biotechnology programme.

Women and Biodiversity Conservation

Conservation is a theme which highlights the state of harmony between land and human beings. The rural women actively participate in protecting health of the soil through organic recycling and promote crop security through the maintenance of varietal diversity and genetic resistance with their intimate knowledge about various species and their growth characteristics. They are particularly keen to maintain biological diversity, as they are the ones who use these genetic resources to develop new varieties according to changing needs. The home gardens of women are perfect models of sustainable land use as they provide sustained yields and yet cause minimal environmental degradation (Saha and Banerjee, 2001).

People's Participation in Biodiversity Conservation

A recent survey suggests that there are more than three million people living inside India's protected areas. It is only an alliance between local communities, government agencies and concerned NGOs and individuals that can save natural habitats and wildlife from the clutches of destructive forces. This realisation has been voiced in a series of meetings and actions in the mid-nineties. In December 1993, conservation groups like Bombay Natural History Society and Sanctuary Asia, environmental/social action groups like Lokayan and Kalpavriksh, mass movements like the Narmada Bachao Andolan and Bharat Jan Andolan and Tribal rights groups like Kashtakari Sanghatana and Ekjoot Sanghatana got together an appeal against the denotification of protected areas. This was organised by the Indian People's Tribunal on Environment and Human Rights (IPT), which later initiated an independent investigation into the people-wildlife crisis in Rajaji National Park (Uttaranchal), culminating in a report by Justice P.S. Poti which argued for a balance between wildlife and people's interests.

In early 1995, several groups jointly organised a *Jungle Jivan Bachao Yatra* (Safe Forest Life Journey) through 15 national parks and sanctuaries, initiating a dialogue between forest officials and local communities. Workshops and consultations at individual protected areas (Bhimashankar, Rajaji, Ranthambhore) or at state level (Rajasthan, Gujarat, Maharashtra) have carried the process further. In October 1995, several conservation groups initiated the *Bagh Bachao Andolan* (Save the Tiger Movement), whose memorandum to the Prime Minister stressed the need to involve representatives of local traditional communities in the planning and management of wildlife programmes, to ensure their customary rights and access to essential livelihood resources which are in consonence with the conservation objectives of the area, and to guarantee employment and other benefits to them.

Benefits of Biodiversity

(a) Germplasm of Wild Species

Crops need to be given new protection every 5 to 10 years because pests and disease causing organisms change their races and physiological specialisations for food requirements. The only effective way to counter it is to inter-breed them with new strains, often wild ones with resistant germplasm. There are several instances where the wild relatives have contributed in the improvement of their cultivated varieties. Rice, Maize, Potato and Sugarcane are prime examples. The wild plant and animal species became the foundation for agriculture and animal husbandry which began 50000 to 10000 years ago. Humanity has since recognised and utilized wildlives through conscious and unconscious selection procedure to develop and spread domesticated plants and animals to its use. Wild relatives of our crop plants and cattle are still needed and are indispensible to maintain their productivity.

(b) New and Alternative Foods from the Wild

The future of human food security is even more dependent on biodiversity and genetic resources. Ancient civilization depended upon a variety of food products with great nutritive value, but with the loss of biological diversity the range of food available for mankind on earth has narrowed down. Just three crop species-wheat, rice and maize provide half the world's food; another four - potato, barley, sweet potato and cassava, bring the total to three quarters. Such overwhelming dependence on few crops could prove dangerous for the civilization. Disease can wipe out these handful of crops, as it happened in the case of Irish potato famine in the 1940's, causing a fifth of the country's people to die.

Some 5000 plant species have been used as food by the civilization across the world and another 75000 unknown species are expected to be edible. They need to be domesticated. A grass called 'job's tears' from tropical forest is an extremely nutritious cereal so far not known to the civilization. Tribals of North-East India grow *Amaranthus polygamous, Fagopyrum exulentum* and 'Buck Wheats', which are 'pseudo-cereals' rich in protein particularly amino acid 'lysine'. Amaranth is all set to make a re-entry into the food chain of human ecosystem as a major food crop of world after 1519. It produces huge quantities of seeds with high lysine content. Other new and promising sources of food for the civilization which can be domesticated from the wild are 'buffalo gourd' (*Cucurbita foetidissima*), 'winged beans' (*Psaphocarpus tetragonolobus*), 'tree tomato', 'yeheb nut', 'pumello' and the 'cope gooseberry' from plant diversity and 'green iguana', 'kouprey', 'pigmy hog' and 'tilapia fish' from the animal diversity. The seeds of *Cicer songaricum* a wild plant from Ladakh Himalaya has high 'protein' and 'phospholipid' contents. It also has about 1 percent 'lecithin'. Paraguayan plant produces 'calorie-free' substance, 300 times sweeter than sugar. A coffee entirely free from 'caffeine' has been discovered on the Comoros Islands near Madagascar. They can enter into our modern food system.

(c) Industrial Raw Materials

We utilize materials from the wild species everytime we apply a 'shampoo' or 'sunscreen lotion', everytime we 'paint' a wall or 'varnish' a table, every time we employ goods containing 'tin plate' or 'glycerine', or every time we get to the doctor to take 'vaccine' or to the dentist to make a 'mould' of our teeth. Wild plant derived industrial materials include fats, oils, waxes, latexes, pectins, resins, gums and other exudates, vegetable dyes and tannins, lignin, cellulose, starch, hydrocarbons and host of biochemical compounds. Palm oil is used in a hundred products from lipstic to tinplate, ice-cream to jet engines.

Raw Materials for Explosive Industries

Candelilla wax' which has great potential in explosive industries has been isolated from *Euphorbia antisyphilitica,* a wild desert plant of Mexican origin.

Raw Materials for the Drug and Phamaceutical Industries

'Diogenin', an important raw material for production of 'Steroid Hormones' and 'oral contraceptives' has been isolated from *Dioscorea deltoidea* and the roots of desert plant *Balanites aegyptiaea*. Nearly 95 percent of all steroids are now being obtained from Mexican yam (Dioscorea) which is the main source of world production of sex hormones (androgens, estrogens and progesterone), oral contraceptives, cortisones and other anti-inflammatory drugs. 'Scoparone' now under clinical trial as a 'hypotensive' and 'tranquillising agent', has been isolated from the inflorescence of *Artemisia scoparia.*

Isohexenylnaphthazarins are considered new class of drugs and some of them possess 'anti-cancer activity'. Five 'isohexenylnaphthazarins' have been isolated from the roots of *Arnebia hispidissima*. 'Withanolide-D' and Withaferin-A two chemical compounds extracted from the leaves of *Withania somnifera* have been found to have significant anti-tumour activity *in-vivo* against Sarcoma-180 cells of mice They also inhibit RNA synthesis in them. The root powder of *Withania somnifera* have been found to be 'anabolic'. It accelerates the growth in children and retards the process of ageing in older people.

Raw Materials for Perfumeries

The essential oil extracted from the leaves and inflorescence of *Cymbopogon martinii* var motia has been found to have great perfumery properties. Jojoba (*Simmondsia chinensis*) oil is in high demand in perfumery industries. Its oil is comparable with 'sperm whale oil'.

Raw Materials for petroleum Industries

Some species of xerophytic plants Euphorbia caducifolia, Jatropha curcus and Calotropis procera are very promising source of rich 'hydrocarbons' (C-15 Compounds) and are classed as 'petro-crops'. The oil obtained from the latex of Jatropha curcus are very close to diesel oil in chemistry.

(d) Life Saving Medicines from Biodiversity

Earth's genetic bank also serves medicine for thousands of years, the indigenous people of the island of Madagascar used an obscure plant, the Rosy periwinkle, in their folk medicine. If this plant, which grows only on Madagascar, had become extinct before 1960, hardly anyone outside Madagascar would have cared. In the 1960s, however, scientists extracted two chemicals called Vincristine and Vinblastine, with medicinal properties from the plant. These chemicals have revolutionized the treatment of childhood leukemia and Hodgkin's disease. Before their discovery leukemia was almost always fatal in children, today, with vincristine treatment, there is a 95% chance of remission. These two drugs now represent a $ 100 million a year industry.

The story of the Rosy periwinkle is just one of hundreds. The venom from a Brazilian pit viper (a poisonous snake) led to the development of the drug capoten, used to control high blood pressure. Paclitaxsel (trade name Taxal), an extract from the bark of the Pacific yew, has proved to be valuable for treating overian, breast and small-cell cancers. To date, some 3000 plants have been identified as having anticancer properties.

According to the WHO, 80% of the world's people depend on non-western medicine that in turn depends on natural products. It is a fact that 25% of pharmaceuticals in the United States contain ingredients originally derived from native plants, representing $ 8 billion of annual revenue for drug companies and better health and longevity for countless people. Table 2 shows a number of well established drugs that were discovered as a result of analysing the chemical properties of plants used by traditional healers (Wright and Nebel, 2004).

Table 2 : Modern drugs from traditional medicines

Drug	Medical Use	Source	Common Name
Aspirin	Reduces pain and inflammation	*Filipendula ulmaria*	Queen of the meadow
Codeine	Eases pain; suppresses coughing	*Papaver somniferum*	Opium, poppy
Ipecac	Induces vomiting	*Psychatria ipecacuanha*	Ipecac
Pilocarpine	Reduces pressure in the eye	*Pilocarpus jaborandi*	Jaborandi plant

Contd.

Pseudoephedrine	Reduces nasal congestion	*Ephedra sinica*	Ma-huang shrub
Quinine	Combats malaria	*Cinchona pubescens*	Cinchona tree
Reserpine	Lowers blood pressue	*Rauwalfia serpentina*	Rauwolfia
Scopolamine	Eases motion , sickness	*Datura stramonium*	Jinsonweed
Theophylline	Opens bronchial passages	*Camellias sinensis*	Tea
Tubocurarine	Relaxes muscles during surgery	*Chondrodendron tomentosum*	Curare vine
Vinblastine	Combats Hodgkin's Disease	*Catharanthus roseus*	Rosy periwinkle

Source : Wright and Nebel (2004)

Worldwide, medicines from the wild products worth some $ 40 billion a year are being utilized by mankind. WHO has listed over 21,000 plants species which have medicinal use around the world. Wild species have provided many of our medicines in the traditional medical practices like Ayurveda, Siddha and Unani. In modern medicine too, around 119 pure chemical substances extracted from about 90 species of plants are used in medicine. The product derived from wild species may be an analgesic, an antibiotic, a diuretic, a laxative, a tranquilizer or a cough postule. A host of microbial antiviral, cardioactive and neurophysiologic substances have been derived from the marine wildlife.

Folgloves (*Digitalis purpurea*) have saved the lives of millions of heart patients by giving 'digoxin' to the modern medicine. The alkaloid from the Australian 'Moreton Bay Chestnut', the turner *Ancistrocladus korupensis* from Korup in Cameroon, Africa yielding the chemical 'Michellamine-B' and the plant *Homolanthus mutans* from the Samoa Island in

South Pacific yielding the chemical 'prostratin' shows greater promise in combating the HIV AIDS virus, the biggest human killer of 20th century (UNEP Report, 1992). *Rauvolfia serpentina* which gave antihypertensive drug 'reserpine', *Gymnema sylvestere* which gave hypoglycaemic drug 'gymnemic acid', *Bacopa monniera* and *Evolvulus alsinoides* which gave mental tonic to increase memory power and relieve from mental anguish, stress and strain; *Phyllanthes nururi* for treatment of viral hepatitis; and *Commiphora wightii*, the gum resins of which have the property to lower serum cholesterol and triglycerides are proving to be boon for modern man.

The importance of alkaloids 'codeine' and 'morphine' obtained from *Papavar bracteatum* and *P. somniferum* respectively; 'ephedrene' from *Ephedra gerardiana* and 'quinine' from *Cinchona officinalis* in human life is already known to the civilization. 'Quinghasu' is a most promising 'anti-malarial' herbal drug discovered in China in 1971. Ginseng (*Panax ginseng*) is emerging as another 'wonder drug'. It is now being actively investigated all over the world for its effects on tumours, corneal opacity and for increasing resistance to infection.

(e) *Biodiversity : The key to Sustainable Agriculture*

Sustainable agriculture is defined as a balanced management system of renewable sources including soil, wildlife, forests, crops fish, livestock, plant genetic resources and ecosystems without degradation and to provide food, livelihood of current and future generations maintaining or improving productivity and ecosystem services of these resources. Sustainable agriculture system has to be economically viable both in the short and long term perspectives. Natural resources not only provide food, fibre fuel and fodder but also perform ecosystem service such as detoxification of noxious chemicals within soils, purification of waters, favourable weather and regulation of hydrological process within watershed. Sustainable agriculture has to prevent land degradation and soil erosion. It has to replenish nutrients and control weeds, pests and diseases through biological and cultural methods.

Sustainable agriculture is also known as *ecofarming* or *organic farming* or *natural farming* or *permaculture*. It is known as ecofarming as ecological balance is given importance. It is also called organic farming as organic matter is the main source for nutrient management. But some scientists consider that it is a misconception to think that sustainable agriculture is farming without chemical inputs. It is considered by some as integrated, low input and highly productive farming system.

The stability of sustainable agriculture depends upon biodiversity. Throughout the world the traditional agro-forestry system which are based on biodiversity contain well over hundred annual and perennial plant species per field which yield diverse plant products from food, fodder to fuel, fertilizer, timber and herbal drugs. Biodiversity renews the soil fertility without the use of chemical fertilizers and controls agricultural pests without the use of pesticides. The intercropping of diverse plant species in a polyculture farming system helps provide habitats for the natural enemies - the benevolent insects and predators for biological control, as well as alternative diversionary host plants for the pests.

The environmentally benign agricultural inputs for sustainable agiculture *i.e.* the herbal 'biopesticides' and 'biofertilizers' are also products of biodiversity. Other indirect benefits of biodiversity to man are : *(i)* Absorption of 'greenhouse' gas carbon dioxide (CO_2) through photosynthesis and regulation of climate *(ii)* Decomposition of 'wastes & pollutants' by diverse micro organisms-bacteria & fungi and cleaning of environment *(iii)* Pollination of flowers of fruits & vegetable plants by insects, bats, birds and butterflies in the absence of which there will be no fruiting. (A million dollar 'durian' fruit industry in Malaysia collapsed in the 1970's when the single species of bat polinating the durian fruit trees migrated from the area due to their habitat destruction). *(iv)* Operation of bio-geochemical cycles in the biosphere *(v)* soil formation, protection and prevention of erosion.

(f) Biodiversity Maintains Environmental Quality

Biodiversity - the variety of plants, animals and the micro-organisms interacting with the surroundings and among one another - is not only the 'bio-indicator' of a healthy and sustainable human environment but also helps in the maintenance of a conducive environment essential for human survival.

National Botanical Research Institute (NBRI) of India has identified several such plants which act as 'natural pollutant sink' intercepting and absorbing various air pollutants and dusts from the atmosphere. There are several aquatic weeds like *Eichhornia, Lemna, Salvinia & Azolla* which accumulates and removes 'heavy metals' and other toxic chemicals like nitrates, phosphorus etc. from waste-water and help in its purification. The water hyacinths (*Eichhorina crassipes*) have also been reported to adsorb radioactive wastes from waste water. The seeds of *Moringa oleifera* and *M. stenopetala* work as 'natural coagunlant' to clean the muddy water.

The diverse species of micro-organisms (both bacteria and fungi) in the soil and air work as the 'decomposer' and 'scavenger' in the natural ecosystem, biodegrading all the wastes including personal excreta created by man and animals and also decomposing their bodies after their death and decay to recycle back the minerals for the continued operations of the ecosystem. In their absence the earth surface would have been stocked with human and animal carcasses and vegetable debris unfit for life to exist. There are number of micro-organisms coming to light which have the capacity to biodegrade even the toxic chemicals and the hazardous wastes in the environment. In Germany, genetically tailored bacteria have been used to clean up polluted soils and oil spills in water. Bacteria eat pollutants, gobble them up, and chemically alter them in their bodies. When pollutants are finished the bacteria die leaving clean soil and a biomass of dead bacteria containing harmless minerals. There are bacteria which can also ingest 'cyanide' from water. It is hoped that in future scientists would be able to genetically tailor such micro-organisms which would also biodegrade the otherwise non-biodegradable plastics.

The earthworms species are emerging as one of the best environmental managers by biodegrading wastes and detoxyfying polluted soils. Earthworms have also been found to ingest several pesticides from soil.

Several species of reptiles and predator birds maintain the environmental quality and a balance in the ecosystem by eating the harmful pests and insects. The role of scavenger birds and animals like vultures and jackals is particularly benevolent as they help clean the human environment by scavenging on dead animal carcasses.

(g) Some Other International Efforts - Gene Banks

A few forest reserves have been set aside to protect wild relatives of crop plants and National Gene Banks (for seed storage) have been set up in some 60 countries. Half of the world's strains of rice are stored at the International Rice

Research Institute, Philippines; nearly 12,000 types of wheat and maize from 47 countries are kept at the International Maize and Wheat Improvement Center in Mexico. Stored seeds can never replicate the species in wild and also can not be kept for long time.

(h) *Biodiversity Conservation in India*

(1) Scientific Institutions for Ex-Situ Conservation

National Bureau of Plant Genetic Resources (NBPGR)

It was established in 1976 by the Indian Council of Agricultural Research, New Delhi for "*Ex-situ*" conservation of plant genetic resources for agri-horticultural and agri-silvicultural activities. Seeds of majority of agri-horticultural crops like cereals, pulses, vegetables, can be dried to low moisture content. Built-in-long term cold storage (Gene Banks) have been installed at the Bureau's Head Quarters in New Delhi to conserve genetic resources at low tempreture at -20° C. At present NBPGR holds about 48.5 thousand accessions of diverse species of economically important plants. About 250 samples of rare cultivars collected from tribal belts of India are deposited in NBGPR, New Delhi. Efforts are also being made to conserve plant germplasm through "cryopreservation". A number of scientific organisations dealing with storage of genetic material of various crops plants have been established in India after Independence. They are "Rice Research Institute", Cuttack; "Potato Research Institute", Shimla; "Plantation Crops Research Institute", Kasargod; "Central Tuber Crops Research Institute", Trivendrum; Indian Grassland and Fodder Research Institute", Jhansi; "Central Research Centre for Spices", Calicut; and "Indian Institute of Horticultural Research", Bangalore.

National Bureau of Animal Genetic Resources (NBAGR)

It was established in the 1980's in Karnal, Haryana for preservation of germplasms of improved species of cattles-cows, buffaloes, goats, sheep, camels and oxen and their various breeds found in different parts of India. Other organizations for "Ex-situ" conservations of animal germplasm are "National Bureau of Fish Genetic Resources", Lucknow and "Wildlife Research Institute of India", Dehradun. At WRI a 'gene bank' of all wild and domesticated animals of India is coming up.

(2) Conservation Through Faith and Tradition of Traditional People

Nature worship, respect and regard for nature's creations is a form of belief practised by the traditional Indian societies, mostly the tribals and the rural folks. The aborigines (tribals) and the traditional people of India, in the North-East, South-West and the Central regions have conserved valuable "primitive germplasms" of important crop plants. The various ethnic groups although isolated from one another practice primitive agriculture and have helped to preserve the local land races and variety of crop plants. The tribals also practice a traditional agriculture called "Shifting cultivation". What is noteworthy is that while shifting the tribals do not raze the whole forest to ground like modern cultivators do, but selectively retain the species like jack fruit (*Artocarpus integrifolia*), mango (*Mangifera indica*), mahua (*Bassia latifolia*) and the myrobalans (*Terminalia and Emblica*), thus enriching the region with native species. The north-eastern Himalayan region has several tribal pockets with enormous biodiversity e.g. citrus, musa, mangifera, oryza, sacceharum and zea mays. There is particularly enormous genetic diversity of citrus in this region (Singh, 1981).

Primitive Cultivars and Their Conservation by the Tribals

Many rare and primitive cultivars of cereals, pseudocereals, millets, pulses and vegetables which probably in modern society have almost disappeared are found still being grown by the primitive tribal communities living in the inaccessible areas of high hills of Himalays or the Western Ghats of India. "The primitive cultivars and wild relatives of crop plants preserved by the tribals are some of the very rare and precious gene pools that hold 'genetic key' of many valuable characters which the plant breeders may require in future for improving the agronomic character of the crop plants. About 250 samples of such rare cultivars collected from tribal belts of India are deposited in the National Bureau of Plant Genetic Resources (NBPGR), New Delhi.

Sacred Groves - The Last Refuge of Endangered Flora and Fauna

Tribal beliefs have survived several virgin forests in its pristine glory called "sacred groves". Human interference into it is a taboo. Such pristine forests rich in biological diversity are found all over India in the tribal belts. In the sacred groves are preserved several wild relatives of our modern crops. There are also several prized medicinal plants such as *Rawolfia serpentina* which have otherwise disappeared from other forests. The traditional people of Rajasthan have preserved village forests in deserts which are called 'orans'. Grazing is totally prohibited in such areas and any interference into them is taboo, punishable by God.

Sustainable Utilization and Conservation of Wild Plant Diversity by the Tribals of India

Over 9500 wild plant species used by tribals for meeting their varied requirements have been recorded. Out of 7500 wild plant species used by the tribals for medicinal purpose, about 950 are found to be new claims and worthy of scientific investigation. Out of 3900 or more wild plant species used as food by tribals, about 800 are new informations and at least 250 of them are worthy of attention to be developed as alternative source of nutritive food that the civilization would need in the near future. Out of over 525 wild plant species used by the tribals for making cordage and fibre, 5 are promising for commercial exploitation. Out of 400 plant species used as fodder, 100 are worth recommending for wider use. The tribals of India have also been using about 300 wild plant species as 'pesticides' and 'pisicides' of which atleast 175 are quite promising to be developed as safe "biopesticides" (Table 3).

Table 3 : Utilization of wild plant diversity by tribals of India

Use of wild plant species		Approx. number of species used
1.	As Food Plants (Cereals, Pulses, Vegetables, Fruits, etc.)	3,900
2.	As Medicinal Herbs	7,500
3.	As Fodder Plants	400
4.	As Fibre and Cordage	525
5.	As Pesticides and Pisicides, etc.	300
6.	As Gums, Resins and Dyes	300
7.	As Incense and Perfumes	100
8.	Miscellaneous and for other cultural requirements.	700

Source : "Ethnobiology in India - A Status Report" by DOEN, Government of India, 1994.

Some of the genetic resources conserved by tribal families are of great value in improving the quality of human life. An extract from the Brahmi plant (*Baccoppa minor*) helps to improve memory in old people. As the average life span continuously increases this could be of great value to mankind.

The Kerala tribes use about 245 wild species of plants as food, fodder, fuel, biofertilizer, medicinal herbs and as construction materials. They also grow 26 different "traditional varieties" of rice crops which have disappeared from the modern agriculture. The tribals of Manipur use as food about 400 species of wild plants ranging from algae to angiosperms.

Wildlife Conservation

According to Kothari (1996) wildlife habitats are the life -support systems for rural populations. If forests are destroyed, so are the people dependent on them. Conservation programmes will be successful only if local people are drawn into management of protected areas.

We are aware of only a few mammals (like the cheetah), birds (like the pinkheaded duck) which have gone extinct. Many of India's natural habitats would otherwise have been gobbled up by commercial forces or excessive local pressure : the world's largest Olive Ridley turtle nesting site has so far escaped rapacious commercial trampling because of the Bhittarkanika Sanctuary, rich rainforests in the Silent Valley National Park continue to be safe from a proposed hydro-electricity project, the Radhanagari Sanctuary in the Western Ghats continues to stand in the way of bauxite mining proposals.

Natural habitats are not only the home of wildlife and rural people but also the repositories of resources which our industries are demanding - minerals, timber, water, hydro-electricity etc. Our "development" strategy has only served to exploit these resources for the enrichment of urban middle-classes and big rural landlords at the expense of wildlife and poor people. As our economy moves on to the fast track in the 21st century, this exploitation is greatly accelerating. Darlaghat in Himachal Pradesh and Narayan Sarovar in Gujarat where denotified to make way for cement factories and limestone mining, iron-ore prospecting was extended in Kudremukh National Park in Karnataka, traveling jetties are being proposed in the Bhittarkanika Sanctuary of Orissa, an oil refinery has been sanctioned adjacent to the Marine National Park in Gujarat.

Wildlife was once remarkable for its abundance in India with tigers haunting the forests in hundreds and antelopes in thousands. It has gradually declined over the centuries and more rapidly after the British took over the country. Today we have reached the critical stage at which most, if not all our wildlife is in danger of extinction. Several species are generally endangered and are fighting a loosing battle for survival. In 1901 there were 30,000 tigers in India which dwindled to some 3000 in 1991. In 1988 IUCN listed 23 species of mammals as endangered or vulnerable. Among the 19 primates 12 are endangered. Among 1175 species of birds 70 species are threatened 63 on the mainland, 4 on the Andaman Islands and 3 on the Nicobar. A number of threatened bird species are from north-east. The ecological status of many invertebrate species are not well known, but Schedule 1 of the Wildlife Protection Act, 1972 of India include the "coconut crab" of Andaman and Nicobar islands, the "Himalayan Dragonfly" and 130 species of butterflies and beetles are also becoming rare or vulnerable due to heavy exploitation and habitat destrucion (Sinha, 1999).

Central Board for Wildlife was set up in India in 1952 and India adopted a National Wildlife Action Plan in 1983. Three types of protected areas were created :

(*i*) Wildlife Sanctuaries (WLS)

(*ii*) National Parks (NP's), and

(*iii*) Biosphere Reserves (BR's)

In 2000, there were 494 WLS, 89 NP's and 14 BR's in India covering about 4 percent of the total geographical area. An all India ban on Tiger hunting in 1980 was soon followed by near total ban on licensed hunting.

The Biosphere Reserves are multipurpose protected areas which preserve the entire ecosystem (plants, animals, man and micro-organism) of India and its genetic diversity. It includes primitive human settlement (cultural diversity) and the adjoining non-forest areas rich in cultivars. In 1979, 14 potential sites were indentified in India for setting up of *Biosphere Reserves* :

1. Niligiri (Karnataka, Kerala, Tamil Nadu)
2. Nanda Devi (Uttaranchal)
3. Nokrek (Meghalaya)
4. Great Nicobar (Andaman and Nicobar Islands)
5. Gulf of Mannar (Tamil Nadu)
6. Manas (Assam)
7. Sundarbans (West Bengal)
8. Namdapha (Arunachal Pradesh)
9. Uttarakhand (Uttar Pradesh)
10. Thar Desert (Rajasthan)
11. Rann of Kutch (Gujarat)
12. North Islands of Andamans

13. Kaziranga (Assam)

14. Kanha (Madhya Pradesh)

The unabated decline of wildlife in India continued until the late 60's, when mounting concern led to a number of conservation steps. The network of National Parks and sancturaries has contantly grown, from 10 National Parks and 127 Sanctuaries covering about 25,000 km^2 in 1970, the network got enlarged in 1994 to 75 National Parks and 421 sancturaries.

(i) Project Tiger

It was launched in 1973 in 13 states of India. There are 18 reserves covering an area of 28609 km^2 which forms 2.1 percent of the total forest area of the country. This has helped in the protection of the 'big cat' which is threatened with extinction. There has been considerable increase in the population of both the prey as well as the predator species. The main objectives for launching of Project Tiger was conservation of entire ecosystem, the flora and fauna, and other biotic components which offer a refuge to the tiger.

(ii) The Gir Lion Project

The project was initiated in 1968 in the Gir Forest of Gujarat to save the last surviving Asiatic Lions. By the turn of the century there were only 20 lions in the Gir forest. The improvement in habitat and removal of biotic pressure have helped in increase in lion population to about 220 today.

(iii) Crocodile Breeding Project

The project was started in Orissa and then extended to several other states in April 1975 with UNDP assistance. The major objectives was to protect the three endangered species of crocodile namely - *Gaveiolis gangeticas, Crocodylus palustric* and the salt water crocodile.

(iv) Lesser Cats Project

The project was launched in 1976 with an assistance of WWF in India for conservation of four species of lesser cats e.g. Felis bengalensis kerr, Felism marmorta martin, Felis lemruinki Horse field,and Felis viverrina bennet, found in Sikkim and Northern part of West Bengal .

(v) The Manipur Brow - Antlered Deer Project

This was launched in 1981 in Manipur to save the Brow - antlered Deer (*Cervus eldi eldi*) which is on the verge of extinction. The habitat includes 35 Km^2 of park and sanctuary. The population of the deer increased from 18 to 23 in just one year.

(vi) Project Elephant

It was launched in 1991 to protect the Asiatic Elephant which is also highly endangered species because of large scale poaching.

(vii) Project Rhino

It was launched in 1987 in Kaziranga Wildlife Sanctuary in Assam to save the lesser one horned Rhinoceros from extinction. It coveres an area of 430 km^2 and it is the natural home of the diwindling rhino.

(viii) Himalayan Musk Deer Project

This was launched in 1981 to save the endangered musk deer which is facing extinction.

(ix) Project Hangul

This project was launched in 1970 in Kashmir valley to save the highly endangered "Kashmir Stag" which is facing extinction.

Some Legal Aspect of Wildlife Conservation

Several laws had been enacted in India even before independence for the protection of wildlife and its habitat. Some of these are :

1. Elephant Preservation Act, 1879
2. The Indian Fisheries Act, 1897
3. The Indian Forest Act, 1927
4. Wild Birds and Wild Animals Protection Act, 1912
5. Bengal Rhinoceros Act, 1932
6. Haily National Park Act, 1936
7. Bombay Wild Animals and Wild Birds Protection Act, 1951
8. The Cruelity Against Animals Act, 1960
9. The Wildlife Protection Act, 1972
10. The Forest Conservation Act, 1980
11. Wildlife (Protection) Amendment Act, 1991

On the other hand, the Wildlife (Protection) Act, 1972 provisions relate to sanctuaries, national parks, game reserves and closed areas. According to this Act, wildlife includes any animal, bees, butterflies, crustacean, fish and moths; and aquatic or land vegetation which forms part of any habitat. National Parks have been given a higher level of protection. According to section 35 (6) of the Act, "No person shall destroy, exploit or remove any wildlife from a National Park or destroy or damage the habitat of any wild animal or deprive any wild animal of its habitat within such National Park.

Neither private land holding nor grazing is permitted within the National Parks. Sanctuaries have been accorded a lesser level of protection. "Game reserves" are those protected areas where hunting of any wild animal is prohibited except under and in accordance with a licence. "Closed areas" are those protected places where hunting of wild animals is totally prohibited during specified periods.

The Wildlife Protection Act, 1972 and the Amendment of 1991 has proved effective in wildlife management. Penalty under Section 51 of the Act is compulsory imprisonment for one year, which could extend to seven years including a minimum fine of Rs. 5,000 for hunting and trading in animal skins, bones, horns and tusks.

International Efforts

Wilderness movement in world can be traced back to the time of poet William Wordsworth (1970 - 1859) in UK and then in US to John Muir (1838 - 1914) who founded the Sierra Club for preserving wilderness. Some of the international conventions made for preserving global wildlife are :-

1. Convention for the Protection of Birds useful to Agriculture, Paris 1902.
2. International Convention for the Regulation of Whaling, Washington, 1946.
3. International Convention for the Protection of Birds, 1950.
4. Convention on the Wet lands of International Importance especially as Water fowl Habitats, Ramsar, Iran, 1971.
5. Convention concerning the protection of the World Cultural and Natural Heritage, Paris, 1972.
6. The Convention on International Trades in Endangered Species of Wild Flora and Fauna

(CITES), Washington, 1973 (Entered into Force July 1, 1975).

7. Convention on the Conservation of Migratory Species of Wild Animals, Bonn, 1979.
8. Convention on Biological Diversity Conservation, Rio de Janeiro 1992 (Entered into force 29 December 1993)
9. Trade Record Analysis of Flora and Fauna (TRAFFIC).

India is signatory to all the above international conventions of wildlife conservation.

Conclusions

Biodiversity contributes a lot to the sustainable development of agriculture, medicine, industry etc. Many species constitute the foundation of community welfare in rural areas by providing food, fuel, fiber etc., and also help in stabilization of climate, protection of watersheds, soil and breeding grounds.

Only a fraction (1%) of the world's total species has been properly studied for its potential value to human as food, medicine and in industry. "Miracle" herbal medicine for incurable human diseases, "miracle super crops" and "super industrial products" wait to be discovered and are being destroyed without even being known. People have to be educated about the enormous socio-economic value of biodiversity and that how our own existence depends upon it. The strategy of biodiversity conservation demands that the introduction of "exotic species" into native lands should be completely prohibited. Widespread destruction of native species can occur by the exotic species against which the local ones do not have any protection.

Biodiversity conservation does not only mean propagation of the given species in a limited protected area. In addition it requires the rehabilitation of given species in ecologically similar habitats still available elsewhere in the biosphere. It is extremely risky to have the sole surviving population of an endangered species in only one area. Any catastrophic event could lead to its extinction.

There is also a need for conservation effort to unite with the many mass movements. The strategies for conservation and sustainable utilization of biodiversity have been providing special protection to biodiversity rich areas by declaring them as National Parks, Wildlife Sanctuaries, Biosphere Reserves and Ecologically fragile areas. Other measures including exploration of alternatives to fuelwood and fodder, afforestation of degraded areas and wastelands, and creation of *Ex-situ* conservation facilities such as gene banks are of immense importance. The environmental education can be instrumental in increasing awareness among people of rural areas. It promotes the economic development which is culturally, socially and economically sustainable at the local level.

Foresters, environmentalists and policy makers have, therefore, a major responsibility to ensure the protection and sustainability of the rich national heritage.

References

Anonymous (2002) Conservation biodiversity of the country. 26 (44) : 1 - 3.

Bedi, D.S. and Pattnaik, S. (1999) Environmental conservation in India. Employment News, 24 (10) : 1-2

Kothari, A. (1996) *Conserving Biodiversity. The Hindu - Survey of the Environment, pp., 129 -137.*

Mayers, N. (1986) "Biological Resources of the Tropics"; *In : Conservation for Productive Agriculture,* ICAR, New Delhi.

McNeely, Jeffrey A. (1994) Lessons from the Past : Forest and Biodiversity. *In : Biodiversity and Conservation, 3, (1) Chapman and Hall, U.K.*

Mishra, R.. and Singh, R.P. (2002) Biosphere Reserve : A Management Concept for Natural Conservation, *26 (46) : 1 - 3.*

Mittermeier, Russell A., Myers, Norman, Mittermeier, Cristina Goettsch (2000). Hotspots: Earth's Biologically Richest and Most Endangered Terrestrial Ecoregions. Conservation International. pp., *432*

Noss, R.F. and Cooperrider, A.Y. (1994) *Saving Nature's Legacy.* Island Press, Washington, D.C.

Oberai, C.P. (2000) *Wildlife Conservation. Employment News, 25 (20) : 4 and 12.*

Priyanka, K.(2000) Natural Resource Management : Towards Sustainable Agriculture in 21st Century. Employment News, 24(46) : 1-3.

Saha, S. and Banerjee, T. (2001) Women : Partners in Development. Employment News, 25 (49) : 1 - 2.

Singh, B. (1981) *Establishment of First Gene Sanctuary in India for Citrus Conservation in Garo Hills.* Concept Publishing House, New Delhi.

Singh, K..K. and Kapoor, B.B.S. (2001) Management of salt-affected and water logged soils in IGNP area of Western Rajasthan, Chapter 3, In : Assessment of Natural Resources of Thar Desert *(Eds. B.B.S. Kapoor, K.K. Singh, Ahmed Ali and R.K. Gehlot),* Madhu Publications, Bikaner (Raj.), India, pp. 25 - 36.

Singh, Y.P and Aggarwal, A. (1998) Environmental Crisis : A Challenge Ahead. *Employment News, 23 (9) : 1-2.*

Swaminathan, M.S. (1994) *Inaugural Address at '4th International Congress of Ethnobiology',* Lucknow, November 17 - 21, 1994.

Tyagi, Anuja, Saxena, Manjula K., Jain, Narendra (2005) *Environmental Studies.* College Book House, Jaipur.

UNEP (1992) UNEP REPORT 1992. United Nation Environment Programme, 1992.

WMO (World Meteorological Organization) (1993). Meteorology and the Transfer of Technology WMO No. 786, Geneva.

Wright, Richard T. and Nebel, Bernard, J.(Eds.) (2004) Wild Species : Biodiversity and Protection, *Chapter 11. In : Environmental Science : Towards a Sustainable Future, 8th. edn., pp. 263 - 285.* Prentice-Hall of India Pvt. Ltd., New Delhi.

CHAPTER 2

RESOURCE CONSERVATION THROUGH LAND TREATMENT OF MUNICIPAL WASTEWATER

P. R. Thawale, Asha. A. Juwarkar, Padma S. Rao and S. K. Singh

Environmental Biotechnology Division,

National Environmental Engineering Research Institute (NEERI)

Nehru Marg, Nagpur – 440020, India.

ABSTRACT

Industrialization and urbanization have been causing tremendous pressure on the water resources, and inturn, to maintain the pace of development. It has become necessary to search for alternative sources of water. Conventional wastewater treatment technologies are cost intensive and often pose financial constraint in developing countries. Therefore considerable attention has been directed towards design and development of low cost wastewater management technologies coupled with recycle and reuse benefits. High Rate Transpiration System (HRTS) is one such technology, which can be implemented for domestic effluent disposal and reuse. This hypothesis was examined in field and laboratory experiments conducted by NEERI, Nagpur, India. This paper highlights the use of HRTS for the removal of pollutants like BOD, nitrogen and phosphorus from primary treated wastewater. The HRTS is a land treatment system where specific plants of transpiration potential are grown on the ridges and wastewater is allowed to flow through furrows.

Laboratory studies carried out at the National Environmental Engineering Research Institute (NEERI) for development of standard design protocol consist of 40 cm diameter cement pipe (having 0.1256 m^2 area) and 0.8 m deep filled with sandy loam soil. The hydraulic loading was maintained at the rate of 5 cm per day. The BOD removal in HRTS was observed to be 86.69 %. The nitrogen content reduced from 33.6 mg L^{-1} to 8.0 mg L^{-1} whereas, phosphate in treated HRTS effluent was 6.3 mg L^{-1} against the mean inflow phosphate content of 16.9 mg L^{-1}. The country's first HRTS was installed at sea beach in Puri in the State of Orissa, India. Two types of plants viz. Dendrocalamus strictus and Casurina equisitifolia were planted. At present 150 – 350 m^3 per day of wastewater is being treated through HRTS. The range of removal of BOD, nitrogen and phosphate was 79.55 % - 93.8 %, 60.7 – 76.2 % and 17.7 – 70.3 % respectively. The HRTS treatment was found to be efficient in wastewater renovation and economically viable. The system, being easy to operate and having low cost, can possibly be an economical viable solution for wastewater management. These low-tech and low-cost wastewater treatment HRTS are showing good performance for reduction of pollutants with minimal soil and plant contamination.

Key Words: *Dendrocalamus strictus; Casurina equisiti-folia;* HRTS; Land treatment; Renovation

Introduction

Land application of domestic sewage effluent is a cost-effective method of treatment and disposal. Rapid infiltration of sewage into sandy soils can result in improvement of its physical, chemical and microbiological quality (Iskandar, 1981). Reduction in nitrates, BOD and bacteria may be achieved after the passage of sewage effluent through a few meters of soil (Bouwer, 1985). Land treatment, especially rapid infiltration of municipal wastewater into relatively permeable soils, is becoming an important treatment method due to the increasing need for water reuse and protection of groundwater in many areas of the world (Asano, 1985). Land application of domestic and industrial wastewater is gaining momentum owing to the fact that it provides primary, secondary and tertiary treatment to the waste, all in a single operation with recycling and reuse benefit of wastewater and nutrients for biomass production (Idlovich and Michail, 1984; Smith and Schroeder, 1985; Witherow and Bledsoe, 1986; Juwarkar *et al.,* 1995) besides preventing the pollution of streams and lakes. In view of the fact that fiscal resources available with the municipal agencies are inadequate, which pose constraints in putting up the conventional facilities, land treatment in conjunction with conventional treatment, or alone in worst case, is an ideal proposition. The in-plant treatment of both domestic and industrial wastewaters, using sophisticated treatment technologies like trickling filters, activated sludge process, aerated lagoons, bio-methanation and incineration etc. are energy and cost intensive and beyond the reach of developing countries. Further, the discharge of treated wastewater enriched with nutrients and with other pollutants causes eutrophication of lakes/rivers, besides creating aesthetic problem. This warrants adoption of an appropriate wastewater management system wherein twin benefits of treatment and recycling and reuse can be achieved, and eco-development can be promoted.

Presently, 6351 million cubic meter of wastewater is being generated per year from 212 class I cities and 242 class II towns in the country, of which only 36% in class I cities and 14% in class II towns are collected due to limited treatment facilities. Hence, conventional approach of wastewater treatment and its disposal in water bodies need to be reviewed. The existing wastewater treatment facilities are mostly confined to primary level, providing treatment to the extent of 20% and 45% of wastewater respectively, in class I cities and class II towns (CPCB Report, 1988). The nutrient value of the available wastewater is estimated to be 317,000 tonnes nitrogen, 140,000 tonnes phosphate and 191,000 tonnes of potash per year. The economic value of the available wastewater is estimated to be Rs. 2592 lakhs. Further, it can also increase the irrigated command area by 1,70,400 hectares in the country. The present practice of land application is disposal oriented and hence the hydraulic and nutrient loading ranges from 22.1 - 336.8 $m^3 ha^{-1} day^{-1}$ and 403 - 6062 kg $ha^{-1} year^{-1}$, respectively which is 2-15 times higher than the normal loading (Juwarkar *et al.,* 1991). The excessive hydraulic and nutrient loading regardless of soil-plant assimilative capacity results in soil sickness, salinity and sodicity problems. Moreover, imbalance in C:N (Carbon: Nitrogen) ratio in plants induced more foliage and less fruiting particularly in case of vegetables and flowering plants (Juwarkar, 1989). The application of wastewater to agricultural crop and forestry plantation with appropriate assimilative capacity based design provides treatment to wastewater through the physico-chemical renovating potential of dynamic multicomponent soil ecosystem. It also promotes recycling and reuse of water, nutrients for biomass generation, replenishment of natural resource and recharge of ground water (Fig. 1). The treatment efficiency of land application and conventional treatment systems given in Table 1, further confirmed the fact that land application provide the highest degree of renovation (Juwarkar *et al.*, 1998).

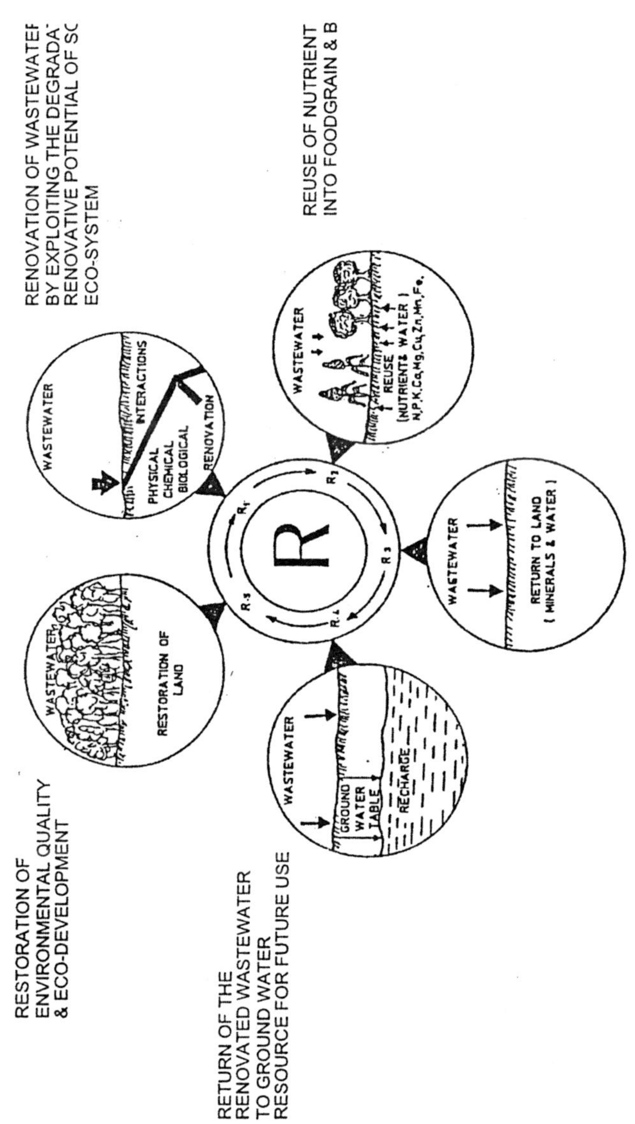

Fig. 1 : 5R Concept of wastewater management and recycling, reuse and eco-development

Table 1 : Typical characteristics of treated wastewater from conventional, advanced wastewater treatment and land treatment systems.

System	Residual Effluent constituent, mg L^{-1}						Pathogens removal, %	
	BOD	SS	NH_3-N	NO_3-N	Total N	Total P	Bacteria	Viruses
Conventional treatment								
Aerated lagoon	35	40	10	20	30	8	90-95	16-94
Activated sludge	20	25	20	10	30	8	85-99	91-98
Advanced Wastewater treatment								
Biological nitrification	12	15	1	29	30	8	--	--
Biological nitrification denitrification	15	16	--	--	3	8	--	--
Tertiary, two stage lime coagulation & filtration	5	5	20	10	30	0.5	99-99.9	90-99.7

Contd.

Tertiary, two stage lime coagulation, filtration, selective ion exchange	5	5	--	--	3	0.5	99-99.9	99-99.9
Land Treatment Systems								
Slow rate	1	1	0.5	2.5	3	0.1	99-100	97-99
Overland flow	5	5	0.5	2.5	3	5.0	90-100	89-99
Rapid infiltration	5	1	--	10	10	2.0	90-99	90-99

Source: *Juwarkar et al.*, (1998).

In disposal of wastewater through crop irrigation, soil works as a living treatment system. Soil and its associated ecosystem components act as physico-bio-chemical reactor capable of treating or stabilizing the pollutants of solid and liquid origin through degradation, adsorption, precipitation and utilization by crop. The wastewater, while passing through the soil matrix provides filtration on the soil surface leading to removal of coarse particles (Primary clarifier). The degradation of soluble organic pollutants in soil profile by microbial action and mixing and aeration extended by macro soil habitants (earthworms and macrofauna) represent the waste treatment process occurring in the aeration tank. The wastewater from the soil reactor is subjected to final polishing / renovation for metals removal through adsorption and ion exchange. The suspended solids and bacterial biomass removal through adsorption, ion exchange and precipitation with hydroxides and carbonate indicates reaction processes as occurring in secondary clarifier. Removal of assailable macro and micronutrients through plant utilization resembles the tertiary waste treatment. All the renovative processes are nature's own treatment process and thus land application is an eco-friendly treatment and disposal system.

The results that are based on limited data of actual systems and designs where alternatives are compared in USA (Overcash and Pal, 1979) substantiates the economic advantages of land treatment. After secondary treatment in a conventional sewage treatment plant, normally some 25-75% of phosphorus, 90% of nitrogen and about 10% of both organic matter and suspended solids remain in the effluent. This treated effluent when discharged to water bodies becomes a potential source of pollution there. To remove nutrients and other pollutants effectively from wastewater, some form of tertiary treatment, which is economical and easy to operate is required. The land treatment systems like HRTS can match with this requirement. The high transpiration capacity of plants grown on soil matrix enables the system to serve as a biopump. The plants such as bamboo (*Bambusa arundinacea*), acacia (*Acacia mangium*), neem (*Azadirachta indica*), shisham (*Dalbergia sissoo*) and eucalyptus (*Eucalyptus hybrid*) transpire water equivalent of 7 to 13 times of potential evapo-transpiration from the soil matrix alone. The HRTS enables the disposal of 350-450 m^3 of wastewater per hectare of land area per day (Juwarkar *et al.*, 1994; 1998 and 2003). As all the wastewater is utilized in this process, the ground water pollution problem is minimized. The nutrients present in the wastewater are used by the plants and partly retained in the soil matrix without affecting the soil ecosystem.

Benefits of HRTS

- ✓ The method works on natural treatment processes and could thus be termed as eco-friendly,
- ✓ Facilitates development of forests and green belts in urban agglomerations,
- ✓ Generates sink potential for air pollutants,
- ✓ Low-energy and low-cost compared to conventional wastewater treatment systems,
- ✓ Ease of installation and simplicity of operations,
- ✓ Reuse of effluent and its nutrient contents for biomass production,
- ✓ Stabilization of organic matter and renovation of effluent,
- ✓ Prevention of ground and surface water pollution.

Constraints of HRTS

- ✓ System is efficient in non monsoon periods, and
- ✓ Evapo-transpiration factor, geology, topograpgy and selection of plant species suitable for systems greatly varies from season to seasons.

NEERI uses many methods to clean up pollution at metal contaminated sites in India. Some of them include phytoremediation, bioremediation and biodegradation which are considered as new or innovative. Such methods can be quicker and cheaper than more common methods. The synergistic action of the plant and the microbes degrade or contain the pollutant of wastewater including heavy metals (Fig. 2).

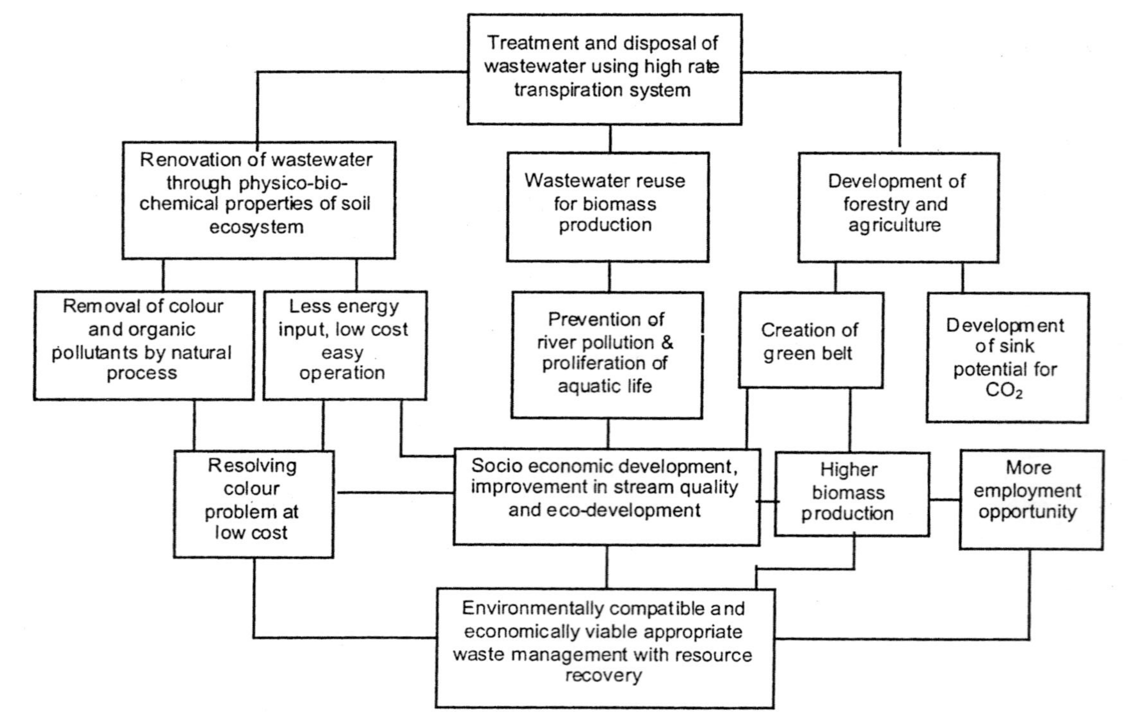

Fig. 2 : Impact network for treatment and disposal of wastewater using high rate transpiration system

Materials and Methods

The laboratory studies were carried out at the National Environmental Engineering Research Institute (NEERI), Nagpur in Maharashtra state of India, representing hot semi arid climate. Cement pipes having a diameter of 40 cm placed at a depth of 80 cm filled with sandy loam soil were employed in the study. The plants of high transpiration potential, *Dendrocalamus strictus* and *Casurina equisitifolia* were grown in one area whereas another area was without plants. Four weeks after planting, primary treated wastewater was applied at the hydraulic loading rate of 5 cm ha^{-1} day^{-1} over the surface of the HRTS adopting a down flow system. The treated effluent was collected from a vertical tube, draining from the bottom of the cement pipe.

HRTS was installed at sea beach, Puri in Orissa state of India. Wastewater was applied in the specially designed field layouts that consist of ridges with plants and furrows laid with filter media. Impact network for treatment and disposal of wastewater of the system is given in Fig. 3. The furrows represent the treatment system resembling shallow oxidation pond. The design of ridges and furrows depend on plants to be grown. In case of *Dendrocalamus strictus* plants ridges were 1.5 m to 2.0 m wide and 0.5 m in height. The furrows were 3 m – 4 m wide and 0.5 m deep. The HRTS with ridges of 0.8 to 1.0 m wide are more suitable for plants like neem, shishum, acacia and *Casurina equisitifolia* etc. Comparative costs of industrial waste management are given in Table 2 and schematic diagram of HRTS is depicted in Fig. 3. Length of the ridge depends on texture and permeability of soil and it varies from 5-20 m. Chabra (1989) recommended ridges of 1 m width and 0.5 m height for *Eucalyptus Hybrid*. The design details of HRTS for some plants were given in Table 3.

Table 2 : Comparative cost of industrial waste management alternatives.

Type of wastewater	Land treatment alternative		Conventional treatment alternative
	Size (ha)	Investment cost (US$)	Investment cost (US$)
Pharmaceutical	49	490,000	745,000
Poultry	--	220,000	720,000
Potato	67	350,000	780,000
Nylon & Polyester	12	140,000	300,000
Refinery	10	6.5/wet ton	11.5/wet ton (Incineration)
Paper mill*	10	20000 $/ m^{3}ha^{-1}	10-1000 $/ m^{3}ha^{-1}
Municipal* wastewater	10	10-100 $/ m^{3}ha^{-1}	20000 $/ m^{3}ha^{-1}

* *Cost estimate of HRTS*

Earthwork for developing ridges and furrows Cost of filter media and its layer Cost of power arrangement at the site Cost towards necessary infrastructure such as motors, pumps etc. Cost of irrigation system development through laying of distribution piping network with control valves and the cost of required civil construction.	**Rs. 1.0 lakh**
Operation and Maintenance cost per month	**Rs. 5.0 lakh**
The cost of land application thus comes out to be	**Rs. 0.90 m^{-3} of effluent**

Source: Juwarkar *et al.,* (1998).

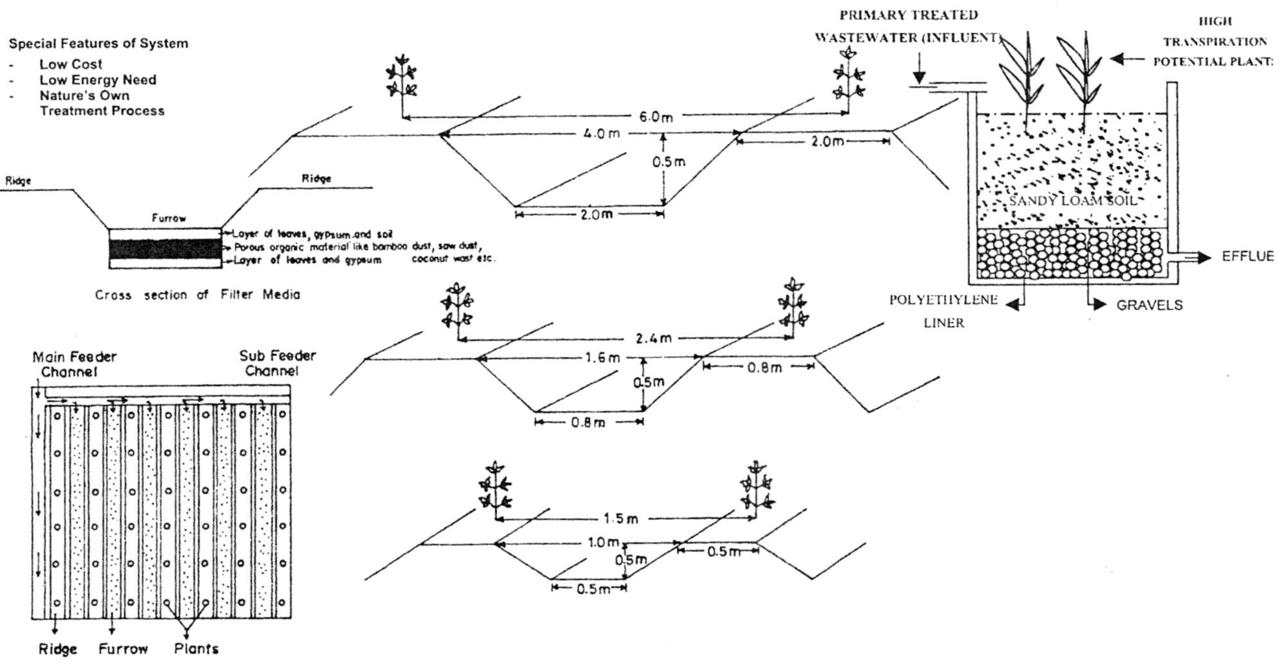

Fig. 3 : Schematics of high rate transpiration system for treatment and disposal of wastewater

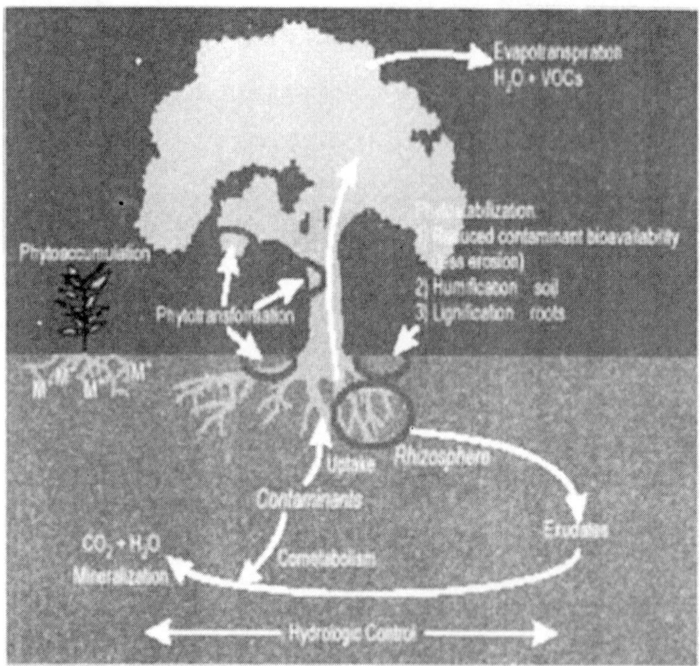

Fig. 4: Phytoremediation : (*i*) in the rhizosphere, exudates stimulate the growth and activity of contaminant – degrading micro-organisms, (*ii*) contaminants are transformed and degraded by plant – specific enzymes in the roots, stems and leaves and may be volatilized via evapotranspiration, (*iii*) a zone of hydrologic control is established that can control the migration of contaminants in the vadose zone and may control and remediate contaminant plumes, (*iv*) by stabilizing the soil, plants minimize erosion and decrease contaminant mobility, and (*v*) hyper-accumulating plants take up and immobilize heavy metals.

Influent and effluent samples were collected regularly and total nitrogen and phosphate were analysed as per Standard Methods for the examination of water and wastewater. Plants height was measured periodically and soil samples collected from HRTS were analysed by standard techniques (Black, 1965 and Jackson 1973).

Results and Discussion

Microbial Activity and Organic Decomposition in the soil

The microbiological processes in the soil are complex, and it is neither possible nor practical to do more than pint out some principles concerning microbial decomposition in the soil in this bulletin. It should be noted that purification of organic effluents applied to the soil, or organic sludge incorporated in the soil, is accomplished by the interrelated activities of the microbial population acting in conjunction with surface adsorption phenomena in much the same manner as in activated sludge units, trickling filters and sewage sand filters. Recent order of magnitude estimates of soil microbial numbers indicate the presence of about 100 million bacteria, 10 million actinomycetes, 1 million fungi, and 100 thousand algae per gram of soil, with a total live weight of 2400 pounds per acre of plow depth. Their activity is shown by the rapid decomposition of crop residues and the differences in composition of such residues and the organic matter of the soil. Of the latter, from 1/3 to 1/2 is estimated to be microbial in origin.

Irrigation Requirements of Various Crops

Blaney and Criddle proposed a method for calculating irrigation requirements based on the premised that consumptive use varies with temperature and number of daylight hours. Empirical consumptive use coefficient K was derived from previous investigations are given below : Consumptive use U is equal to $K\Sigma f$, where $f = tp/100$

t = mean monthly temp. ^{0}F

p = monthly percent of yearly daylight hours

High transpiration capacity of plants renders the system to consume more water and thus minimizes the leaching problem. It has been reported that *Casurina equisitifolia* plants can transpire water equivalent to 8-12 times of potential evapotranspiration and thus very useful to grow using domestic wastewater (Chabra, 1989; Juwarkar *et al.*, 1994 and Juwarkar *et al.*, 2003).

Nutrient and Pathogens Removal

The mean concentrations of nitrogen, phosphate and BOD in the inflow and the outflow from the HRTS which received primary treated wastewater at the rate 5 cm day^{-1} are presented in Table 3. The results showed that the HRTS removed N by 60 to 76.2 % and concentration of N in the outflow from HRTS varied from 8.3 to 9.5 mg L^{-1} with respect to *Dendrocalamus strictus* and 8.0 to 9.0 mg L^{-1} in the case of *Casurina equisitifolia*. Further, it was observed that the removal efficiency of N was greater in the case of *Casurina equisitifolia* due to profuse growth as compared to *Dendrocalamus strictus*. Removal of phosphate in the HRTS was comparatively less than nitrogen and it ranged from 17.7

Table 3 : Design details of HRTS for some plants

Type of plants	Ridges		Furrows		Plant to plant distance on ridges, m
	Width (m)	Height (m)	Width (m)	Depth (m)	
Dendrocalamus strictus (Bamboo)	1.5	0.5	3.0	0.5	3.0
Bambusa arundincea (Bamboo)	2.0	0.5	4.0	0.5	2.0
Azadiractha indica (Neem)	0.8	0.5	1.6	0.5	2.0
Casurina equisitifolia (Casurina)	0.8	0.5	1.6	0.5	2.0
Delbergia sissoo (Shishum)	0.8	0.5	1.6	0.5	2.0
Acacia mengium (Acacia)	0.8	0.5	1.6	0.5	2.0
Eucalyptus hybrid (Eucalyptus)	0.8	0.5	1.6	0.5	2.0
Eucalyptus robusta (Eucalyptus)	1.0	0.5	2.0	0.5	1.5

Source: Juwarkar *et al.*, (1998)

to 70.3 %. Bouwer, *et al.* (1980) also reported nitrogen removal to the extent of 30 to 65 % and phosphorus removal 40 to 80 % in a soil aquifer treatment system. However, nitrogen and phosphate removals by 70 and 95% respectively through soil, are reported by Gupta and Nema (1991). The removal of nitrogen is mostly attributed to nitrification/denitrification followed by plant removal. Coprecepitation of phosphate along with plant are considered to be the major processes for phosphate removal. The BOD removal efficiency in the present study was observed to be 80.0 to 94.3%. The BOD of the outflow effluent ranged from 10.0 to 43.3 mg L^{-1} as against the inflow BOD of 160 to 235 mg L^{-1}. These results are well supported by the findings reported by Sepp (1971) who observed 85 to 92% BOD removal in a soil aquifer treatment system. The comparative study of nitrogen and phosphate removal from vegetated and unvegetated HRTS shows that the presence of plants makes a difference in nutrient removal as shown in Table 4. The nitrogen removal in the unvegetated HRTS was 25.0 to 32.0 % as compared to 60.7 to 76.2 % in the vegetated HRTS system. Similarly, phosphate removal in vegetated system was more than the unvegetated. Lance *et al.*, (1978) found that nitrogen removal was increased by 10 – 18.5% when vegetation was used. Levine (1980) reported that there was 30% reduction in infiltration rates during second 34 weeks of flooding indicating some cultivation is necessary for maintenance of infiltration rates. Kaur and Singh (2002) recommended that in long term use of soil aquifer treatment system, some cultivation is necessary to maintain through infiltration rate and enhance pollutant/contaminant removal efficiency of system. Similar type of results were also reported by the other workers (Sepp, 1971; Igbounamba, 1972; Bose *et al.*, 1973; Patra and Behara, 1974; Hansen *et al.*, 1980; Thawale *et al.*, 1999 and Hongve *et al.*, 2000).

Table 4 : Mean concentration of BOD, nitrogen and phosphate in influent and effluent from HRTS planted with *Dendrocalamus strictus* and *Casurina equisitifolia*

Months	**Treatments**	**Parameters, mg L^{-1}**					
		Total Nitrogen		**Total Phosphate**		**BOD, 20°C**	
		B	**C**	**B**	**C**	**B**	**C**
3	I	27.4	27.4	11.6	11.6	183.3	183.3
	E	9.1	9.0	8.1	7.8	34.2	34.3
	R	66.8	67.2	30.2	32.8	81.3	81.3
6	I	30.3	30.3	12.4	12.4	205	205
	E	9.2	9.0	7.8	10.2	41	42
	R	69.6	70.3	37.1	17.7	80.0	79.5
9	I	24.3	24.3	11.8	11.8	160	160
	E	9.2	8.4	7.2	7.5	10.1	10
	R	62.1	65.4	39.0	36.4	93.7	93.8
12	I	33.6	33.6	16.9	16.9	232	232
	E	8.3	8	9.7	9	20.5	20.6
	R	75.3	76.2	42.6	46.7	91.2	91.1
15	I	33.5	33.5	15.8	15.8	211	211
	E	8.8	8	9.3	8.2	20.3	18.8
	R	73.7	76.1	41.1	48.1	90.4	91.1
18	I	24.2	24.2	16.2	16.2	235	235
	E	9.5	8.8	9.8	9.1	43.3	44.6
	R	60.7	63.6	39.5	43.8	94.3	81.0
21	I	26.7	26.7	13.5	13.5	216	216
	E	9.3	8.6	6.8	6.3	33	31.8
	R	65.2	67.8	49.6	53.3	84.7	85.3
24	I	32.5	32.5	15.8	15.6	233	233
	E	9.2	8.7	9.7	8.8	19.6	18.5
	R	71.7	73.2	70.3	43.6	91.6	92.1

B : *Dendrocalamus strictus*; C : *Casurina equisitifolia*;

I : Influent; E : Effluent; R : Removal Percent

Conclusions

The HRTS found to be a cost effective and reuse alternative to conventional treatment processes, which involve huge energy and cost. The experimental results conducted at NEERI showed that HRTS at a hydraulic loading of 5 cm day^{-1} produced an effluent with BOD, nitrogen and phosphate content of 10 to 44.6 mg L^{-1}, 8 to 9.5 mg L^{-1} and 6.3 to 10.2 mg L^{-1}, respectively. *Casurina equisitifolia* plant was more efficient in nitrogen removal compared to *Dendorcalamus strictus*. The plants irrigated with wastewater show increase in growth than irrigated with well water without affecting soil productivity and fertility. Further, the plants got established quickly and grow profusely. Being simple in installation and operation HRTS for wastewater treatment can be adopted in small towns and villages. HRTS performance is affected by rainfall, temperature etc. Since it is not site specific, the system can be implemented near the wastewater source. The evaluation of the hazards associated to this kind of contamination would require a good understanding of the different phenomena involved not only the chemical equilibria, but also the hydrodynamics and the contact between the soil and the contaminant solution.

References

Apha (1995) Standard methods for the examination of water and wastewater, 19th edn. Publ. American Public Health Association, Washington, DC, USA.

Asano, T. (1985) Overview: Artificial recharge of groundwater. *In: Artificial recharge of groundwater,* (Ed. T. Asano) : Butterworth Publ., Boston, MA 3-19.

Black, C.A. (1965) *Methods for Soil Analysis,* Am. Soc. Agro. Inc. Publ. Madison, Wisconsin, USA.

Blaney, H.F. and Cridle, W.D. (1950) Determining water requirements in irrigated areas from climatological and irrigation data. US Dept. of Agric., Soil Conservation Service Tech. Paper 96.

Bose, T.K., Basu, S. and Basu, R.N. (1973) Changes in rooting on cutting of Bongainvielea and Hibiscus, Indian J. Pl. Physiol 16: 127-139.

Bouwer, H. (1985) Renovation of wastewater with rapid infiltration land treatment systems. *In: Artificial Recharge of Groundwater*, (Ed. T. Asano) Butterworth Publ., Boston, MA. pp., 249-282.

Bouwer, H., Rice, R.C., Lance, J.C., Gilbert, R.G. (1980) Rapid in filtration research at Flushing Meadows Project. Arizona, J.W., PCF52, pp. 2457- 2470.

CPCB Report (1988) Status of water supply and wastewater collection treatment and disposal in class I & II cities, CUPS/31/1988-90, New Delhi.

Crites, R.W. (1985) Nitrogen Removal in Rapid Infiltration System. J. Environ. Engg. 111(6): 865 – 873.

Gideon, O., Demalach, Y., Hoffman, Z., and Manor, Y. (1985) Effluent reuse by trickle irrigation. Water Sci. Tech. 24 (9); 103 – 108.

Gupta, S.K. and Nema, P. (1997) Conservation and renovation of wastewater, National meet on S&T Issue to water Resource Management held at IIT, New Delhi, pp. 133 – 144.

Hansen, E.A., Dawson, H.D. and Tolsted, N.D. (1980) Irrigation of intensively cultured plantation with paper mill effluent. Tappi, 63 (11) : 1385 - 1395.

Hongve, D., VanHees, P.A.W. and Lundstrom, U.S. (2000) Dissolved components in precipitation water percolated through forest litter, European J. of Soil Sci., 51 : 667-677.

Idelovitch, E. and Michael, M. (1984) A new approach to an old method of wastewater reuse. J. Water Pollut. Control : 56 (8) : 9294 - 9300.

Igbounamba, O. (1972) Exchangeable reserve potassium and other cation reserves in agodi and ado soils. Soil Sci. 113 : 394 - 409.

Iskandar, I.K. (1981) Introduction, in Modeling Wastewater Renovation: *Land Treatment,* (Ed. I.K. Iskandar) John Wiley & Sons, New York, pp. 3 – 19.

Jackson, M. L. (1973) *Soil Chemical Analysis*, Publ. Practice Hall of India Ltd, New Delhi.

Juwarkar, A.S. (1987) A case study on the use of sewage for crop irrigation - Indian experience. Food and Agriculture Organization Rome. pp., 63 - 68.

Juwarkar, A.S., Juwarkar, A., Deshbratar, P.B. and Bal, A.S. (1990) Exploitation of Nutrient Potential of Sewage and Sludge Through Land Application. Report of the Expert Consultation of the Asian Network on Bio and Organic Fertilizers, Bangkok, Thailand, 18-21 Sept., 1990.

Juwarkar, A.S., Thawale P.R. Juwarkar, A.A. and Khanna, P. (1995) A case study of environmental problems in the use of wastewater for crop irrigation. National Workshop on Health, Agriculture and Environmental Aspects of Wastewater use, unep-who-NEERI, Nagpur.

Juwarkar, A.S., Thawale, P.R., Jambulkar, H.P. and Juwarkar, A.A. (1998) Management of Wastewater through crop irrigation – An ecofriendly approach. *In : Ecotechnology for Pollution Control & Environment Management*. Enviro Media, pp. 25 – 48.

Juwarkar, A.S. Thawale P.R., Padole L.M., Pande M.C. , Singh S.K. and Juwarkar, Asha A. (2003) An Eco-friendly Approach for Treatment and Disposal of Pulp and Paper mill wastewater through land Management - a case study. *In proc. of Nat. Conf. "Innovative Approaches in the Management of Environment (IAEM)"* pp. 21

Kaur, S. and Singh, M. (2002) Soil aquifer treatment system: A Case Study. Indian J. Environ. Health, 44 (3) : 244 – 246.

Lance, J.C. and Whisler, F.D. (1976) Stimulation of denitrification in soil columns by adding organic carbon to wastewater, J. Water Pollut. Control Fed., 48 (2) : 346-356.

Lance, J.C., and Whisler, F.D. and Rice, R.C. (1976) Maximizing denitrification during soil filtration of sewage water, J. Environ. Qual. 5(1) : 102-107.

Lance, J.C., Rice, R.C. and Whisler, F.D. (1978) Effect of vegetation on denitrification and phosphate movement during rapid infiltration on soil columns J. WPCF 50 : 2183 – 2187.

Leach, L.E. and Enfield, C.G. (1983) Nitrogen control in domestic wastewater rapid infiltration Systems, J. Water Pollut. Control, 55(9) : 1150-1157.

Levine, P.E., Crites, R.W., and Olson, J.V. (1980) Soil chemistry changes at rapid infiltration site. J. Environ. Engg. 106 : 869 – 883.

Overcash, M.R. and Pal, D. (1979) *Design of land treatment systems for industrial waste,* Theory and Practices, Ann. Arber Science Publication, USA.

Patra, S.K. and Behera, S. (1974) Effect of paper mill sludge on mineralization of soil nitrogen. Agra Univ. J. Res. 4 : 111-113.

Sepp, E. (1971) *The use of sewage for irrigation.* A literature review - California State Department of Public Health, Bureau of Sanitary Engineering, Sacramento.

Smith, R.G. and Schroeder, E.D. (1985) Field studies of the overland flow process for the treatment of raw and primary treated municipal wastewater. J. Water Pollut. Control Fed., 57 (7) : 785 - 790.

Thawale, P.R., Juwarkar, A.S., Kulkarni, A.B. and Juwarkar, A.A. (1999) Lysimeter studies for evaluation of changes in soil properties and crop yield using wastewater, intern. J. trop. agric., 17 (1-4) : 231-244.

WHO (1989) *Health Guidelines for the use of wastewater in agriculture and aquaculture.* WHO, Geneva.

Wilson, I.G., Amy, G. L., Gerba, C.P., Gordon, H., Johnson, B. and Miller, J. (1986) Quality changes during soil aquifer treatment of tertiary effluent. Water Environment Research, 67 : 371 – 376.

Witherow, J.L. and Bledsoe, B.E. (1986) *Design model for overland flow process.* J. Water Pollut. Control Fed. 58(5) : 381 – 385.

CHAPTER 3

ADVANCED BIOTECHNOLOGY PROCESS 'THE BIOREMEDIATION' TO RESTORE THE HEALTH OF AQUACULTURE POND ECOSYSTEM

A. Venkateswara Rao

Manager - Technical Services, Aquaculture Products Division
Neospark Drugs & Chemicals Pvt. Ltd., 241 B.L. Bagh
Panjagutta, Hyderabad-500 082, A.P., India.

ABSTRACT

Aquaculture is concerned with 'the propagation and rearing of aquatic organisms under complete human control involving manipulation of atleast one stage of an aquatic organism's life before harvest, in order to increase its production'. Fish catches from the marine environment have been steadily declining in many parts of the world due to over-exploitation and pollution, many people are turning to aquaculture to improve the food production and to contribute in economic development. Aquaculture, in India, has made encouraging progress in the past two decades producing significant quantities of food, income and employment. Aquaculture, particularly, tiger shrimp (*Penaeus monodon*) culture, has extensively been practiced all along coastal regions of India. Increased production is being achieved by expansion of culture areas and the use of modern methods. This development of aquaculture in our country has led to not only severe disease problems but also alteration of the quality of our natural habitats through increased effluent discharges from aquaculture systems, which contains high quantities of hither-to-non-existent materials of both organic and inorganic forms. Since recent past, it has been observed that the sustainable development of aquaculture sector can be achieved by adopting eco-friendly aquaculture practices by minimizing impact on the surrounding environment. To maintain healthy ecosystem in aquaculture ponds and hatchery tanks, bioremediation is the best biotechnology process. Many researchers has been demonstrated that the pathogens can be eliminated or minimized through this bio-control process and hence, can achieve good yield by maximizing both survival rate and growth rate and by minimizing the disease problems in aquaculture systems.

Key Words: Aquaculture; Over-exploitation; Pollution; *Penaeus monodon*; Sustainable development; Eco-friendly; Bioremediation; Probiotics; Enzymes; Feed additives; Water Quality; Disease control.

Introduction

During the past 20 years, aquaculture industry has been growing tremendously, especially that of marine fish, shrimps and bivalves in addition to freshwater fish and prawn. Penaeid shrimps are among the most important and extensively cultured crustaceans in the world (> 60 countries). In 2002, the world's shrimp farmers produced an estimated more than 1.0 million metric tons of whole shrimp and feed mills around the world produced approximately 1.5 million metric tons of shrimp feed.

Shrimp culture all over the world has been frequently affected by viral and bacterial diseases inflicting huge losses and annual losses due to disease has been estimated to be more than US $5 billions. Pathogenic micro-organisms implicated in these outbreaks were viruses, bacteria, algae, fungi and protozoan parasites. Although, diseases pose a serious threat to penaeid shrimp aquaculture, the production of these highly valued crustaceans continue to grow. For preventing and controlling diseases, particularly in aquaculture, the best method is the improving health of culture organisms and elimination of pathogens by improving aquatic environment. Thus, how to improve the ecological environment of aquaculture has become the focus of attention of international aquaculture. Now, researchers have proved the use of probiotic bacteria in aquaculture to improve water quality by balancing bacterial population in water and reducing pathogenic bacterial load. Researchers are increasingly paying more attention to this new approach (ecological aquaculture), and have made considerable headway. In addition to this, microbial pathogens cause millions of cases of foodborne disease and result in many hospitalizations and deaths each year globally. (Jordan, *et al.*, 2005).

Competition for survival can be strong, even on a scale invisible to the human eye. Indeed, aquaculture pond bacteria is so small that 10,000 fit on a pinhead are subject to the same law of evolution as that Darwin documented on the Galapagos, that is, survival of the fittest or competitive exclusion. Competitive exclusion is one species out-competing another in a natural search for habitat dominance. As old as time, competitive exclusion is providing science with a neat new means of addressing health and environmental challenges now. The use of competitive exclusion for improving a specific ecology is called "probiotics" (Parkar, 1974). Probiotics therapy, intentionally introduces strains of beneficial bacteria in order to replace bad bacteria. The first application of probiotics in aquaculture seems relatively recent (Kozasa, 1986), but the interest in such environment-friendly treatments is increasing rapidly.

Aquatic animals are quite different from the land animals for which the probiotic concept was developed, and a preliminary question is the pertinence of probiotic applications to aquaculture. Man and terrestrial livestock undergo embryonic development within an amnion, whereas the larval forms of most fish and shellfish are released in the external environment at an early ontogenetic stage. These larvae are highly exposed to gastro-intestinal microbiota-associated disorders, because they start feeding even through the digestive tract is not yet fully developed (Timmermans, 1987), though, the immune system is still incomplete (Vadstein, 1997). Thus, probiotic treatments are particularly desirable during the larval stages.

The transience of aquatic microbes is legitimate the extension of the probiotic concept to living microbial preparations used to treat aquaculture ponds. Moriarty (1997, 1998) proposed to extend the definition of probiotics to microbial water additives.

In 1991, Porubcan reported on two attempts at bacterial treatments to improve water quality and production yield of Penaeus monodon. (1) Pre-inoculated with nitrifying bacteria decreased the amounts of ammonia and nitrite in the rearing water. This treatment increased shrimp survival (Porubcan, 1991a) . (2) The introduction of Bacillus spp. in proximity to pond aerators reduced chemical oxygen demand, and increased shrimp harvest (Porubcan, 1991b). Moriarty (1998) noted an increase of shrimp/prawn survival in ponds where some strains of *Bacillus* spp. were introduced. The actual data of Moriarty (1998) showed the inhibitory activity of *Bacillus* spp. against luminous vibrio sp. in pond sediment, but the effect on shrimp/prawn survival might be due either to a probiotic effect, or to an indirect effect on animal health. For instance, the degradation of organic matter by *Bacillus* spp. might improve water quality.

The probiotic treatments may be considered as methods of biological control, the so-called "biocontrol" that termed the limitation or the elimination of pests by the introduction of adverse organisms, like parasites or specific pathogens. Maeda *et al.* (1997) proposed to designate as biocontrol the methods of treatment using "the antagonism among microbes through which pathogens can be killed or reduced in number in the aquaculture environment". Another terminology should designate the applications of nitrifying bacteria that are related to the bioremediation concept. This concept refers to the treatment of pollutants or waste by the use of micro-organisms that break down the undesirable substances.

Sugita *et al.* (1998) isolated a strain of *Bacillus* spp. that was antagonistic to 63% of the isolates from fish intestine. Pathogenic strains of *Vibrio* or *Aeromonas* have been targeted in most in vitro tests. Treatment with *Lactobacillus brevis* and lactic acid reduced the load of *Vibrio alginolyticus* in the *Artemia* culture water (Villamil *et al.*, 2003). Some bacteria are antagonistic to viruses (Kamei *et al.*, 1987, 1988; Direkbusarakom *et al.*, 1998), and they may be efficient for the biocontrol of viral diseases (Maeda *et al.*, 1997) and some other probiotics are effective in controlling bacterial diseases in fishes (Aubin, *et al.*, 2005).

The resistance cause by probiotics to infections to shrimp, prawn and fish is due to – Bacterial antagonism, bacterial interference, barrier effect, colonization resistance and competitive exclusion in addition to improving biodegradation of waste organic matter through nitrogen cycle.

To best determine, which bacteria make good probiotics for aquaculture production, scientists scoop up quantities of water from healthy habitat in the ocean where species (aquaculture organisms like shrimp) perform at peak capacity. They analyze the water's makeup and culture single or mixed bacteria they find there to use as probiotics. Their culture does not involve any sort of chemicals or toxins. These are fortified with naturally occurring phytoplankton, amino acids, a wide range of vitamins and minerals, an important variety of anti-oxidants and proteolytic enzymes, as well as an array of nucleic acids. These are the paramount keepers of the code of life, which appears to be in charge of growth and continuous cell repair.

The hypothesis of stimulation of the immune system of aquatic organisms may be also considered. Many immunostimulants have been tested on fish and shellfish, and some of the originated from microbial cell walls, eg. glucans (Anderson, 1992; Huang and Song, 1999; Song and Huang, 2000; Bricknell and Dalmo, 2005). It is possible that autochthonous microbiota may stimulate the immune response of aquatic animals to enteric pathogens, as reported in shrimp (Gullian *et al.*, 2004) and in land animals (Gaskins, 1997).

Bioremediation – Concept

The newest attempt being made to improve water quality in aquaculture is the application of probiotics and/or enzymes to the ponds. This type of biotechnology is known as *"bioremediation"*, which involves manipulation of micro-organisms in ponds to enhance mineralization of organic matter and get rid of undesirable waste compounds.

Probiotics and Enzymes

Probiotics

The concept of biological disease control, particularly using microbiological modulator for disease prevention, has received widespread attention. A bacterial supplement of a single or mixed culture of selected non-pathogenic bacterial strains was termed probiotics.

'Probiotics' the term was, first coined by Parker (1974) and originated from two Greek words 'pro' and 'bios' which mean 'for life'. Organisms -- be they human, cattle, chicken, fish, prawn or shrimp -- require good bacteria to break down nutrients for digestion. Living systems require bacteria to decompose waste. "Probiotics" generally includes bacteria, cyanobacteria, fungi, etc. They may be called as "Normal micro biota" or "Effective micro biota". In literature, probiotic bacteria are generally called the bacteria, which can improve the water quality of aquaculture, and (or) inhibit the pathogens in water thereby increasing production. "Probiotics", "Probiont", "Probiotic bacteria", "Beneficial bacteria", or "Friendly bacteria" are the terms synonymously used for probiotic bacteria.

The theory of ecological prevention and cure in controlling the insect pest of terrestrial higher-grade animals and plants has been in practice for long time, and has achieved remarkable success. The bio-controlling theory has been applied to aquaculture and many researchers attempt to use some kind of probiotics in aquaculture water to regulate the micro flora of aquaculture water, control pathogenic micro-organisms, to enhance decomposition of the undesirable organic substances in aquaculture water, and improve ecological environment of aquaculture. In addition, the use of probiotics can increase the population of food organisms, improve the nutrition level of aquacultural animals and improve immunity of cultured animals to pathogenic micro-organisms.

According to some recent publications, in the aquaculture the mechanism of action of the probiotic bacteria have several aspects.

- probiotic bacteria competitively exclude the pathogenic bacteria or produce substances that inhibit the growth of the pathogenic bacteria (eg. Bacitracin and polymyxin produced by *Bacillus* Spp.).

- provide essential nutrients to enhance the nutrition of the cultured animals.
- provide digestive enzymes to enhance the digestion of the cultured animals.
- probiotic bacteria directly uptake or decompose the organic matter or toxic material in the water improving the quality of the water.

Hence, the probiotics can decompose the excreta of fish or prawns, remaining food materials, remains of the plankton and other organic materials to CO_2, nitrate and phosphate. These inorganic salts provide the nutrition for the growth of micro algae, while the bacteria grow rapidly and become the dominant group in the water, inhibiting the growth of the pathogenic micro-organisms.

The photosynthesis of the micro algae provide dissolved oxygen for oxidation and decomposition of the organic materials and for the respiration of the microbes and cultured animals. This kind of cycle improves the nutrient cycle and it can create a balance between bacteria and micro algae and maintaining a good water quality environment for the cultured animals.

Types of Probiotics

Non-viable probiotics	These are dead.
Freeze-dried probiotics	These will die rapidly upon leaving refrigeration.
Fermentation probiotics	These are produced through fermentation.
Viable probiotics	This is live with guaranteed shelf life, guaranteed number of organisms, have a protocol for counting and to be very stable and efficacious. (produce many benefits).

Probiotics and their Role

Bacillus sp.	Mineralization and Breakage of proteins
Nitrosomonas sp.	Oxidation of ammonia
Nitrobacter sp.	Oxidation of nitrites
Aerobacter sp.	Reduction of organic matter
Cellulomonas sp.	Breakage of plant material

Beneficial effects of probiotics may be mediated by:

- Neutralization of toxin
- Suppression of viable count
- Production of antibacterial compounds
- Competition for adhesion sites
- Alternation of microbial metabolism
- Stimulation of immunity in the host
- Accelerate the sediment decomposition by producing organic acids
- Production of hydrogen peroxide
- Production of enzymes

Application of Probiotics in Aquaculture

- To regulate the microflora of aquaculture water.
- To control pathogenic micro-organisms.
- To enhance decomposition of the undesirable organic substances in aquaculture water and improve ecological environment of aquaculture by minimizing the toxic gases like ammonia, nitrite, hydrogen sulfide, methane etc.

- To increase the population of food organisms.
- Improve the nutrition level of aquaculture animals and improve immunity of cultured animals to pathogenic micro-organisms.
- The frequent outbreaks of diseases can be prevented.

Enzymes

Enzymes are organic catalysts formed naturally in living cells. They are compounds, which accelerated the rate at which chemical reactions occur and they remain unchanged after the reaction is completed. Thousands of enzymes exist in nature and are responsible for life.

Enzymes work by breaking the chemical bonds that hold compounds together, releasing smaller, more readily absorbed compounds (Julio *et al.*, 2004). For example, proteases work on proteins, amylases work on starches, celluloses work on cellulose and lipases work on lipids or fats. Recall that, cellulose is the major cell wall material in plants and is therefore, quite durable.

Nitrogen Cycle

Ammonia is the principal excretory product of most aquatic organisms. Inputs of ammonia cannot be eliminated from the water body. But ammonia is toxic, acutely and chronically, to fish and invertebrates and thus, it is a critical water quality factor. Ammonia should be maintained below 0.1 mg L^{-1} (total ammonia). The most efficient way to do this is by the establishment of a biological filter. A biological filter is a collection of naturally occurring bacteria, which oxidize ammonia to nitrite, and other bacteria, which then convert nitrite to nitrate. Nitrite is formed either by the oxidation of ammonia (nitrification) or the reduction of nitrate (denitrification). Nitrite is toxic to fish and some invertebrates and should be maintained below 0.1 mg L^{-1}. It is also a critical water quality factor.

Nitrate is the end product of nitrification. The vast majority of aquaculture ponds accumulate nitrate as they do not contain a denitrifying filter. In general, nitrate should be maintained below 50 mg L^{-1} (measured as NO_3-N) but it is not a critical water quality factor.

The most common ways to reduce nitrate are water changes and growing live plants. More sophisticated systems such as denitrifying filters are also available. A denitrifying filter creates an anaerobic region where anaerobic bacteria can grow and reduce nitrate to nitrogen gas. But they can be complex and easily disturbed which kills the anaerobic bacteria. A poorly run denitrifying filter does not convert nitrate all the way to nitrogen gas but instead produces nitrite.

The nitrogen 'cycle' is the oxidation of ammonia to nitrite by bacteria of the genus *Nitrosomonas* and the subsequent oxidation of the nitrite to nitrate by bacteria belonging to the genus *Nitrobacter*. It is easiest to visualize the nitrogen cycle as an endless loop divided into four phases, as follows:

- Fish, prawn and shrimp excrete ammonia as waste from their gills, kidneys and normal respiration. Ammonia also develops from unconsumed feeds, shell moults of prawn and shrimp, dead algae, zooplankton etc. by the microbial activity.
- A species of bacteria called *Nitrosomonas* converts this ammonia into nitrite

$$(2NH_4^+ + 3O_2 = 2NO_2^- + 4H^+ + 2H_2O).$$

- A second species of bacteria called *Nitrobacter* converts this nitrite into nitrate

$$(2NO_2^- + O_2 = 2NO_3^-).$$

- Algae and aquatic plants utilize nitrate to produce chlorophyll, which are in turn consumed by zooplankton and then by fish, prawn and shrimp. Thence the cycle repeats.

These bacteria are important to aqua farmers because without them it is difficult to maintain healthy environmental conditions in the aquaculture ponds.

The biochemical reaction of *Nitrosomonas* sp.: Energy generation in Nitrosomonas by two enzymes, Ammonia monooxygenase (AMO) and Hydroxylamine oxidoreductase (HAO) are involved in the oxidation of ammonia to nitrite.

$$NH_3 + O_2 + 2H^+ \xrightarrow{AMO} NH_2OH + H_2O$$

$$NH_2OH \xrightarrow{HAO} NO_2^-$$

The biochemical reaction of *Nitrobacter* is a very simple reaction, involving the cytochrome system as follows:

$$NO_2^- \longrightarrow NO_3^-$$

Nitrobacter sp. is facultatively mixotrophic and capable of growing anaerobically with nitrate as electron acceptor, producing nitrite, nitric oxide and nitrous oxide and then to nitrogen gas. Aerobically, it oxidizes nitric oxide to nitrite and thence to nitrate. All tricarboxylic acid cycle enzymes are present (eg. Carboxysomes, poly-beta-hydroxybutyrate (PHB) and polyphosphate granules).

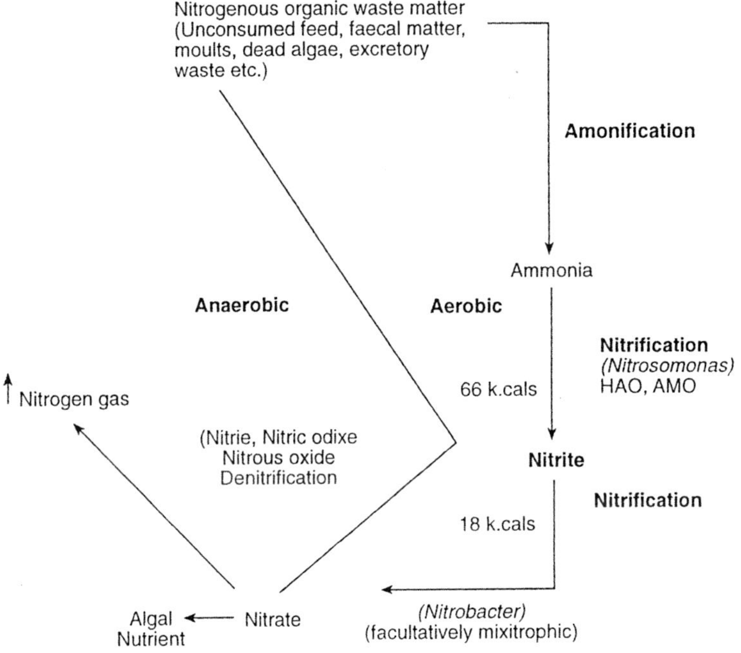

Fig. 1 : Nitrification : Nitrogen cycle

The nitrifying bacteria are gram-negative, non acid-fast rods, which may be pleomorphic or coccoid (*Nitrobacter*). They may be motile. The main component of the gram-negative cell wall is lipopolysaccharide (LPS). Additionally, there is present phospholipid, protein, lipoprotein and a small amount of peptidoglycan. Hence, the component of cell wall of most gram-negative bacteria is associated with endotoxic activity, with which are associated the pyrogenic effects of gram-negative infections like vibriosis. Sixty-six kilocalories of energy are liberated per gram atom of ammonia oxidized. Eighteen kcal of energy is liberated per gram atom of nitrite oxidized.

Nitrification is an obligate aerobic, oxidizing process. This means that it can only occur in an environment, which contains oxygen and the process produces electrons. In general **denitrification** is a process of bacteria converting nitrate to other substances. It is an anaerobic, reducing process. This means that, it occurs in environments without oxygen and the process accepts electrons.

Denitrification is defined as the transformation of nitrate to dinitrogen. Dinitrogen is a gas that is harmless and will bubble out of the system. Between the starting product (nitrate) and the end product (dinitrogen) there are three intermediate products, these are in the order in which they are produced nitrite (NO_2^-), Nitric Oxide (NO) and nitrous oxide (N_2O).

Hence, denitrification, like nitrification, is a multi-step process with many intermediate compounds produced before the final product is generated. In most cases, these intermediate products are toxic like ammonia and nitrite. Thus, denitrification does proceed to complete its process and to expel dinitrogen gas.

It is worth to mention that the nitrate, which is the end product of nitrification process is the major nutrient for the growth of primary producers i.e. phytoplankton as well as the microbes. Hence, the micro flora and fauna for their growth will utilize the nitrate and makes limit the process of denitrification.

Another difference between nitrification and denitrification is the type of bacteria, which perform the processes. Nitrification is done by what are called autotrophic bacteria. This term means the bacteria get the carbon they need for cell growth from carbon dioxide. Denitrifying bacteria are heterotrophic bacteria. This means they get their carbon from organic carbon sources such as methane, sucrose or glucose.

In addition, these probiotics controls the formation of toxic hydrogen sulfide by eliminating the *Desulfovibrio desulfuricans*, the hydrogen sulfide producing bacteria, through antagonism. The probiotics converts the toxic sulfide to nutritive sulphate.

Conclusions

The probiotics can decompose the excreta of shrimp, prawn or fish, remaining food materials, remains of the plankton and other organic materials to CO_2, nitrate and phosphate. These inorganic salts provide the nutrition for the growth of micro algae, while the bacteria grow rapidly and become the dominant group in the water, inhibiting the growth of the pathogenic micro-organisms. The photosynthesis of the micro algae provide dissolved oxygen for oxidation and decomposition of the organic materials and for the respiration of the microbes and cultured animals. This kind of cycle may improve the nutrient cycle, and it can create a balance between bacteria and micro algae, and maintaining a good water quality environment for the cultured animals.

Probiotics reduce the level of infection and mortality in aquaculture organisms. Probiotics compete with the disease-causing bacteria for food. Customarily, ponds have indigenous bad bacteria that leisurely eat on an abundance of undigested food, faecal matter, and dead algae. When farmers suddenly introduce a large quantity of these good bacteria -- probiotics -- into a pond, the newcomers eliminate the pre-existing bad bacteria out of the nutrient queue. The old bacteria, often-bad bacteria, never having had to compete for food, cannot keep pace with the aggressive probiotics.

Probiotics excretions make the pond medium less inhabitable for bad bacteria. Not only do probiotics bacteria have terrific appetites; they excrete enzymes -- exoenzymes -- as a natural byproduct of their metabolic activity, just as human's sweat. The enzyme excretions infuse and spread throughout the pond medium, changing its chemistry, resulting destroy of bad bacteria. Hence, probiotics therapy greatly improves pond water quality and reduces the pollution level of effluent before its release into the environment.

Probiotics speed the breakdown of organic waste fragments (dissolved proteins and unused feed), thus lessening sludge build-up. If sludge is not removed or does not decompose, dangerous concentrations of sulfide, nitrite, ammonia and various organic acids can occur. While the exo-enzymes of good bacteria go to work on larger waste particles and breaking them down through chemical reaction. As a result, there are fewer harmful chemicals in the medium.

Probiotics balance algae growth through providing nutrients by their bio-degradation activity. Probiotics utilizes phosphate for their body metabolic activities and hence prevents over growth (heavy blooms) of algae by limiting the phosphate. Dead algae are one of bacteria's favorite foods. Also, probiotics diminish nutrients normally consumed by algae and results less slime in the ponds.

Probiotics make better habitat for culture organisms. With less accumulation of organic matter on the pond bottom, more oxygen can penetrate the sediment. For eg. Prawn and shrimp characteristically burrow in the sediment. By loosening the sediment, probiotics make this burrowing easier. Moreover, they diminish the toxin level in the sediment itself.

Probiotics maximize fish, prawn and shrimp nutrition. In addition to consuming the feed administered by farmers, prawn and shrimp graze on tiny zooplankton that is present in the water supply. Zooplankton eats bacteria. Probiotics are another nutrient for existing zooplankton in the pond medium, thus invigorating the zooplankton population, and strengthen up the food supply to culture organisms.

Probiotics optimize the immune systems of culture organisms, increasing their resistance to disease. By upgrading the pond environment, augmenting the food supply, and making habitat more comfortable, probiotics fortify fish, prawn and shrimp immune system.

The application of probiotics in aquaculture shown promise, but further investigations may be expected with propagation of molecular approaches to analyse bacterial communities (Raskin *et al.*, 1997; Wallner *et al.*, 1997; Hugenholtz *et al.*, 1998; Gatesoupe, 1999).

References

Anderson, D.P. (1992) Immunostimulants, adjuvants and vaccine carriers in fish: applications to aquaculture. Annu. Rev. Fish Dis. 2 : 281-307.

Aubin, J., *et al.*, (2005) Trial of probiotics to prevent the vertebral column compression syndrome in rainbow trout (*Oncorhynchus mykiss* Walbaum). Aquaculture Research 36 : 758.

Bricknell, I., and Dalmo, R.A. (2005) The use of immunostimulants in fish larval aquaculture. Fish and Shellfish Immunology, 19 : 457-472.

Direkbusarakom, S., Yoshimizu, M., Ezura, Y., Ruangpan, L., Danayadol, Y., (1998) *Vibrio* spp., the dominant flora in shrimp hatchery against some fish pathogenic viruses. J. Mar. Biotechnol., 6 : 266-267.

Gaskins, H.R., (1997) Immunological aspects of host/microbiota interactions at the intestinal epithelium. In: Mackie, R.I., With, B.A., Isaacson, R.E. (Eds.), Gastrointestinal Microbiology, Vol. 2, Gastrointestinal Microbes and Host Interactions. Chapman & Hall Microbiology Series, International Thomson Publishing, New York, pp. 537-587.

Gatesoupe, F.J. (1999) The use of probiotics in aquaculture, Aquaculture, 180 : 147-165.

Gullian, M., Thompson, F., Rodriguez, J. (2004) Selection of probiotic bacteria and study of their immunostimulatory effect in *Penaeus vannamei*. Aquaculture, 233 : 1-14.

Huang, C.C., Song, Y. L., (1999) Maternal transmission of immunity to white spot syndrome associated virus (WSSV) in shrimp (*Penaeus monodon*). Developmental and Comparative Immunology, 23 : 545-552.

Hugenholtz, P., Pitulle, C., Hershberger, K. L., Pace, N. R. (1998) Novel division level bacterial diversity in a Yellowstone hot spring. J. Bacteriol, 180 : 366-376.

Jordan Lin, C. T., *et al.*, (2005) Awareness of foodborne pathogens among US consumers. Food Quality and Preference 16, 401-412.

Julio, H. Cordova-Murueta, *et al.*, (2004). Effect of stressors on shrimp digestive enzymes from assays of feces: an alternate method of evaluation. Aquaculture, 233 : 439-449.

Kamei, Y., Yoshimizu, M., Ezura, Y., Kimura, T. (1988) Screening of bacteria with antiviral activity from fresh water salmonid hatcheries. Microbiol. Immunol. 32 : 67-73.

Kamei, Y., Yoshimizu, M., Ezura, Y., Kimura, T. (1987) Screening of bacteria with antiviral activity against infectious hematopoietic necrosis virus (HNV) from estuarine and marine environments. Bull. Jpn. Soc. Sci. Fish, 53 : 2179-2185.

Kozasa, M. (1986) Toyocerin (*Bacillus toyoi*) as growth promoter for animal feeding. Microbiol. Aliment. Nutr. 4 : 121-135.

Maeda, M., Nogami, K., Kanematsu, M., Hirayama, K. (1997) The concept of biological control methods in aquaculture. Hydrobiologia, 358 : 285-290.

Moriarty, D.J.W. (1997) The role of microorganisms in aquaculture ponds. Aquaculture, 151 : 333-349.

Moriarty, D.J.W. (1998) Control of luminous *Vibrio* species in penaeid aquaculture ponds. Aquaculture, 164 : 351-358.

Parker, R.B. (1974) probiotics. The other half of the antibiotics story. Anim. Nutr. Health, 29 : 4-8.

Porubcan, R.S. (1991a) Reduction of ammonia nitrogen and nitrite in tanks of *Penaeus monodon* using floating biofilters containing processed diatomaceous earth media pre-inoculated with nitrifying bacteria. Program and Abstracts of the 22nd Annual Conference and Exposition, 16-20 June 1991, San Juan, Puerto Rico. World Aquaculture Society.

Porubcan, R.S. (1991b) Reduction in chemical oxygen demand and improvement in *Penaeus monodon* yield in ponds inoculated with aerobic Bacillus bacteria. Program and Abstracts of the 22nd Annual Conference and Exposition, 16-20 June 1991, San Juan, Puerto Rico. World Aquaculture Society.

Rao, A. V. (1999) Studies on some Ecological and Pathological aspects in shrimp farms of *Penaeus monodon* (Fabricius) at Vakapadu, Visakhapatnam District", Ph.D. Thesis. Andhra University, India.

Raskin, L., Capman, W. C., Sharp, R., Poulsen, L. K., Stahi, D. A. (1997) Molecular ecology of gastrointestinal ecosystems *In: (Eds. R.I. Mackie, B.A. With, R.E. Isaacson, Gastrointestinal Microbiology),* Vol. 2, Gastrointestinal Microbes and Host Interactions. Chapman & Hall Microbiology Series, International Thomson Publishing, New York, pp. 243-298.

Song, Y. L. and Huang, C.C. (2000) Application of Immunostimulants to Prevent Shrimp Diseases, Recent Advances in Marine biotechnology, Vol.5, Immunobiology and Pathology, 173-187.

Sugita, H., Hirose, Y., Matsuo, N., Deguchi, Y. (1998) Production of the antimicrobial substance by *Bacillus* sp. strain NM 12, an intestinal bacterium of Japanese coastal fish. Aquaculture 165, 269-280.

Timmermans, L. P. M. (1987) Early development and differentiation in fish. Sarsia, 72 : 331-339.

Vadstein, O. (1997) The use of immunostimulation in marine larviculture: possibilities and challenges. Aquaculture 155, 401-417.

Villamil, L., Figueras, A., Planas, M., Novoa, B. (2003) Control of *Vibrio alginolyticus* in *Artemia* culture by treatment with bacterial probiotics. Aquaculture, 219 : 43-56.

Wallner, G., Fuchs, B., Spring, S., Beisker, W., Amman, R. (1997) Flow sorting of micro-organisms for molecular analysis. Appl. Environ. Microbiol., 63 : 4223-4231.

CHAPTER 4

PROBIOTIC IN FOOD-OPPORTUNITIES

U.Sivakumar, S.Karthikeyan, K.R.Arun Kumar, G.Kalaichelvan and K.Ramasamy

Fermentation Lab, Tamil Nadu Agricultural University, Coimbatore—641 003 (T.N), India.

ABSTRACT

In prehistoric period, the only probiotic products such as milk fermented by lactic acid bacteria were used world wide with different names. After the introduction of probiotic concept, researchers gave more attention towards application of probiotics. Though many applications are claimed, some of them are proved with experimental evidence. Such applications can be of two broad categories.

1. Nutritional applications which include alleviation of lactose mal-digestion, improved digestion, vitamin synthesis, increased mineral absorption etc.

2. Clinical applications that includes prevention of types of diarrhoea, gastroenteritis, constipation, food allergy, immune mediated gastrointestinal disturbances and disorders and fast recovery from the radio-damage of intestinal mucosa etc.

These activities of probiotic strains are due to their antagonistic properties. Probiotics compete for adhesion sites and nutrients with other microbes in the niches. They antagonise other microbes by producing antimicrobial substances like organic acids, bacteriocins, bacteriocin-like substances, hydrogen peroxide, non-proteinaceous inhibitory metabolites like diacetyl, reuterin and other compounds. They also induce the host defence by inducing the production of antimicrobial proteins like defensins. Probiotics help in improving immune activity of host by improving barrier properties of mucosa, sampling and modulating production of cytokines. Other beneficial effects of probiotic cultures are hypolipidemic, hypocholesteremic effects. They are shown to exert anti-mutagenic, anti-carcinogenic and anti-oxidative effects on host. This paper, besides, narrating the beneficial effects of probiotics, their mechanisms for health benefits and prevention of diseases, products safety, evaluation and future prospects are also dealt.

Key Words : Probiotics, microorganisms, food and enzymes, beneficial effects on human beings

Introduction

Currently, there is huge interest in the use of foods which may exert a positive functional effect on our health. Two of these 'functional foods' are known as probiotics and prebiotics, both of which have a favourable effect on the 'good' bacteria that reside in our digestive systems, also known as our gut microflora. These 'good' bacteria live naturally in our intestines and are essential to good health having a number of positive effects, primarily helping our digestive systems work efficiently. We traditionally, view bacteria as being 'bad'; however, in reality, there are relatively only a small number of strains which are pathogenic and most microbes are harmless and contribute to well-being (Gibson, 2003).

The use of live microbial food supplements dates back to thousands of years. Fermented milks containing living micro-organisms were recorded in Old Testaments, Ramayana and Mahabharatha. In the past century, various micro-organisms were tested for their ability to prevent and cure diseases in animals and humans. Nearly a century ago, the longevity of Caucasians were attributed to their consumption of large quantitites of fermented milk containing lactobacilli (Metchnikoff, 1907). In the nineteenth century, Elie Metchnikoff working at the Pasteur Institute in Paris, played a key role in the process. He had long recorded the microflora of the lower gut as having an adverse effect on the health of the human adult. First he advocated the surgical removal of the colon (Fuller, 1992). Later, he was convinced to less invasive therapy after learning that Bulgarian peasants, who ingested large amounts of soured milks, also lived to a ripe old age (Fuller, 1992).

Metchnikoff was convinced that the human colon acted as a reservoir of proteolytic bacteria that generated substances toxic to the host's tissues. He advocated the consumption of milk products that had undergone a lactic fermentation. Milk fermented by bacteria producing lactic acid, did not provide a suitable medium for proteolytic microbes. Colonization of the colon by bacteria capable of producing lactic acid fermentation, it was reasoned, would inhibit the proliferation of putrefactive microbes in that site, thus protecting the host from toxins produced by proteolytic bacteria (Tannock, 1983). Metchnikoff was the first one who quoted the relationship between consumption of fermented milks and long life (Fuller, 1992). Metchnikoff's work can be regarded as the birth of probiotics, *i.e.* microbes ingested with the aim of promoting good health. The habit was given added support by the publication in 1911 of a book "The Bacillus of Long life" by Louden Douglas. In that book, the connection between fermented milks and longevity was reinforced (Fuller, 1992).

Around 1920, *L. acidophilus* was isolated and named as Scavano strain by Yale University investigators. The Yale University investigators were leaders in the new fields of *Lactobacillus* and fermented milk products (Gorbach, 1996).

Lactobacillus GG was one of the first and best scientifically documented probiotic strains with significant health effects. After this discovery, probiotic bacteria and their health benefits became focus of intensive research in European Union, Japan and United States. Modification of intestinal microflora and barrier effects by probiotic bacteria or probiotic substances can form a basis for special dietary and clinical foods for prevention and treatment of intestinal disturbances (Salminen *et al.*, 1998). Now, probiotic products are available not only for human use but for animals and birds too.

The ready availability of antibiotics in the 1950s resulted in their widespread use as therapeutic agents and growth stimulants for farm animals. The use of antibiotics as growth promoters resulted in the development of resistant populations of bacteria, which made subsequent therapeutic use of antibiotics difficult. After banning antibiotics in food, research in probiotics for animals took a development. Nurmi concept led to the development of probiotics for chickens and other birds.

Definitions for Probiotic

The word 'probiotic' was first used by Lilley and Stillwell in 1965 to describe 'substance secreted by one micro-organism which stimulated the growth of another'. It thus meant the exact opposite of antibiotic, which is defined as substances secreted by one micro-organism that inhibit the growth of another. In 1971, Sperti referred probiotics as "tissue extracts which stimulated microbial growth". In 1974, Parker gave a new definition to probiotic as 'organisms and substances which contribute to intestinal microbial balance'. He was the first to include cells of organisms as probiotics. Nevertheless, the inclusion of 'substances' gave it a wider usage which could include antibiotics, vitamins and other substances.

A proper shape of the definition was given by Fuller in 1989. He redefined probiotics as a live microbial food supplements that beneficially affect the host animal by improving its intestinal microbial balance. Hose and Sozzi (1991), further explained the word 'balance' as the balance between the beneficial bacteria and the harmful bacteria. Though, Fuller's definition is frequently used, it has been expanded to cover examples of treatment with live bacteria, yeast and other organisms. According to Salminen *et al.* (1998), 'Probiotics are commonly defined as viable micro-organisms such as bacteria or yeast that exhibit a beneficial effect on the health of the host when they are ingested'.

"Pure or mixed cultures of live micro-organisms that applied to animals and humans, benefit the host by improving properties of indigenous microflora" was definition given by Havenaar and Huis in't Veld in 1992, to cover live microbial cultures that are not administered by mouth and that do not exert their effect through the intestinal microflora. This definition includes probiotic products containing live micro-organisms (e.g. freeze dried cell or in a fermented product) and improve the health status of the host by exerting beneficial effects in the mouth or gastrointestinal tract (taken as capsules or food), in the upper respiratory tract (administered as an aerosol to protect against *Salmonella* infections in chicks) or in the urogenital tract (local applications) (Havenaar *et al.*, 1992).

In all these definitions, probiotics are understood to exert some beneficial effects. Such effects are attributed to biochemical, physiological and antimicrobial effects as well as competitive exclusion in the intestinal and urogenital tract *etc.* (Goldin and Gorbach, 1992). Prebiotics and synbiotics are terms related to probiotics. 'A prebiotic is defined as a non-digestable food ingredient that beneficially affects the host by selectively stimulating the growth and/or activity of one or limited number of bacteria in the colon, and thus improves host health'. Synbiotic is a combination of a probiotic and prebiotic that beneficially affects the host by improving the survival and implantation of live microbial dietary supplements in the gastrointestinal tract through selective stimulation of growth and/or through metabolic activation of one or a limited number of health promoting bacteria, and thus improving host welfare (Gibson and Roberfroid, 1995). Of late, the Joint FAO/WHO Working Group Report on Drafting guidelines for the Evaluation of Probiotics in Food (2002) defined probiotics as livè micro-organisms that confer a beneficial physiological effect on the host when administered in adequate amounts. So, probiotics are generally live preparations of individual or mixtures of bacterial species which, when ingested, have a beneficial effect on the consumer. The claimed health benefits of probiotic- containing foods include improving general gut hèalth, lowering blood cholesterol and improving the body's natural defenses. Moreover, there is growing evidence that probiotics may be useful in managing irritable bowel syndrome, lactose intolerance, chronic liver disease, pancreatitis and even certain forms of cancer. Furthermore, the increasing use of probiotic products both in humans and livestock can reduce the requirement of antibiotics.

Intestine and Gut microflora

The intestine contains millions of bacteria, many of them friendly and essential for good health. They aid in digestion, stimulate the immune system and inhibit the growth of food-poisoning and disease-causing bacteria. However, because some bacteria are not good for us, keeping the vaious kinds of bacteria in balance plays an important role in our general health and well-being. Healthy people have a good balance of intestinal bacteria. Source of intestinal micro-organisms in the wild and domesticated animal is shown in fig. 1.

The gastrointestinal tract normally contains large numbers of bacteria (natural microflora) including $10^{7\text{-}8}$ organisms in the oral cavity (predominantly *Streptococcus, Veillonella, Neisseria*), $10^{2\text{-}3}$ organisms in the stomach and small intestine (*Lactobacillus, Streptococcus*), and $10^{10\text{-}11}$ organisms in the large intestine and colon (*Bifidobacterium, Bacteroides, Eubacterium, Peptostreptococcus*).

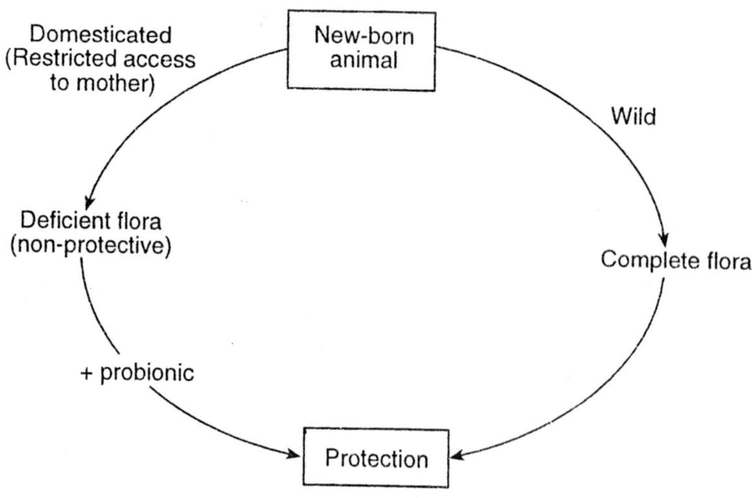

Fig. 1 : Source of intestinal microorganisms

Micro-organisms in the right side (proximal) of the colon grow at a fast rate due to a good supply of nutrients, resulting in short chain fatty acid (SCFA) production thereby causing a decrease in pH. In contrast, in the left side (distal) colon bacteria grow more slowly due to a restricted supply of nutrients and therefore the pH often approaches neutrality. Several factors (such as poor diet, stress, antibiotics, aging) can tip the scales in the direction of the pathogenic bacteria and perhaps probiotic bacteria can help in this situation.

Factors affecting the human colonic microflora

(I) Host factors

Acids (hydrochloric, lactic and fatty acids)

Enzymes (gastric, pancreatic and epithelial)

Bile salts

Peristalsis

Local immune mechanisms

Villous contraction/epithelial turnover

Redox potential

(II) Microbial factors

Bacterial interactions (antagonistic, symbiotic or synergistic)

Traits of the micro-organism (e.g. growth requirements and adhesion properties)

(III) Environmental factors

Diet

Drugs

Probiotic Bacteria and Products

The most frequently used species of intestinal origin are : *Bifidobacterium bifidum, Bifidobacterium infantis, L. casei, L. acidophilus, Enterococcus faecium and Propionibacterium freudenreichii* sub sp. *shermanii*. A more comprehensive list of bacteria that have been used either in dairy or pharmaceutical probiotic preparations is presented.

Strains currently used in probiotic products are :

***Lactobacillus* sp.**	***Bifidobacterium* sp.**
L. acidophilus	*B. fidum*
L. plantarum	*B. longum*

L. casei subsp. rhamnosus

L. brevis

L. delbrueckii subsp. bulgaricus

L. helveticus

L.fermentum

B. infantis

B. breve

B. adolescentis

Others

Streptococcus salivarius subsp. thermophilus

Lactococcus lactis sub sp. lactis and cremoris

Enterococcus faecium

Leuconostoc mesenteroides sub sp. dextranium

Propionibacterium freudenreichii

Pediococcus acidilactici

Saccharomyces boulardii

Escherichia coli

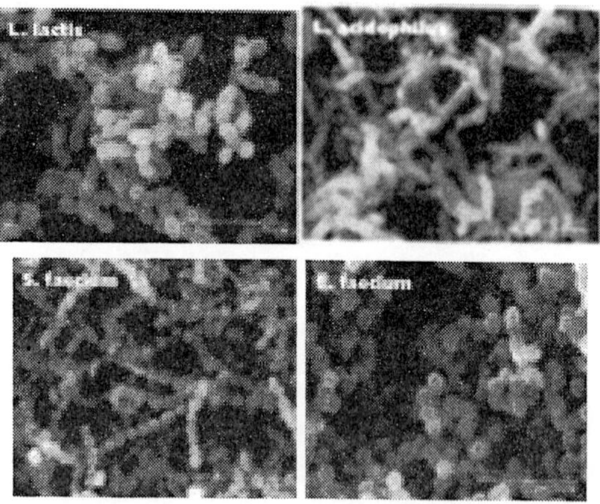

Fig. 2: Scaning electron micrographs of certain probiotic bacteria

Bifidobacteria are the predominant intestinal organisms of breast-fed infants. Since, Tissier advocated in 1906 the administration of *B. bifidum* to infants suffering from *diarrhoea*, there has been tremendous commercial interest in the incorporation of bifidobacteria in baby foods and also in the developement of 'bifidus milk' containing growth-promoting bifidogenic factors such as lactulose and fructo-oligosaccharides. Products that have been developed for the baby-food market include dried preparations such as 'Lactana-B' and 'Femilact'. Lactana-B (developed in Germany in 1964) contains lactulose and viable *B. bifidum.* Femilact (developed in Czechoslovakia in 1984) contains *B. bifidum, L. acidophilus* and *Pediococcus acidilactici*.

The following are the descriptions of various bacteria and yeasts used as probiotics:

Bifidobacterium

Bifidobacteria are normal inhabitants of the human and animal colon. Newborns, especially those that are breast-fed, are colonized with bifidobacteria within days after birth. Bifidobacteria were first isolated from the feces of breast-fed infants. The population of these bacteria in the colon appears to be relatively stable until advanced age when it appears to decline. The bifidobacteria population is influenced by a number of factors, including diet, antibiotics and stress. Bifidobacteria are gram-positive anaerobes non-motile, non-spore forming and catalase-negative. They have various shapes, including short, curved rods, club-shaped rods and bifurcated Y-shaped rods. Their name is derived from the observation that they often exist in a Y-shaped or bifid form. The guanine and cytosine content of their DNA is between 54 mol% and 67 mol%. They are saccharolytic organisms that produce acetic and lactic acids without generation of CO_2, except during degradation of gluconate. They are also classified as lactic acid bacteria (LAB). To date, 30 species of bifidobacteria have been isolated. Bifidobacteria used as probiotics include *Bifidobacterium adolescentis, Bifidobacterium bifidum, Bifidobacterium animalis, Bifidobacterium thermophilum, Bifidobacterium breve, Bifidobacterium longum, Bifidobacterium infantis* and *Bifidobacterium lactis*. Specific strains of bifidobacteria used as probiotics include *Bifidobacterium breve* strain Yakult, *Bifidobacterium breve* RO7O, *Bifidobacterium lactis* Bb12, *Bifidobacterium longum* RO23, *Bifidobacterium bifidum* RO71, *Bifidobacterium infantis* RO33, *Bifidobacterium longum* BB536 and *Bifidobacterium longum* SBT-2928.

Lactobacillus

Lactobacilli are normal inhabitants of the human intestine and vagina. Lactobacilli are gram-positive facultative anaerobes. They are non-spore forming and non-flagellated rod or coccobacilli. The guanine and cytosine content of their DNA is between 32 mol% and 51 mol%. They are either aerotolerant or anaerobic and strictly fermentative. In the homofermentative case, glucose is fermented predominantly to lactic acid. Lactobacilli are also classified as lactic acid bacteria (LAB). To date, 56 species of the genus *Lactobacillus* have been identified. Lactobacilli used as probiotics include *Lactobacillus acidophilus, Lactobacillus brevis, Lactobacillus bulgaricus, Lactobacillus casei, Lactobacillus cellobiosus, Lactobacillus crispatus, Lactobacillus curvatus, Lactobacillus fermentum, Lactobacillus* GG *(Lactobacillus rhamnosus* or *Lactobacillus casei* subspecies *rhamnosus), Lactobacillus gasseri, Lactobacillus johnsonii, Lactobacillus plantarum* and *Lactobacillus salivarus. Lactobacillus plantarum* 299v strain originates from sour dough. *Lactobacillus plantarum* itself is of human origin. Other probiotic strains of *Lactobacillus* are *Lactobacillus acidophilus* BG2FO4, *Lactobacillus acidophilus* INT-9, *Lactobacillus plantarum* ST31, *Lactobacillus reuteri,*

Lactobacillus johnsonii LA1, *Lactobacillus acidophilus* NCFB 1748, *Lactobacillus casei Shirota, Lactobacillus acidophilus* NCFM, *Lactobacillus acidophilus* DDS-1, *Lactobacillus delbrueckii* subspecies *delbrueckii*, *Lactobacillus delbrueckii* subspecies *bulgaricus* type 2038, *Lactobacillus acidophilus* SBT-2062, *Lactobacillus brevis, Lactobacillus salivarius* UCC 118 and *Lactobacillus paracasei* subsp *paracasei* F19.

Lactococcus

Lactococci are gram-positive facultative anaerobes. They are also classified as lactic acid bacteria (LAB). *Lactococcus lactis* (formerly known as *Streptococcus lactis*) is found in dairy products and is commonly responsible for the souring of milk. Lactococci that are used or are being developed as probiotics include *Lactococcus lactis, Lactococcus lactis* subspecies *cremoris (Streptococcus cremoris), Lactococcus lactis* subspecies *lactis* NCDO 712, *Lactococcus lactis* subspecies *lactis* NIAI 527, *Lactococcus lactis* subspecies *lactis* NIAI 1061, *Lactococcus lactis* subspecies *lactis* biovar diacetylactis NIAI 8 W and *Lactococcus lactis* subspecies *lactis* biovar diacetylactis ATCC 13675.

Saccharomyces

Saccharomyces belongs to the yeast family. The principal probiotic yeast is *Saccharomyces boulardii. Saccharomyces boulardii* is also known as *Saccharomyces cerevisiae* Hansen CBS 5296 and *S. boulardii.* is normally a non-pathogenic yeast, which has been used to treat *diarrhoea* associated with antibiotic use.

Streptococcus thermophilus

Streptococcus thermophilus is a gram-positive facultative anaerobe. It is a cytochrome-, oxidase- and catalase- negative organism, nonmotile, non-spore forming and homo-fermentative. This species is an alpha-hemolytic variant of the *viridans* group. It is also classified as a lactic acid bacteria (LAB). *Steptococcus thermophilus* is found in milk and milk products. It is a probiotic and used in the production of yogurt. *Streptococcus salivarus* subspecies *thermophilus* type 1131 is another probiotic strain.

Enterococcus

Enterococci are gram-positive, facultative anaerobic cocci of the Streptococcaceae family. They are spherical to ovoid and occur in pairs or short chains. Enterococci are catalase-negative, non-spore forming and usually nonmotile. Enterococci are part of the intestinal microflora of humans and animals. *Enterococcus faecium* SF68 is a probiotic strain that has been used in the management of diarrhoeal illnesses.

Table 1 : Commercial products containing probiotic bacteria

Product	**Country of origin**	**Probiotic bacteria**
Dairy products Acidophilus milk	Many countries	*L. acidophilus*
Bifidus milk	Many countries	*B. bifidum or B. longum*
ACO-yoghurt	Switzerland	*S. thermophilus; L. bulgaricus; L. acidophilus*
Cultura AB-yoghurt	Denmark	*L. acidophilus; B. bifidum*
Biogarde	Germany	*L. acidophilus; B. bifidum; S. thermophilus*
Bifighurt	Germany	*B..longum; S. thermophilus*

Contd.

Gefilac	Finland	*L. casei* subsp. *rhamnosus*
Yakult	Japan	*L. casei*
Biokys	Czechoslov-akia	*B. bifidum; L. acidophilus; P. acidilactici*
Ofilus	France	*L. bulgaricus; L. acidophilus; S. thermophilus; B. bifidum and/or B. longum*
Pharmaceutical preparations Infloran Berna	Switzerland	*L. acidophilus; B. infantis*
Euga-Lein	Germany	*Bifidobacterium spp.*
Lactopriv	Germany	*Bifidobacterium spp.*
Ominiflora	Germany	*L. acidophilus; B. longum; E. coli*
Synerlac	France	*L. acidophilus; B.bifidum; L. bulgaricus*
Lactana-B	Germany	*Bifidobacterium spp.*
Bacelac	India	*L. acidophilus*
Ozolab DT	India	*L. sporogenes*
ViBact	India	*L. sporogenes, Bacillus mesentricus, Clostridium butyricum, Streptococcus faecalis*

Many products of dairy origin containing probiotic bacteria are in the market (Table 1). These include sour cream, ice cream, buttermilk, yoghurt, powdered milk and frozen desserts. The probiotic culture may be added during fermentation with normal yoghurt starters, to the final fermented product, or to the fresh product before shipment. For example, 'Cultura' (made in Denmark) is made by fermenting protein-enriched whole milk with *B. bifidum* and *L. acidophilus*, has a shelf life of at least 20 days after production. Also, a drink is obtained by fermenting partially skimmed milk. 'Biogarde', which is produced by more than 45 dairies in Germany, is made by fermenting milk with

Streptococcus thermophilus, B.bifidum and *L. acidophilus.* Biogarde is used in the manufacture of other products such as buttermilk, sauces, breakfast cereal, ice cream and beverages. Two dairy products (yoghurt and a fruit-flavoured fermented whey drink) made with lactobacillus GG ('Gefilac') have been reported to have clinically proven health benefits in intestinal disturbances such as infantile *diarrhoea* caused by rotavirus and traveller's *diarrhoea*, and in the treatment of side effects of antibiotic therapy.

In addition to food products containing probiotic bacteria, there are various health food adjuncts and pharmaceutical preparations containing probiotics on the market. These are generally encapsulated freeze-dried bacterial preparations, and are used in the treatment of gastrointestinal disturbances (diarrhoea, or the side effects of antibiotic or radiation therapy), constipation and certain hepatic diseases.

Selection of functional Probiotics

The perceived desirable traits for selection of functional probiotics are many. Table 2. presents a list of selection criteria. All the detailed criteria fall into four basic categories – Appropriateness, Technological suitability, Competitiveness, Performance and functionality.

Many of these criteria are sensibly based on extensive experience with microbial selection, propagation (viability, technological suitability), and safe use of lactic acid bacteria in foods (non-pathogenic; non-toxic, genetically stable, normal inhabitant of target species, viability). However, those selection criteria that address competitiveness and performance issues remain controversial because the underlying mechanisms by which probiotics exert functional roles *in vivo* are not generally understood. Three excellent examples of these are (i) Bile tolerance and bile salt hydrolase (BSH) activity (ii) Adjuvant activity and immunostimulation and (iii) Antimicrobials. Understanding the mechanisms of how these criteria impact in vivo functionality will present one of the major scientific challenges for probiotics in the coming decade. It has become clear that defining and screening important genetic traits, which confer functional probiotic activities, offers considerable promise to attack the insurmountable task of selecting superior strains and building combinations that can elicit unique or multiple effects.

Table 2 : Selection criteria for probiotic strains

a. Appropriateness	
(i)	Accurate taxonomic identification
(ii)	Normal inhabitant of the species targeted; human origin for human probiotics
(iii)	Nontoxic, nonpathogenic, GRAS status
b. Technological suitability	
(iv)	Amenable to mass production and storage; adequate growth, recovery, concentration, freezing, dehydration, storage, and distribution
(v)	Viability at high populations (preferred at $10^6 - 10^6$)
(vi)	Stability of desired characteristics during culture preparation, storage, and delivery
(vii)	Provides desirable organoleptic qualities (or no undesirable qualities) when included in foods or fermentation process
(viii)	Genetically stable
(ix)	Genetically amenable
c. Competitiveness	
(x)	Capable of survival, proliferation, and metabolic activity at the target site in vivo
(xi)	Resistant to bile
(xii)	Resistant to acid

Contd.

(*xiii*)	Able to compete with the normal microflora, including the same or closely related species; potentially resistant to bacteriocins, acid, and other antimicrobials produced by residing microflora
(*xiv*)	Adherence and colonization potential preferred
d. Performance and functionality	
(*xv*)	Able to exert one or more clinically documented health benefits (*e.g.* lactose tolerance)
(*xvi*)	Antagonistic toward pathogenic/carcinogenic bacteria
(*xvii*)	Production of antimicrobial substances (bacteriocins, hydrogen peroxide, organic acids, or other inhibitory compounds)
(*xviii*)	Immunostimulatory
(*xix*)	Antimutagenic
(*xx*)	Anticarcinogenic
(*xxi*)	Production of bioactive compounds (enzymes, vaccines, peptides)

Source : Klaenhammer and Kullen, (1999)

Characteristics of a Good Probiotic

Although, positive results were demonstrated experimentally with probiotics, the results obtained in field trials have been variable. One of the problems is the nature of the phenomenon itself. It is bound to be variable because it operates by reversing stress factors, which may or may not be present. This is particularly likely in the case of growth stimulation when the organism responsible for the growth depression is not always present in the gut. This sort of variation occurs with antibiotics and other chemical growth promoters. The practical consequence is that probiotics may work on one farm but not on another and in one occasion but not in the next. The other problem which has occurred with some of the commercial preparations is poor quality control.

Features of a good probiotic are :

- Should be a strain which is capable of exerting a beneficial effect on the host animal, e.g. increased growth or resistance to disease
- Should be non-pathogenic and non-toxic
- Should be present as viable cells, preferably in large numbers, although we do not know the minimum effective dose
- Should be capable of surviving and metabolizing in the gut environment, e.g. resistant to low pH and organic acids
- Should be stable and capable of remaining viable for long periods under storage and field conditions

Such a probiotic with all these features has considerable advantages over antibacterial supplements currently in use. They do not induce resistance to antibiotics, which will compromise therapy. They are not toxic and therefore will not produce undesirable side effects when being fed and, in the case of food animals, will not produce toxic residues in the carcass. They may stimulate immunity, whereas the immune status remains unaffected by antibiotics. They may be cheaper; at present we do not know what the minimum effective dose. Establishing minimal dosing will reduce the cost since at this moment probiotics tend to consist of number of bacteria with continuous feeding.

Although, the production of a probiotic, which would permanently colonize the gut and thus would require only a limited administration, would be ideal, it may be difficult to achieve practically. Certainly, in the adult where the intestinal *Lactobacillus* niche is already occupied by naturally acquired strains, permanent establishment of a probiotic strain would require their displacement and would be difficult to induce. Even in neonates, where the flora is in a more unstable condition, it would be necessary to administer the probiotic very soon after birth if it is to compete with the acquired flora. It would seem, therefore, that the best method of administration is continuous feeding. This would ensure that the probiotic is always present in the gut in large numbers and is able to metabolize and produce its probiotic effect. However, even with continuous administration, it is important to select strains with the maximum ability to survive in the intestine, and attention to colonization factors such as epithelial adhesion and growth rate is still recommended.

Mechanisms of protective action of Probiotic cultures

The three essential mechanisms proposed for the mode of action of probiotic is furnished below :

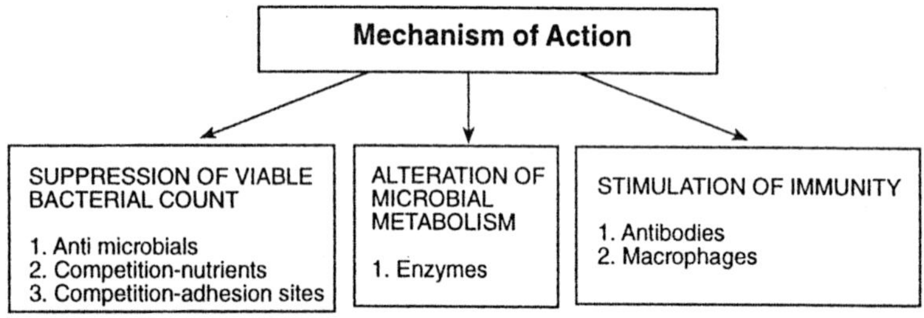

It is evident that all the probiotic strains protect the host by one or many mechanisms. These protective mechanisms are responsible for their health beneficial effects. These mechanisms can be classified into *three* categories.

1. Immunomodulation
2. Antagonism

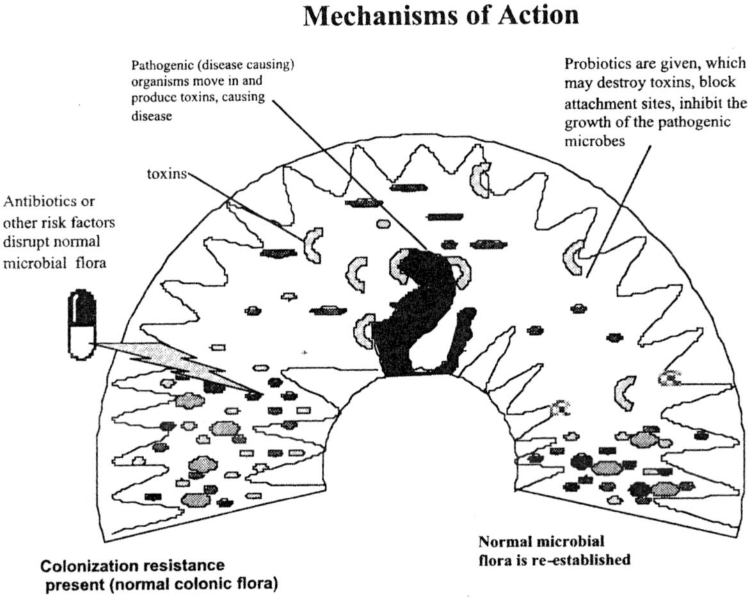

Fig. 3 : Other protective mechanisms which includes antitumorogenic, hypocholesteremic, antimut-agenic, anticarcinogenic properties, etc.

Immunomodulation

Probiotics can prevent and promote recovery from infectious diseases, particularly intestinal infections such as *diarrhoea*. Immunological mechanisms behind this may include:

1. Stimulation of specific antibody secreting cell response (Kaila *et al.*, 1992).
2. Enhancement of pathogen phagocytosis and (Schiffrin *et al.*, 1997).
3. Modification of cytokine production (Miettinen *et al.*, 1996).

Consequently, probiotic bacteria may influence both specific and non specific immune responses. Dietary antigens, such as protein in cow's milk can induce inflammation in food hypersensitive subjects. Probiotic reverses the increased intestinal permeability induced by antigens.

Stimulation of Antibody Secretion

The intestinal mucosa is the most important barrier against pathogenic micro-organisms and dietary antigens. The predominant mucosal IgA, particularly secretary IgA, has an essential role in this defense system, providing an immunological barrier. The role of IgA is to eliminate invading pathogens from the gastrointestinal tract. IgA acts in the first line of defense against penetration of microbes and other antigens. Unlike IgG and IgM, it does not induce powerful inflammatory reactions (Oksanen *et al.,* 1990). In a study conducted by Malin *et al.* (1996) oral bacteriotherapy with *Lactobacillus* GG appeared to act as an immunotherapeutic agent promoting the antigen specific IgA immune response, especially in Crohn's disease and irrespective of its activity possibly indicating an intrinsic defect in the immunological barrier of the gut. *Lactobacillus* GG promoted the antigen specific IgA immune response and shortened the duration of the diarrhoeal phase. *Lactobacillus* GG enhanced the gut immune response, normalized the gut permeability to macromolecules, and simultaneously, increased the proportional transport of macromolecules across Peyer's patches. Therefore, the immune system enhancing effect, particularly in the IgA class, may be explained by the role of Peyer's patches as the major IgA inductive site of the body (Doe, 1989).

Modification of Cytokine Production

The augmentation of the immune response by probiotic bacteria seems to be similar to that of cholera toxin (Mowat, 1987). Therefore, as adherence of food antigen with cholera toxin B may enhance the intestinal immune response (Van-der Heijden *et al.*, 1991). A similar phenomenon may also occur in adherence with gut-associated lymphoid tissue (GALT) and may therefore directly affect leukocytes by stimulating phagocytosis (De Simone *et al.*, 1987). Probiotic bacteria may also hydrolyse milk proteins, producing bioactive peptides which may trigger gut immune responses (Sutas *et al*, 1996). Alternatively, probiotic bacteria can further induce receptor expression. For example, interferon gamma (IFN-γ) can increase the expression of FcγRI and FcγRIII but no alter the expression of FcαRII, CR1 and CR3. Oral allergen challenge reduces production of IFN-γ by peripheral blood mononuclear cells in hypersensitive subjects (Buckle and Hogg, 1989). Lipopolysaccharide (LPS) of gram negative bacteria induces production of proinflammatory cytokines, tumour necrosis factor alpha (TNP-α) and interleukin-6 (IL-6), as well as IL-10, which is known to inhibit the synthesis of the former two cytokines (Maxer *et al.*, 1991). These cytokines contribute to defense mechanisms of the host in response to bacterial colonization or invasion, and when secreted in excess, they may induce immunopathological disorders. Many component of gram positive bacterial cell wall for example, capsular polysaccharides, peptidoglycans and lipoteichoic acids, have been shown to be involved in cytokine induction (Miettihen *et al.*, 1996). Several live LAB (*Bifidobacterium longum, B. animals, Lactobacillus paracascei, L. acidophilus, Lactobacillus* GG, *Lactococcus lactis, Lactobacillus plantarum*) are potent inducers of TNF-α release from human peripheral are potent induces of in quantities even high than those induced with LPS.

Anti-inflammatory Effects

In health, mucosal processing of external antigens modifies most of their antigenic properties, thus rending them particularly inert to the systemic immunity (Peng *et al.*, 1990). Environmental factors particularly those associated with mucosal inflammation, may interfere with this particular phenomenon of hyporesponsiveness, the result being induction of a systemic immune response to some antigens (Macpherson *et al.*, 1996). This is hypothesized to perpetuate the damage to the mucosa and impairment of mucosal barrier function. Disruption of the mucosal barrier and the consequent increase in permeability to bystander antigens in the gut implies a positive feed back on mucosal inflammation (Wyatt *et al.*, 1993). An increase in the uptake of luminal antigens stimulate the immune compartment of the gut mucosal barrier and induces the local secretion of proinflamnatory cytokines can directly disrupt the tight junctional integrity and thus have the potential cause a leakage of macromolecules in their intact forms (Maramo *et al.*, 1993). *Lactobacillus* GG administered together with unhydrolysed antigen increased the transport of degraded macromolecules, but when administered with hydrolysed antigen, it reduced the transport. Increased degraded macromolecular absorption, after administered *Lactobacillus* GG with unhydrolysed antigen, was not associated with dysfunction of the gut mucosa or tissue damage, since absorption of intact protein was not increased and electrical parameters remain unchanged. Increased absorption may have pronounced the immuno-stimulatory effect of probiotics as an adjuvant, adherence of adjuvant to the epithelium enhances antigen absorption and antigen specific immune responses to antigen encountered (Lyke and Holmgran, 1986). Administrated degraded macromolecular absorption was seen in nude mice, where the limiting step is not intracellular degradation but rather occurs at the lamina membrane (Heman *et al.*, 1986). The contrary effect of *Lactobacillus* GG on absorption with hydrolysed antigen may be due to reduced antigensity. Lack of antigen stimulus, the complex of hydrolysed antigen and *Lactobacillus* GG may have similar immunomodulatory activity in dietary peptides generated *using Lactobacillus GG i. e.* the down regulation of proliferative (Sutas *et al.*, 1996) and interleukin-4 producing immune responsiveness. This kind of suppressive effect of *Lactobacillus* GG may be a useful tool for alleviating hyper responsiveness in the gut.

Lactobacillus GG reverses increased intestinal permeability induced by cow milk in suckling rats (Isolauri *et al.*, 1993). Results of experiments of Pelto *et al.*, (1998) demonstrate that milk increased the expression of phaocytosis receptors (CR-1, CR-3, FcγRI and IgαR) while *Lactobacillus* GG prevented the increase in milk hypersensitive subjects. This indicates that the probiotic bacteria can down regulate the milk induced immunoinflammatory effect seen as increased receptor expression when consuming milk with *Lactobacillus* GG. Therefore, probiotic bacteria can modulate the immune response differently in healthy and hypersensitive subjects (Pelto *et al.*, 1998).

Beneficial Effects of Probiotic Bacteria

The history recording the probiotic properties of live microbial (particularly lactic acid bacteria) food supplements is long. As early as 76 BC, the Roman historian Plinio advocated the use of fermented milk in the treatment of various pathological forms of gastrointestinal infections.

Metchnikoff first provided a scientific explanation of the beneficial effects of lactic acid bacteria present in yoghurts at the beginning of this century (Metchnikoff, 1907). He proposed that the consumption of large quantities of yoghurts containing *Lactobacillus* sp. would result in the replacement of toxin-producing bacteria normally present in the intestine, and would thus result in longevity-without-ageing – better health and increased lifespan (Fuller, 1992). Similarly, Tissier (1906) recommended the administration of bifidobacteria to infants suffering from diarrhoea, believing that the bifidobacteria displace putrefactive bacteria responsible for gastric upset, while re-establishing themselves as the dominant intestinal micro-organism. During the past 80 years, there have been numerous claims advocating therapeutic benefits of probiotics in humans. These claimed health and nutritional effects are listed below:

Beneficial Effects

- Maintenance of normal intestinal and urogenital microflora
- Alleviation of lactose intolerance
- Reduction of serum cholesterol levels
- Anticarcinogenic activity
- Stimulation of the immune system
- Improved nutritional value of food

Therapeutic Applications

- Prevention of urogenital infection
- Alleviation of constipation
- Protection against traveller's *diarrhoea*
- Prevention of infantile *diarrhoea*

- Reduction of antibiotic-induced *diarrhoea*
- Prevention of hypercholesterolaemia
- Protection from colon/bladder cancer
- Reduction of side effects of hepatic encephalopathy
- Aid in cases of hypo- and hyperchlorohydria
- Prevention of osteoporosis

Inhibition of Microbial Pathogens

It is now recognized that probiotic bacteria such as the bifidobacteria and lactobacilli have antimicrobial properties. These have been demonstrated against a variety of undesirable enteric pathogenic bacteria such as *Salmonella typhimurium, Clostridium difficile, Campylobacter jejuni, Escherichia coli* and *Shigella* spp. There are also many reports in the literature demonstrating that lactobacilli can provide an important defense against urogenital colonization by pathogens such as *Gardnerella vaginalis, Bacteroides bivius, Candida albicans and Chlamydia trachomatis.* Mechanisms responsible for the inhabitation of pathogens include; competition for nutrients and adhesion sites; the production of inhibitory metabolites such as organic acids, hydrogen peroxide, bacteriocins and deconjugated bile acids; and stimulation of the immune system (Juven *et al.*, 1991). Consumption/application of probiotic bacteria has been reported to be effective in the treatment of a number of disorders such as infantile, traveller's and antibiotic-induced *diarrhoea* and candida vaginitis. The systemic treatment of acquired immuno deficiency syndrome (AIDS) patients with orally administered live lactobacilli has also been proposed (Klebanoff and Coombs, 1991). It has been suggested that hydrogen peroxide produced by lactobacilli acts either alone or in conjunction with a halide and peroxidase of leukocytic or uterine origin to inactivate the human immunodeficiency virus (HIV).

Alleviation of Lactose Intolerance

Lactose intolerance can be due to either a congenital deficiency of the intestinal mucosal enzyme β-galactosidase (lactase; EC 3.2.1.23) or a reduction in lactase activity during intestinal disorders such as gastroenteritis. Lactose intolerance is very prevalent in populations of Oriental or African ancestry. After consuming unfermented dairy products, lactose-intolerant individuals suffer from flatulence, abdominal pain and diarrhoea as a result of the action of the colonic bacteria on undigested lactose. These people may often avoid milk and other dairy products because of the intolerance symptoms, and therefore may consume suboptimal levels of calcium. However, there is evidence that fermented dairy products such as yoghurt and lactose-intolerant individuals can digest fermented milks more easily. This improved tolerance is believed to be due to partial fermentation of lactose by the starter bacteria before ingestion, and release/production of lactose in the intestine by the culture consumed in the fermented product. Furthermore, it has also been suggested that lactase synthesis in the gut mucosa may be induced by live bacteria ingested in cultured products (IDF, 1991).

Reduction in Serum Cholesterol Levels

Results from several clinical studies indicate a positive correlation between elevated serum cholesterol levels and increased incidence of coronary heart disease. However, literature reports of a reduction in serum cholesterol levels following the consumption of skim milk and fermented products have been variable and controversial. It has been suggested that any hypocholesterolaemic effect of these products may be due to the presence in fermented milk or organic acids such as uric, orotic and hydroxymethylglutaric acids, which inhibit cholesterol synthesis. Furthermore, using *in vitro* studies, Gilliland *et al.* (1985) has shown that, in the presence of bile and under anaerobic conditions, some strains of lactobacilli and bifidobacteria can assimilate cholesterol from laboratory media. Gilliland has also suggested that deconjugation of bile acids by probiotic bacteria results in less efficient absorption of cholesterol from the intestine. From the experimental data available, it is not possible to make definite conclusions as to whether cultured products have a hypocholesterolaemic effect because many of the studies involved too few subjects and did not establish whether the subjects had elevated or normal serum cholesterol levels at the beginning of the study. Although there are, some positive experimental animal studies attributing cholesterol-lowering characteristics to probiotic strains (Gilliland *et al.* (1985), results cannot be transferred to humans since there are differences in the regulation of cholesterol metabolism among animals and humans. Considerable research is still required to establish whether there is a definite link between the consumption of probiotic bacteria and reduced serum cholesterol levels.

Anticarcinogenic Activity

In several countries, a positive correlation between dietary factors such as the consumption of red meat and fat and the incidence of colon cancer has been established. However, Finland is an exception, with a high per capita fat consumption and a relatively low incidence of large-bowel cancer. The Finnish people consume large amounts of dairy products, especially yoghurt, and it has been suggested that they harbour high numbers of intestinal lactobacilli that have anticarcinogenic properties (Goldin and Gorbah, 1984).

Some of the mechanisms by which large-bowel cancer may be prevented are:

- metabolic conversion/degradation/absorption of carcinogenic compounds;
- reduction in levels of faecal bacterial enzymes;
- stimulation of the immune system.

Lactic acid bacteria (LAB) have been reported to inactivate dietary and intestinally generated mutagenic compounds such as azo dyes and *N*-nitrosamines. It has been proposed that peptidoglycan and polysaccharide components of bacterial cell walls have strong binding affinities for mutagens. LAB can also mediate anticarcinogenic activities by reducing the activity of faecal bacterial enzymes such as nitroreductase(s), azoreductase(s) and β-glucuronidase (EC 3.2.1.31), which have the ability to convert procarcinogens to carcinogens in the colon (Goldin and Gorbah, 1984).

Enhancement of the Immune System

Stimulation of the immune system by LAB has also been reported to play an important role in the suppression of tumour formation in animal models. This activity is predominantly macrophage mediated. Although, there is evidence to suggest that LAB reduce the risk of cancer in animal models, there is insufficient clinical evidence available to extrapolate these results to humans. However, there are literature reports of the disappearance of colon carcinomas during prolonged periods of *Lactobacillus acidophilus* therapy (Sellers, 1991).

In recent years, a number of in *vivo* and in *vitro* studies have investigated the interaction between dietary LAB and immunocompetence. By increasing the host's specific and non-specific immune mechanisms, LAB can protect the host against infection by enteric pathogens, and tumour development. The factors reported to be involved in stimulation of the immune system by probiotic bacteria are macrophage and lymphocyte activation, enhanced immunoglobulin A (IgA) levels and production of γ-interferon.

Perdigon and Alvarez (1992), observed an increase in macrophage and lymphocytic activity in mice fed lactobacilli. The stimulated macrophages exhibited increased secretion of lysosomal hydrolases, plasminogen activator, collagenase and lysozyme. Recently, Tomioka *et al.* (1992) showed that intraperitoneal injection of mice with *Lactobacillus casei* YIT 0003 either 2 or 13 days before infection with *Listeria monocytogenes* protected against the infection. However, injection with attenuated *Streptococcus pyogenes* OK-432 or Bacillus Calmette-Guerin (BCG) did not. The authors suggested that the lack of protective activity by BCG or OK-432 might have been due to inability to induce recruitment of blood monocyte-derived macrophages to the site of infection.

Experiments with human subjects fed with a diet supplement with lyophilized lactobacilli and plain yoghurt showed a progressive increase in blood levels of natural killer cells and γ-interferon relative to those of control group (fed skim milk with no lactobacilli). Earlier, in *vitro* experiments with human peripheral blood lymphocytes showed that the addition of small quantities (a few microlitres) of yoghurt containing lactobacilli increased the production of γ-interferon by T lymphocytes three-to fourfold relative to control lymphocytes (heat-treated yoghurt added). Since, immunoglobulin E (IgE) synthesis is antagonized by γ-interferon, which is a cytokine with anti-infective and immunomodulating properties, it has recently been suggested that yoghurt consumption can boost the antiallergic response.

Improved Nutritional Value in Food

The nutritional benefits of probiotics have been mostly studied in milk products fermented with lactobacilli. These products have a lower lactose content and higher levels of free amino acids and certain vitamins than products fermented by other means, and often contain the more easily metabolized (+)-L form of lactic acid. Lactobacilli and bifidobacteria have been reported to produce folic acid, niacin, thiamine, riboflavin, pyridoxine and vitamin K. There is still considerable controversy as to whether fermented dairy products increase the bioavailability of minerals such as calcium, zinc, iron, manganese, copper and phosphorus. Recker *et al.* (1988), showed that there was no difference in calcium absorption when ten healthy post menopausal women were fed either supplementary yoghurt or whole milk. It has been suggested that a lowering of the gastric pH following the consumption of fermented products improves mineral absorption by the host.

In summary, claims have been made regarding the effectiveness of probiotic bacteria in the treatment of a number of disorders. However, it must be concluded that there is still not adequate and consistent scientific evidence to substantiate some of the proposed health benefits of probiotic bacteria incorporated into commercial products. This has been due to poorly designed experimental studies, inadequate statistical analysis of the results, poor choice of probiotic strain(s), and poor quality control of culture and product.

Clinical Applications of Probiotics

1. Lactose Malabsorption

Alleviation of lactose intolerance has been reviewed in earlier sections.

2. Intestinal Flora in Infants and Probiotics

Breast-feeding infants are protected by probiotics from infectious diseases. Multiple mechanisms can explain such protection. However, given the fact that the cellular and humoral components of human milk may have an effect in modulating the composition of the intestinal flora, a fair amount of attention has been given to the differences in intestinal flora between breast-fed and bottle-fed children. Although, there are wide individual and population variations, bifidobacteria generally constitute a significant component of normal intestinal flora in breast-fed infants. Some factors in breast milk that may enhance the selective growth of bifidobacteria include the presence of N-acetylglucosamine, glucose, lactoferrin, galactose, and fructose, and other not as well-described bifidogenic factors (McKeller and Moddler, 1989). Breast-feeding can also affect the occurrence and virulence of colonizing pathogens. Thus, though the mechanisms have yet to be fully elucidated, it appears that a combination of increased bifidobacterial counts and decreased concentrations of other enterobacterial counts and luminal host factors may play a role in protecting premature babies and newborns from diarrhoeal disease.

Modification of the intestinal flora by increasing the predominance of specific nonpathogenic bacteria would seem a reasonable means of attaining a prophylactic or therapeutic effect against enteropathogens. *Lactobacillus* GG can colonize the gut of premature infants, but had little effect on enterobacteria, yeasts, or staphylococci in small observational studies. A recent trial documented a reduction of necrotizing enterocolitis in a population of premature newborns given a supplement of *Lactobacillus* GG daily compared with historical control subjects. Prospective studies examining this possible application are in progress.

3. Diarrhoea

(i) Clostridium difficile diarrhaea

Several investigators reported the resolution of recurrent *Clostridium difficile* diarrhoea with oral supplementation of *Lactobacillus* GG and *Saccharomyces boulardii* in adults and children ; other *Lactobacillus* strains did not have the same effect. Prospective controlled studies are needed to confirm the efficacy of probiotics for this application.

(ii) Traveler's diarrhoea

Lactobacillus GG was found to be effective in the prevention of traveler's diarrhoea in some studies but the effect may not be uniform or consistent, depending on the geographic area or populations studied. Other lactobacilli preparations have not produced any significant, positive results and *S. boulardii* may have only a marginal effect. The many variables and varied populations involved in these studies do not allow for any generalizations. Although, the evidence may suggest a protective effect, the variety of agents used, the difficulties involved with measuring compliance, and the lack of etiologic documentation of diarrhoea in several of these studies make forming recommendations or conclusions difficult.

(iii) Antibiotic-associated diarrhoea

Antibiotics can severely disrupt gut microbial ecology. Ingestion of a probiotic with a prescribed antibiotic can reduce the effect of such microbial alteration and any resulting changes in stool consistency and frequency. Several reports and more recently a few controlled studies, showed the efficacy of several agents in the management of non-*C. difficile,* antibiotic associated diarrhoea. Agents used included *Enterococcus faecium, L. acidophilus, L. bulgaricus* and

S. boulardii. In decreasing the changes in stool consistency and the duration of loose stools associated with antibiotic use.

(iv) Treatment of diarrhoeal disease in children

The best-established benefit of using probiotic agents has been in the management of acute pediatric diarrhoeal disease. Several large and well-controlled studies showed a significant decrease in the duration of diarrhoea in children who received *Lactobacillus* GG, either as a supplement or in fermented milk, early in the course of the condition (Guandalini *et al.*, 2000). In a large multicenter trial in which *Lactobacillus* GG was added to an oral rehydration solution and given to children during a diarrhoeal episode, there was also a significant reduction in the duration of illness; similar results were also observed with *Lactobacillus reuteri*. *Lactobacillus* GG was shown to be more effective when compared with *Lactobacillus rhamnosus* or a combination of *S. thermophilus* and *Lactobacillus delbruckii*.

In general, depending on the definitions used for diarrhoea and duration of illness, the use of probiotics during an episode resulted in a shortened course of illness of 1-3d, with varying decreases in purge. In addition, the efficacy appears to be greater in diarrhoea of viral etiology. The beneficial effect (as it refers to clinical indexes) was shown to be accompanied by a greater immunoglobulin A-antibody secreting response and less rotaviral shedding in children treated with these agents than in children treated with placebo.

(v) Prevention of diarrhoeal disease in children

The regular consumption of specific probiotic agents over extended periods of time (weeks to months) was shown to decrease the incidence of acute diarrhoea in several well-designed trials. Supplementation of an infant formula with bifidobacteria and *S. thermophilus* resulted in a decreased incidence of diarrhoeal disease and rotaviral shedding in a population of chronically hospitalized children over 17 months.

Bacteria compared with viruses

The fact that these orally ingested bacterial agents show a prophylactic and therapeutic effect against intestinal viruses suggests that this effect is most likely mediated through the stimulation of gut-associated lymphoid tissue, which results in an increased humoral antigenic response. The increased immunogenicity of rotavirus vaccine when administered with lactobacilli (Isolauri *et al.*, 1995) and the clinical observations of decreased rotaviral shedding in populations receiving probiotics, therapeutically or prophylactically, suggests this type of response.

These findings of improved antiviral response were also demonstrated in animals. Furthermore, passive protection against rotavirus-induced diarrhoea in mouse pups born to and nursed by dams fed *Bifidobacteria breve* was shown. This passive protection was associated with increased concentrations of antirotavirus immunoglobin A in the milk of the dams fed bifidobacteria and immunized orally with rotavirus. These observations suggest numerous potential applications for probiotic use, such as to heighten the immunologic response to vaccines, potentially decreasing the necessary number of boosters, and to further enhance the natural passive protection of breast feeding by maternal ingestion of probiotics.

Atopic disease

The traditional approach to food hypersensitivity, of which atopic disease is a manifestation, has been the elimination of potential protein offenders in the diet. This has lead to the use of elimination diets and to the development of increasingly elemental formulations for this purpose. Both approaches are difficult to implement and as costly. Intestinal microflora can contribute to the processing of food antigens in the gut and antibiotics could modify the structure of potential antigens reduce their immunogenicity. Moreover, gut microflora contribute to the generation of a T helper population amenable to oral tolerance induction (Isolauri, 2001). This offers a new therapeutic approach to the management of hypersensitive disorders. The results of the first prospective studies are now available, which show a significant improvement of atopic dermatitis in children and markers of allergic response in children and adults with the use of lactobacilli and bifidobacteria.

'Good' Bacteria Controls Pouchitis

Italian researchers are reporting that high doses of probiotics can help inflammation in the small intestine known as pouchitis. People who undergo surgery for ulcerative colitis may develop pouchitis. Symptoms can include more frequent and urgent bowel movements, abdominal cramping, bleeding and fever. Pouchitis usually responds well to treatment with antibiotics, but can recur in about two thirds of patients. The cause of pouchitis is unknown, but has been linked to low levels of bacteria normally found in the intestine.

Dr. Paolo Gionchetti and colleagues at the University of Bologna, Italy, tested probiotics as a treatment for pouchitis. A control group of twenty patients received a placebo, and another twenty patients with chronic pouchitis received probiotics. 85% of the probiotic group did not have symptoms during the 9 months of the study, but all 20 of the placebo group relapsed within 4 months. Within 4 months of stopping treatment, all 20 patients in the probiotic group relapsed. Gionchetti maintains that long-term probiotic use is safe.

Probiotic yoghurt for infant feeding

Breast milk is considered superior over other modified milk formulas due to its inherent properties and advantages. Technological innovations made in the commercial infant milk powder have not been able to meet the critical nutritional and physiological needs of infants (Thompkinson and Mathur, 1995). In the absence of nutritionally competent infant foods and inadequate production of breast milk, cultured milk products could be a suitable and practical substitute for infants owing to its nutritional and therapeutic properties.

Yoghurt, a cultured milk product is generally fermented with a mixture of two species, *Lactobacillus delbrueckii* subsp. *bulgaricus* and *Streptococcus thermophilus*. In recent years, yoghurt has become a popular vehicle for incorporating the probiotic species, *Lactobacillus acidophilus* (Hull *et al.,* 1984) and *Bifidobacterium bifidum* (Holcomb *et al.,* 1991). Yoghurt, being capable of restoring the normal lactic intestinal flora and inhibiting undesirable proteolytic organisms, has been recommended for infant nutrition. Yoghurt could be used for infant feeding owing to its higher calcium content in protein and higher calcium/sodium ratio as compared to Recommended Dietary Allowance value for infants in USA. Recently, researchers have made an attempt to develop probiotic yoghurt containing probiotic cultures like *Bifidobacterium bifidum* and other beneficial culture such as *Propionibacterium freudenreichii* sub sp. *shermanii* for feeding infants and children.

Dietic Characteristics of Cultures

Dietic characteristics of yoghurt cultures, *B. bifidum* and *P. freudenreichii* sub sp. *shermanii* which led to suggestions for their use as dietary supplements are highlighted below:

1. Yoghurt cultures and *B. bifidum* are known to retain

their viability through the digestive tract and thus can afford a means of implantation in the intestine.

2. *L. delbrueckii* subsp. *bulgaricus* and *S. thermophilus* are reported to produce substances, inhibitory to pathogens, the former organism being considerably stronger than the latter (Mel'nikova and Koreleva, 1974). Elaboration of bacteriocins or bacteriocin like compounds such as bifidin by *B. bifidum* (Anand *et al.*, 1984), and microgard by *P. fredudenreichii* subsp. *shermanii* (Al-Zoreky *et al.*, 1993), proved to be inhibitory towards undesirable micro-organisms of public health. Inhibition of coliforms, *Bacillus cereus, Shigella dysenteriae* and *Salmonella typhimurium* by antimicrobials elaborated by mixed cultures of yoghurt organisms, *B. bifidum* and *P. freudenreichii* subsp. *shermanii* have been observed by the authors.

3. Synthesis of niacin, folic acid and vitamin B12 by yoghurt cultures, vitamin B1, B6, folic acid by *B. bifidum* (Hamad.., 1966) and thiamine, vitamins B6, B12 and nicotinic acid by *P. freudenreichii* subsp. *shermanii* induce an improvement in the nutritional qualities of cultured milks.

4. Fermented milk containing both D(+) and D(-) lactic acid and both isomers improved the digestability of casein and retention of calcium in the intestine. Ballabriga *et al.* (1970) suggested that infants should be given only L (+) lactic acid to prevent acidosis. Yoghurt is reported to contain 47 – 60% L (+) lactic acid. However, in bifidobacteria-based fermented milks, the amount of desired L (+) lactic acid dominated to a level of 90%. Therefore, milk cultured with these cultures would be safe of infant feeding.

5. Proteolytic activity has been demonstrated by yoghurt cultures, B. *bifidum* and P. *freudenreichii* subsp. *shermanii*. Proteolysis induces an increase in free

amino acid content, improves the digestibility of proteins and absorption of calcium, phosphorus, magnesium and zinc.

6. Presence of galactosidase enzyme, responsible for hydrolyzing the naturally occurring (1-6) linked galactosidase in yoghurt cultures; *B. bifidum* and *P. freudenreichii* subsp. *shermanii* have been reported. A decline in lactose content and an increase in lactose activity due to β-galactosidase activity of starter cultures make fermented milk more suitable for lactose-intolerant infants.

7. Serum cholesterol levels are important for a public health standpoint because high levels are associated with a greater risk to cardiovascular disease. Hypocholesterolemic effect in yoghurt cultures and Bifidobacteria have been registered. Deeth and Tamime (1981), reported hypocholesterolemic effect of yoghurt is either due to presence of heat stable enzyme system or a bacterial metabolite, which is not present or present in low levels in milk.

Manufacture of Probiotic Yoghurt

A schematic diagram conceptualizing the procedure employed for the manufacture of probiotic yoghurt is shown:

Formulated milk was obtained by fortifying standard cowmilk (2.5% fat, 10.46% SNF) with 500 IU vitamin A, 80 IU vitamin D and 750 milligram vitamin E. Milk was sweetened by admixturing 12% sucrose as suggested by Misra and Kuila (1992). The milk was then heat treated at 95°C./30 min and cooled to 42 ±1°C for starter inoculation. Yoghurt-YH-3/ *B. bifidum* NDRI and *P. freudenreichii* subsp. *shermanii* MTCC 1371 were inoculated at 1% level, individually and incubated at 42±1°C for 4 hours to obtain probiotic yoghurt. Probiotic yoghurt retained all its desirable properties up to 7 days of storage at 8±1°C.

***IN VITRO* INTESTINAL MODEL**

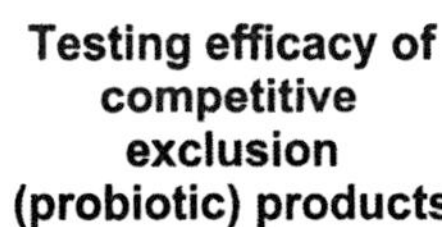

Chemical and Technological Characteristics

Freshly prepared probiotic yoghurt at 2.33% fat, 4.53% protein, 8.14% carbohydrate, 0.63% ash and 0.612% titrable acidity. The diacetyl and acetoin contains along with the volatile acids contribute to the characteristic aroma and flavour of the products. Both volatile acidity and diacetyle and acetoine contents of probiotic yoghurt increased and reached the peak values after 3 days followed by the decline after 7 days of storage (Table 3).

Nutritional Characteristics

Nutritional characteristics evaluated through rat bioassay technique revealed higher weight gains, feed efficiency ratio, protein efficiency ration and net protein ratio in rats receiving probiotic yoghurt than those fed with laboratory stock diet (Table 4). Improved digestion and absorption of amino acids have been reported as growth stimulating effect due to yoghurt. Better nutritional status of probiotic yoghurt was due to presence of easily assimilable proteins resulting from proteolytic activity of starter cultures. Thus, probiotics yoghurt is nutritionally adequate for feeding infants and children.

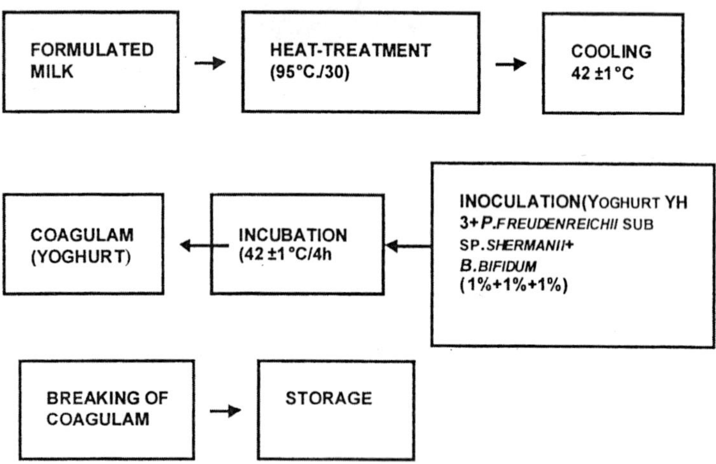

Table 3 : Technological and chemical characteristics of probiotic yoghurt

Characteristics	Days of storage at 8 ± 1°C		
	0	3	7
1. Titrable acidity (% lactic acid)	0.612	0.797	0.825
2. Volatile acidity(ml 0.1N NaOH/50 g curd)	2.0	2.9	2.5
3. Diacetyl and acetoin	40.0	101.0	43.0
4. Proteolytic activity (µg tyrosine/ml)	170	230	125
5. Lactic acid (µg/ml)	225	225	225
6. D-galactosidase activity(µg ONP/ml)	80	120	110
7. *Propionnibacteria* count X108 (cfu/ml)	2.10	2.17	2.26
8. *Lactobacilli* count X108 (cfu/ml)	1.83	2.05	1.96
9. *Bifidobacteria* count X108 (cfu/ml)	1.57	1.66	1.63

Contd.

Antibacterial activity (diameter of inh.zone in mm)			
11. *Solmonella typhimurium*	8.5	6.5	6.5
12. *Escherichia coli* 03	7.0	7.5	7.5
13. *Bacillus cereus*	9.0	9.0	8.0
14. *Shigella dysenteriae*	8.0	8.5	6.5

Table 4 : Nutritional characteristics of probiotic yoghurt

Nutritional attributes	**Types of feed**					
	Laboratory stock feed			**Probiotic yoghurt**		
	Intervals of analysis					
	10	**20**	**30**	**10**	**20**	**30**
Average gain in body weight (g)	20	2	6	31	16	8
Feeding efficiency ratio	0.066	0.008	0.018	0.074	0.024	0.019
Net protein ratio	0.006	0.002	0.002	4.22	1.43	1.36
Protein efficiency ratio	0.004	0.001	0.001	3.16	1.01	—

Safety of Probiotics

Most probiotics have been designated as GRAS based on their long history of use in food fermentation. However, there have been occasional reports of bacteraemia and endocarditis associated with Lactobacillus generally in severely immuno-compromised individuals. This prompted the suggestion that some type of surveillance be instituted for probiotics. Blood cultures isolated from bacteraemia patients in southern Finland were studied. A total of 5192 blood culture isolates were recovered from patients with bacteraemia. Twelve isolates contained lactobacilli. None of these lactobacilli corresponded to Lactobacillus or any other Lactobacillus used in dairy products or pharmaceutical preparations. These data found in bacteraemial infections and that the current probiotics lack a pathogenic potential (Saxelin *et al.*, 1996).

Negative results do not totally rule out the possibility that current or future probiotics can cause infection. However, to date the probiotics currently used appear to be safe (Goldin, 1998).

The safety of probiotics strains has been of prime importance and new guidelines have been developed. The significance of human origin has been debated recently, but most if not all current, successful strains are indicated to be of human origin. Similarly, the role of the ability to colonize the human gastrointestinal tract has been questioned. However, most current strains are reported to al least temporarily colonize humans as measured by faecal counts following ingestion. At least some strain specific properties are known to exist (Mattila-Sandholm and Salminen, 1998).

Before their incorporation into food and therapeutic products, probiotic strains of lactic acid bacteria should be carefully assessed and tested for the safety and efficacy of their proposed used. Yet, no general guidelines exist for the safety testing of probiotics. However, some publications have proposed outlines for safety assessment of lactic acid bacteria (Donohue and Salminen, 1996). Different aspects of the safety of probiotic bacteria can assessed using a panel of in vitro methods, animal models and human subjects with epidemiological studies to monitor extensive exposure via food products.

Members of the genus Lactobacillus are most commonly given safe or generally recognized as safe (GRAS) status, whereas members of the genera Streptococcus and Enterococcus contain many opportunistic pathogens.

Safety of Novel Probiotics

It cannot be assumed that these novel probiotic organisms share the historical safety of traditional strains. Before their incorporation into products, new strains should be carefully assessed and tested for the safety and efficacy of their proposed use. The following suggestions and recommendation have been proposed as suitable models and methods to test the safety of probiotic bacteria (Adams and Marteau, 1995).

1. Determine the intrinsic properties of bacteria and strains selected for probiotic use. For example: adhesion factors, antibiotic resistance, plasmid transfer, enzyme profiles.
2. Assess the effects of the metabolic products of the bacteria.
3. Assess the acute and sub acute toxicity of ingestion of extremely large amounts of the bacteria.
4. Estimate the in vitro infective properties of probiotic bacteria using cell lines and human intestinal mucus degradation.
5. Assess infectivity in animal models like immuno-compromised animals or lethally irradiated animals.
6. Determine the efficacy of ingested probiotic bacteria as measured by does response (minimum and maximum dose required, consequent health effects); assess the effects of massive probiotic doses on the composition of human intestinal microflora.
7. Carefully assess side effects during human volunteer studies and clinical studies in various disease specific states.
8. Epidemiological surveillance of people ingesting large amounts of newly introduced probiotic bacteria for infections.
9. The most rigorous safety testing along the above lines to be undertaken for genetically modified strains and strains derived from animals.

Table 5 : Acute toxicity of certain probiotic bacterial strains

Acute Toxicity of Probiotics	**LD50(g kg^{-1} body wt.)**
Streptococcus faecium AD1050 (HT)	>6.6
Streptococcus equinus (HT)	>6.39
Lactobacillus fermentum AD002 (HT)	>6.62
L. salivarius AD0001 (HT)	>6.47
Lactobacillus GG (ATCC 53103)	>6.00
L. helveticus	>6.00
L. bulgaricus	>6.00
Bifidobacterium longum	25

Table 6 : Classification of probiotic organisms and their safety status (Donohue and Salminen, 1996)

Organisms	**Infection Potential**
Lactobacillus	Mainly non-pathogens some Opportunistic infections (usually in immunocompromised patients
Lactococcus	Mainly non-pathogens
Leuconostoc	Mainly non-pathogens, some isolated case of infections
Streptococcus	Oral streptococci mainly non-pathogen (including Streptococcus thermophilus); some may cause opportunistic infections
Enterococcus	Some strains are opportunistic pathogens with haemolytic activity and antibiotic resistance.
Bifidobacterium	Mainly non-pathogens, some isolated cases of human infection.
Saccharomyces	Mainly non-pathogens, some isolated cases of human infection.

Guidelines for evaluation of Probiotic in food

Criteria and methodology for the evaluation of probiotics ad to identify and define what data need to be available to accurately substantiate health claims are given jointly by FAO/WHO working group meeting held at London, on 30.04.2002-01.05.2002

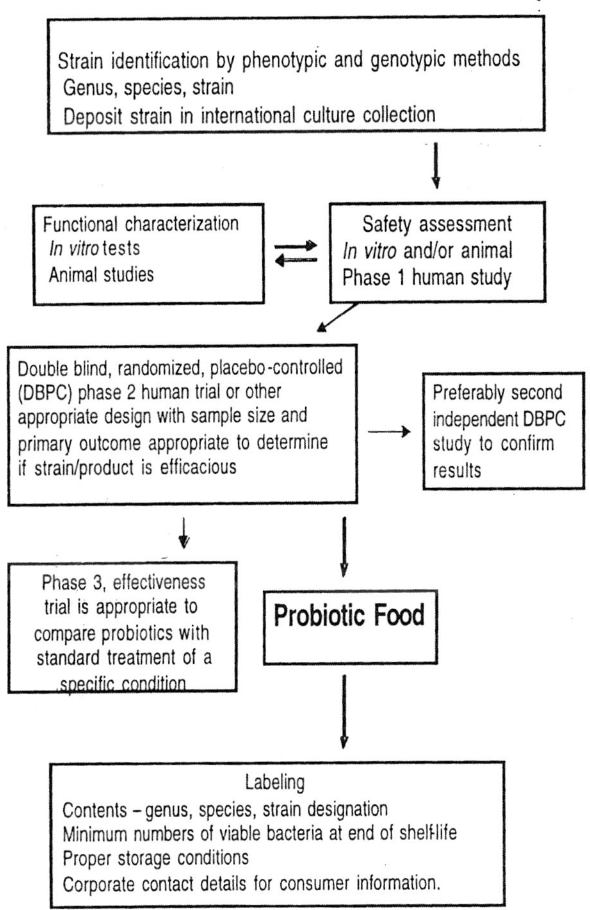

Future of Probiotics

Evidence has accumulated to support an important role for intestinal microflora in gastointestinal function in maintaining health and preventing diseases. Although, some effects are now well documented and acknowdeged, many questions still remain regarding the accuracy of studies used to claim such effects.

One of the main questions that needs to be answered is the anatomical site at which probiotic strains adhere (or would be) most efficient. For example, the colon contains 1011 bacteria per gram and this resident microflora cannot be out-numbered or modified under the influence of ingested probiotic micro-organisms. In this organ, the modulation of the composition of the microflora might be more easily obtained by ingesting prebiotics that will favour the production of antibacterial metabolites such as short-chain fatty acids (or) bacteriocins that are implicated in the control of new comers into a stable existing microflora (Gibson and Roberfroid, 1995).

Disturbances of the intestinal microflora may lead to other disturbances and dysfunctions of the gut. Thus, understaning the normal microflora with regard to their metabolic activities and influences on the immune and endocrine system remains a key area for future research. In this regard, Salminen *et al.*(1998), recommended that future research requires to cover the following areas:-

- Develop and validate robust methods that are applicable to large scale human studies of the intestinal micoflora.
- Characterize the normal microflora and their activities in healthy persons of all ages.
- Identify changes in composition of microflora and activity associated with major dysfunctions of the gut.

- Identify dietery factors that lead to changes in gut microflora and the mechanism that bring about improvement in health.

In spite of considerable progress in 'Probiotic' research over the last ten years, not all probiotic bacteria available in the market have a solid scientific record. If nutritional and health benefits are to be derived from products containing probiotic bacteria, it is imperative that we understand the mechanisms underlying these benefits.

The 'probiotic' concept will only be accepted by regulatoty bodies and authorities if these mechanisms are elucidated and appropriate selection criteria for probiotic micro-organisms are defined. It is clear that the selection of strains for probiotic use must be based on criteria, which are coherent with the claim the probiotic is used for (Holzapfel *et al.,* 1998).

Rational selection and validation of promising microbial strains should be based on evidence obtained in *in vitro* models with a reliable predicted value or function, and followed by studies in humans. Acceptance of the probiotic concept by both the scientific world and regularoty bodies must be based on evidence obtained from fundamental research with respect to the three M's: Mechanisms to verify, Models to certify and Methods to quantify especially controlled studies in humans (Holzapfel *et al.,* 1998).

Conclusions

There is a general agreement on the role of the gastrointestinal microflora in the health status of men and animals. Probiotic strains alter the properties of indigenous microflora by affecting the balance between pathogenic and harmful microbes and beneficial microbes. To give all the said beneficial effects, probiotic strains are required to have certain important characters such as: tolerance to gastric acidity and bile salts, resistance to digestive enzymes, adherence to enterocytes, production of antimicrobial substances and ability to grow and survive in the gastrointestinal environment. Above all these, for industrial production, they need very fast growth rate, survival in product and during processing of preparations. Besides these requirements, safety of these strains is very important. Though, there is no perfect system to quantify the level of safety of these strains, the important factors looked for on are: mucus non-degradative, non-toxigenic, non-infectious, less active or inactive in genetic material transfer.

Traditionally, the most popular food delivery systems for these cultures have been freshly fermented dairy foods, such as yogurts and fermented milks, as well as unfermented milks with cultures added. However, in the development of functional foods, the technological suitability of probiotic strains poses a serious challenge since their survival and viability may be adversely affected by processing conditions as well as by the product environment and storage conditions. Moreover, the bacterial strain is the core of the probiotic action; it is mandatory, for the future, to have a more in depth knowledge of each single strain used as probiotic supplementation. A second area of research will be the molecular ecology of the intestinal tract. Combining these two areas, we will have to obtain information on the molecular mechanisms used by probiotic bacteria to exert the observed beneficial effects, an area which is still a black hole.

Lots of health beneficial claims were made and many products also came to the market with probiotic strains. Still, there is no perfect procedure for quality and safety testing. Acceptance of probiotic concept by regulatory bodies will be possible only if the mechanisms of action of probiotics are well explained. Fundamental research has to be done to develop mechanisms to verify, models to certify and methods to quantify the beneficial effects of probiotics.

References

Adams, M.R. and Marteau, P. (1995) On the safety of lactic acid bacteria from food. Int. J. Food Microbiol. 27: 263-264.

Al-Zoreky, N, Ayres, J.W. and Sandline, W.E. (1993) Characterization of propionibacterial growth metabolites inhibitory for Gram negative bacteria. Cultured. Dairy Product J., 28:4-13.

Anand, S.K., Srinivasan, R.A. and Rao, L.K. (1984) Antibacterial activity associated with *Bifidobacterium bifidum* II. Cultured Dairy Products J., 2: 21-23.

Ballabriga A., Conde C., and Gallart-Catala A.(1970) Metabolic response of prematures to milk formulas with different lactic acid isomers or citric acid. Helv. Paediat Acta., 25: 25-34.

Buckle, A.M. and Hogg, N. (1989) The effect of IFN-gamma and colony stimulating factors on the expression of neutrophil cell membrane receptors. J. Immunol., 143: 2295-2301.

De Simone, C., Vesely, R. and Negri, R. (1987) Enhancement of immune response of murine Peyer's patches by a diet supplement with yoghurt. Immunopharmacol. Immunotoxicol., 9: 87-100.

Deeth, H.C. and Tamime, A.Y. (1981) Yoghurt: Nutritive and therapeutic aspects. J. Food. Protect. 44:78-86.

Doe, W.F. (1989) The intestinal immune system. Gut. 30: 1679-1685.

Donohue, D.C. and Salminen, S. (1996) Safety of probiotic bacteria. Asia Pacific J. Clin. Nutr., 5 : 25-28.

Fuller, R. (1989) Probiotics in man and animals. J. Appl. Bacteriol., 66: 365-378.

Fuller, R. (1992) History and development of probiotics. In *Probiotics: Scientific basis* (Ed. R. Fuller). Chapman and Hall, London. 1-8.

Gibson, G.R. (2003) Probiotics & Prebiotics and their Function. Functional Nutrition 2 (2): 11-13

Gibson, G.R. and Roberfroid, M.B. (1995) Dietery modulation of the human colonic microbiota: Introducing the concept of prebiotics. J. Nutr., 125:1401-1412.

Gilliland, S.E., Nelson, C.R. and Maxwell, C. (1985) Assimilation of cholesterol by Lactobacillus acidophilus. Appl. Eviron. Microbiol., 49:377-381.

Goldin, B.R. (1998) Health benefits of probiotics. British J. Nutr., 80: (Suppl.2)S203-207.

Goldin, B.R. and Gorbach, S. (1984) The effect of milk and *Lactobacillus* on human intestinal bacterial enzyme activity. Am. J. Clin. Nutr., 39(5): 756-761.

Goldin, B.R. and Gorbach, S.L. (1992) Probiotics for humans. In *Probiotics: Scientific Basis* (Ed. R. Fuller) Chapman and Hall, London. pp., 355-376.

Gorbach, S.L. (1996) The discovery of Lactobacillus GG. Nutr. Today Suppl. 31(6): 2S-4S.

Guandalini, S. Pendsabene L, Sikri, M.A. (2000) *Lactobacillus* GG administered in oral dehydration solution to children with acutediarrhoea: a multicenter European trial. J Pediatr Gastroenterol Nutr. 30:54-60.

Hamada, K. (1966) Preparation of lactic bacteria. *Studies on lactic acid bacteria*. (Ed. K. Kitchara) University of Tokyo Press, Tokyo, pp. 476.

Havenaar, R., and Huis in't Veld, J.H.J., (1992) Probiotics: a general view. In: *The Lactic Acid Bacteria,* (Ed. B.J.B. Wood)., Chapman and Hall, New York, pp., 209-224.

Havenaar, R., ten Brink, B. and Huis in't Veld, J.H.J.(1992) *Probiotics: The Scientific Basis* (Ed. R. Fuller), pp. 209-224, Chapman & Hall.

He-man, M., Crain-Denoyelle, M., Corthier, G. and Desjeux, J.F. (1986) Postnatal development of protein absorption in conventional and germ-freemice. Am. J. Physiol., 251: G326-G331.

Holcomb, J.E., Frank, J.F. and McGregor, J.U. (1991) Viability of *Lactobacillus acidophilus* and *B. bifidum* in soft serve frozen yoghurt. Cult. Dairy Prod. J., 26: 4-5.

Holzapfel, W.H., Haberer, P., Snel, J., Schillinger, U. and Huis in't veld. (1998) Overview of gut flora and probiotics. Int. J. Food Micrbiol., 41: 85-101.

Hose, H. and Sozzi, T. (1991) Probiotics, fact or fiction. J. Chemical Technol. Biotechnol., 51: 539-570.

International Dairy Federation. (1991) *Bull. Int. Dairy Fed.255*: 2-24.

Isolauri, E. (2001) Probiotics in human disease. Am J Clin Nutr., 73(suppl): 1142S-6S.

Isolauri, E., Majamaa. H., Arvola, T., Rantala, I., Virtanen, E. and Arvilommi, H. (1993) *Lactobacillus casei* strain GG reverses increased intestinal permeability induced by cow milk in suckling rats. Gastroenterol., 105: 1643-1650.

Juven, B.J., Meinersmann, R.J. and Stern, N.J. (1991) Antagonistic effects of lactobacilli and pediococci to control intestinal colonization by human enteropathogens in live poultry. J. Appl. Bacteriol. 70: 95-103.

Kaila, M., Isolauri, E., Soppi, E., Virtanen, E., Laine, S. and Arvilommi, H. (1992) Enhancement of the circulating antibody secreting cell response in human diarrhoea by a human Lactobacillus strain. Pediatr. Res., 32: 141-144.

Klaenhammer, T.R. and Kullen, M.J. (1999) Selection and design of Probiotics. Int. J. Food Microbiol. 50: 45-57.

Klebanoff, S.J. and Coombs, R.W. (1991) Exp. Med., 174: 289-292

Lycke, N. and Holmgren, J. (1986) Strong adjuvant properties of cholera toxin on gut mucosal immune responses to orally presented antigens. Immunol., 59: 301-308

Macpherson, A., Khoo, U.Y., Forgacs, I., Philpott-Howard, J. and Bjamason, I. (1996) Mucosal antibodies in inflammatory bowel disease are directed against intestinal bacterial. Gut. 38: 365-375.

Malin, M., Suomalainen, H., Saxelin, M. and Isolauri, E. (1996) Promotion of IgA immune response in patients with Crohn's disease by oral bacteriotherapy with *Lactobacillus GG.* Ann. Nutr. Metab., 40: 137-145.

Maramo, C.W., Laughlin, K.V., Russo, L.M., Peralta-soler, A. and Mullin, J.M. (1993) Long term effects of tumor necrosis factor on LCC-PK1 transepithelial resistance. J.Cell Physiol., 157-527.

Mattila-Sandholm, T. and Salminen, S. (1998) Up-to-date on probiotics in Europe. *Gastroenterology International.* 5(Suppl.1): 8-16.

Maxer, B.D., Renz, H. and Gelfand, E.W. (1991) An ELISA spot assay for quantification of human immunoglobulin secreting cells. J. Allergy Clin. Immunol., 88: 235-243.

McKeller, R.C. and Moddler, H.W. (1989) Metabolism of fructoligosaccharides by *Bifidobacterium* sp. Appl. Microbiol. Biotechnol. 31:537-41.

Metchnikoff, E.(1907) The Prolongation of Life. Heinemann.p.

Miettihen, M., Vuopio-Varkila, J. and Varkila, K(1996) Production of human tumor necrosis factor alpha, interleukin-6 and interleukin-10 is induced by lactic acid bacteria. Infect. Immunol., 64: 5403-5405.

Misra, A.K. and Kuila, R.K.(1992) Use of Bifidobacterium bifidum in the manufacture of bifidus milk and its antibacterial activity. *Lait.,* 72: 213-220.

Mowat, A.M. (1987) The regulation of immune responses to dietary protein antigens. Immunol. Today., 8: 93-98.

Okasanen, P.J., Salminen, S. and Saxelin, M. (1990) Prevention of traveler's diarrhoea by *Lactobacillus* GG. Ann. Med., 22: 53-56.

Peng, H.J., Tumer, M.W. and Strobel, S. (1990) The generation of a tolerogen after ingestion of ovalbumin is time dependent and unrelated to serum levels in immunoreactive antigen. Clin. Exp. Immunol. 81: 520-525.

Pelto, L., Isolauri, E., Lilius, E.M., Nuutila, J. and Salminen, S. 1998. Probiotic bacteria downregulate the milk induced inflammatory response in milk hypersensitive subjects but have an immunostimulatory effect in healthy subjects. Clin. Exp. Allerhy, 28: 1474-1479.

Perdigon, G and Alvarez, S. (1992) Bacterial interactions in the gut. In: *Probiotics: The Scientific Basis*, (Ed R. Fuller), Chapman and Hall, London, UK., pp., 146-180.

Recker , R.R., Bammi, A., Barger-Lux, J. and Heaney, R.P. (1988) Am. J. Clin. Nutr. 47: 93-95

Salminen, S., Bouley, C., Boutron-Raualt, M.C., Cummings, J.H., Franck, A. (1998) Functional food science and gastrointestinal physiology and function. Br. J. Nutr., 80(Suppl.1): S147-S171.

Saxelin, M., Rautelin, H. and Makela, P.H.(1996) Safety of commercial products with viable *Lactobacillus* strains.*Infectious* Diseases in Clinical Practice., 5: 331-335.

Schiffrin, E.J., Brassart, D., Servin, A.L., Rochat, F., Donnet-Hughes, A. (1997) Immune modulation of blood leukocytes in humans by lactic acid bacteria: Criteria for strain selection. Am. J. Clin. Nutr., 65: 515S-520S.

Sellers, R.L. (1991) In : *Therapeutic Properties of Fermented Milks* (Ed. R.K. Rokinron), Elsevier, pp. 81-116.

Sutas, Y., Soppi, E. and Kohonen, H. (1996) Suppression of lymphocyte proliferation *in vitro* by bovine casein hydrolyzed with *Lactobacillus casei* GG derived enzymes. J. Allergy Clin. Immunol., 98: 216-224.

Tannock, G.W. (1983) Effect of dietary and environmental stress on the gastrointestinal microbiota. In *Human intestinal microflora in health and disease* (Ed. D.J. Hentges) Academic Press, New York., pp., 517-539.

Thompkinson, D.K., and Mathur, B.N.(1995) Compositional developments for infant foods. Indian Food Industry, 14(2): 23-27.

Tomioka, H., Sato, K. and Saito, H. (1992) J. Med. Microbiol., 36: 112-116.

Tissier, H. (1906) C.R. Soc. Biol., 60: 359-361

Van der Heijden, P.J., Bianchi, A.T., Dol, M., Pals, J.W., Stok, W. and Bokhout, B.A. (1991) Manipulation of intestinal immune responses against ovalbulin by cholera toxin and its B sub unit in mice. Immuno., 72: 89-93.

Wyatt, J., Vogelsang, H., Hubl. W., Waldhoer, T. and Lochs, H. (1993) Intestinal permeability and the prediction of relapse in Crohn's disease. Lancet., 341: 1437-1439.

CHAPTER 5

MICROBIAL PHYTASES IN COMBATING ENVIRONMENTAL PHOSPHORUS POLLUTION

Parvinder Kaur, Bijender Singh and T. Satyanarayana

Department of Microbiology, University of Delhi, South Campus, Benito Juarez Road, New Delhi-110 021

ABSTRACT

Phosphorus (P) is critical to all life forms and has a number of indispensable biochemical roles as it forms the basic component of nucleic acids and ATP. This element does not, however, have a rapid global cycle like that of C or N. In nature, mobilization of P is slow. Furthermore, the low solubility of phosphates and their rapid transformation to insoluble forms make the element a growth-limiting nutrient, particularly in aquatic ecosystems. Nonetheless, human activities have intensified the release of P into aquatic ecosystems, which is commonly the main cause of eutrophication, the undesirable process that affects fresh and ocean waters in many parts of the world.

Microbes play important roles in the management of P pollution. Most plants contain 50-80 % of their phosphorus content in the form of phytate, the organic form of phosphorus. This is largely unavailable to monogastric animals as well as humans, due to the lack of adequate levels of phytases (phytate-hydrolyzing enzymes). This necessitates the need for supplementation of animal and human diets with inorganic P. The release of phytates as well as the excess P into the environment in turn leads to phosphorus pollution problems. Various microbes including fungi, yeasts and bacteria are known to produce phytases. As long-term prospects of inorganic-P supply and its environmental consequences remain a matter of concern, concerted efforts to exploit microbial phytases for the management of P in animal feeds, human foods and agriculture are in progress.

Key Words: Phytase, phytic acid, phosphorus, eutrophication.

Introduction

Phosphorus is a naturally occurring element that is an essential nutrient for all living organisms. It is a vital component of the genetic material i.e. DNA and RNA found in all cells, involved in energy transfer reactions in the form of ATP and ADP, and it is also present in phospholipids. Though, P is absent from amino acids, the building blocks of proteins and from carbohydrates, it is essential for their synthesis as ATP; the biospheric currency of metabolism is required. Thus, no life is possible without P (Deevey, 1970).

Phosphorus cycle is one of the slow biogeochemical cycles in nature, and thus it tends to be the growth-limiting element in most soils and aquatic systems. It stimulates plant growth and in most agricultural situations, additional phosphorus improves productivity. But in rivers, streams and lakes, phosphorus can cause problems by stimulating excess plant and algal growth leading to deterioration in the quality of the water (Bali and Satyanarayana, 2001; Kaur *et al.*, 2003).

Though, P is abundant in the soil, it is not in a readily available form for uptake by plants. Throughout the globe, 70 % of the cultivable land has either acid or alkaline soils (Lopez-Bucio *et al.*, 2000). In these soils, P tends to form compounds that are not readily available for plant use

(Marschner, 1995). As P can form a component of organic compounds and can interact with a number of divalent and trivalent cations in the soil, it becomes the least readily available nutrient in the rhizosphere (Raghothama, 2000). To compensate for the low availability of P in agricultural soils, fertilizers are often used and the excess P is washed off to water bodies, leading to eutrophication problems. Two other problems are associated with the use of P fertilizers: firstly they are prepared from non-renewable resources and secondly, a considerable proportion of the applied P fertilizer gets lost due to interactions in the soil (Vance, 2001).

Biogeochemical Cycling of Phosphorus

Phosphorus cycle is the slowest and the least extensively studied element cycle. Though, living organisms play crucial role in P cycle, it is not as dominated by biota as carbon and nitrogen cycles. The natural global P cycle is so slow that it appears to be more or less a one-way flow with mineralization, weathering, erosion and run-off transfer of soluble and particulate P into the ocean sediments acting as sinks. There may be minor interruptions in flow owing to temporary absorption of a small fraction of P by the living organisms. The recycling of the sedimented mineral depends on the slow reshaping of the earth's surface which re-exposes the P-containing rocks to weathering and denudation (Smil, 2000).

There is also a secondary land and water based cycling of organic P, which is relatively rapid. This is more or less a soil-plant cycle, whereby, phosphates present in soil are absorbed by plants and returned back via mineralization of plant litter, dead microbes and other biomass, thus again becoming available for absorption. However, some of it is also lost to sediments, thus entering the grand cycle. Very minute amounts of P are present in the atmosphere, where they enter as phosphine gas (PH_3) produced by microbial activity or due to wind erosion (Smil, 2000).

The role of biota in the P cycle constitutes microbial decomposition of dead biomass, solubilization of unavailable soil phosphates like phytates by various bacteria and fungi, and enhanced release of P from soil apatites by acid-producing mycorrhizal fungi (Walker & Syers, 1976; Frossard *et al.*, 1998). The ultimate sources of phosphorus in the environment are primary mineral rocks like rock phosphate/ apatite – $Ca_{10}(PO_4)_6X_2$ (X being F in fluorapatite, OH in hydroxyapatite, or Cl in chlorapatite) and others, which comprise about 95 % of all the P in the earth's crust (Smil, 2000). The P is usually present in poorly soluble form, and hence, unutilizable form in the rocks. The P released by weathering is very reactive in the environment and it is found in solution as one of the several orthophosphate forms (PO_4^{3-}, HPO_4^{2-} or $H_2PO_4^-$) depending on the acidity of the solution. If this is not quickly taken up by living organisms, it is rapidly fixed into insoluble forms by reacting with cations like Ca^{2+}, Fe^{2+}, Al^{3+}, Mn^{2+} etc. associated with soils (Khasawneh *et al.*, 1980). Fertilizers, plant residues and agricultural wastes also contribute to P addition to the soil. Organically bound P, mainly as phytates and in nucleic acids can constitute between 5-95 % of the element present in soils, while P in the soil solution of most agricultural soils ranges from <0.01 to 1 ppm. Thus, only a small fraction of P present in soils is available to plants. Phosphorus is removed or lost from the soil by crop uptake and removal, run-off and erosion and leaching. Hence, P is generally the growth-limiting nutrient in terrestrial systems and similarly in freshwater bodies, scarcity of P is the main factor limiting photosynthesis and thus growth. There are three major sources of phosphorus in water: a) mineral P released from weathering of phosphate minerals in river beds, b) organic and inorganic P in the runoff from lands adjacent to the surface waters, and c) organic P from animal feces and urine, or from wastewater treatment plants. It is the P from agricultural sources, which is considered to be an important threat to water quality (Smil, 2000).

Though, P is a scarce element in the biosphere, it is very abundant in vertebrate bodies as hydroxyapatite that makes upto 60 % of bone and 70 % of teeth; P is also present in fibrous collagen (Marieb, 1998).

Certain human activities have led to interference in the P cycle, and these include:

(*i*) Accelerated erosion, run-off and leaching due to the conversion of forests and grasslands into agricultural land that are more susceptible to erosion effects.

(*ii*) Recycling of organic wastes has led to greater concentration of P in the soils and thus higher wash-off and losses into the sediments.

(*iii*) Untreated human waste comprising sewage and P containing synthetic detergents are released into water bodies, adding to their P loads.

(*iv*) Enhanced application of inorganic P in fertilizers and feed of monogastric animals has further added to the P load of the soil and water that has resulted in rapid decline in the natural mineral reservoir.

Thus, anthropogenic role in mobilization of P has enhanced several-folds over the last few centuries. The best way to reduce the impact of P on the biosphere is to minimize the initial inputs in agriculture and animal husbandry. The use of well-tested management practices to lower the inputs of P-fertilizers and addition of phytases in feeds to enhance the utilization of phytates by monogastric animals are some of the areas with immense potential for research. Other areas include sewage treatment practices for removal of P before disposal into water-bodies and even recovery and reuse of P present in high concentrations in sewage and animal wastes in the form of calcium phosphate.

Environmental Impacts of Excess Phosphorus

In the past few decades, excessive usage of P-containing fertilizers in deficient agricultural soils as well as intensive usage of P in feeds for livestock rearing has led to severe environmental pollution problems due to build-up of phosphorus. The high P levels are a threat to the water quality due to run-off from such P-rich soils polluting the water bodies. As in unfertilized soils, P is often the limiting nutrient in aquatic systems as well and hence, its excess tends to promote the growth of algae and other aquatic microbes and plants. This in turn, leads to higher oxygen requirement and growth continues till either oxygen or phosphorus becomes limiting. Limitation of dissolved oxygen tends to affect the aerobic organisms in the ecosystem and leads to death of fish, and other aquatic fauna resulting in further increase in demand for oxygen required for decomposition, until it eventually depletes (anoxia). Blooms of blue-green algae produce neurotoxins and hepatotoxins, thus causing further death in aquatic ecosystems and serious public health problems (Martin and Cooke, 1994). This changes the entire system from aerobic to anaerobic leading to more unpleasant changes like surface scums, odors, and increased population of insect pests. Thus, phosphorus pollution leads to eutrophication, which is essentially the process of a lake's biological death due to depleted bioavailable oxygen.

One pound of P can result in the growth of 350-700 lbs of green algae. These include blooms of cyanobacteria (*Anabena*,

Aphanizomenon, *Oscillatoria*), siliceous algae (*Asterionella*, *Melosira*), scum-forming algae (*Phaeocystic pichetii*) and potentially toxic algae like *Dinophysis* and *Gonyaulux* (Smil, 2000). So, enrichment of surface waters with phosphorus is clearly undesirable. The harmful effects of eutrophication on economy includes increased water treatment costs to remove odor, turbidity and color, and negative impact on navigational and recreational activities like fishing, boating and swimming, and thus generally affecting tourism and property values. Reversal of eutrophication is a very tedious process requiring phosphorus reduction of 70-90 % to cause any significant change. As P is the key nutrient to manage water bodies as 'clean' or 'green', controlling the amount of phosphorus entering the aquatic systems is important to prevent excessive growth. In the US, the USEPA (United States Environmental Protection Agency) has recommended a limit of 0.05 ppm and 0.1 ppm of total P in lakes and flowing streams, respectively, as the critical values to control eutrophication (USEPA, 1986).

Methods to Reduce Phosphorus Load

To reduce the impact of P on the biosphere, the best strategy is to minimize the initial inputs. In agriculture, inputs of P fertilizers can be lowered by using various well-tested best management practices, while application of P fertilizers may be altogether omitted for several years on soils with high P content without affecting yields. Environmental management of P by using acid-producing bacteria to increase the solubility of phosphates in soils, or inoculation with suitable mycorrhizal fungi are other options being explored (Smil, 2000).

A major field of research interest for environmentalists these days is microbial phytases. The bulk of P in most cereals and legumes is organically bound in the form of phytic acid, and hence is indigestible by monogastric animals lacking the requisite enzyme i.e. phytase for the release phosphate. This necessitates the addition of inorganic P to animal diets resulting in large losses of P in excreted manure. Addition of phytase to enhance utilization of phytate could substantially reduce P excretion by monogastrics (Vohra and Satyanarayana, 2003; Satyanarayana *et al.*, 2004).

Phytic Acid, the Organic Phosphorus

The organic form of P is phytic acid, which is chemically myo-inositol hexakisdihydrogen phosphate (IP_6). It is an abundant plant constituent, comprising 1 to 5 % by weight of edible legumes, cereals, oil seeds and nuts. Phytic acid was discovered by Pfeffer as early as 1872 in the subcellular particles of wheat endosperm, but its structure was first described by Posternak in 1903. There are several terms associated with phytic acid; the term phytates refers to the salts of phytic acid, while phytins are the calcium/magnesium salts of phytic acid.

Phytates are the primary source of inositol and major storage form of phosphorous in the mature seeds of monocot as well as dicot plants (Maga *et al.*, 1982). The phytate-P constitutes 60-74% of total phosphorus in some cereals (Tyagi *et al.* 1998). Initially, it was speculated that phytin-P mainly acts as a storage product, large amount of which is stored in the seed, and the phosphorus is liberated on germination and incorporated into ATP (Wodzinski and Ullah, 1996). The later investigations, however, highlighted the importance of inositol phosphate intermediates in several cellular functions such as in transport as secondary messengers and in signal transduction in plant and animal cells (Sasakawa *et al.*, 1995), in ATP metabolism (Safrany *et al.*, 1999), as therapeutic agents in controlling cancer and preventing the effects of heart disease and diabetes (Potter, 1995; Shamsuddin and Vucenik, 1999); and further, they were also found to form important constituents of phospholipids in plant and animal tissues.

In monogastrics, the dietary phytate is mostly unutilizable due to lack/ low levels of phytase, thus necessitating supplementation with external utilizable P sources. This adds to the cost of feeds and at the same time, inorganic phosphate is a fast depleting source (Abelson, 1999). Moreover, phytate tends to act as an antinutrient in more than one ways. The molecular structure of phytic acid is the basis for its antinutritive effect, since the six reactive groups make it a strong chelating agent that binds cations such as Ca^{2+}, Mg^{2+}, Fe^{2+}. At gastrointestinal pH, stable and insoluble metal phytate complexes are formed, thus making the divalent cations unavailable for absorption in the intestinal tract of animals (Maga, 1982). Under acidic conditions, a negative influence of phytic acid on protein solubility and inhibition of digestive enzymes like trypsin, pepsin, amylase and others has also been reported (Harland and Morris, 1995).

The combined negative effect of phytate as an antinutrient and unavailable source of P makes it a very lucrative target for investigations to overcome these problems. Several methods such as soaking, fermentation, cooking and germination of seeds have been suggested to eliminate phytates from foods. Harsh treatments like autoclaving, chemical treatment, and ion-exchange techniques have also been attempted (Urbano *et al.*, 2000). These methods have a negative affect on the nutritional quality of the foodstuffs, and hence, the search for a mild but effective alternative approach led to the application of phytases.

Phytase, the Hydrolytic Enzyme

Phytases are acid phosphohydrolases that catalyse the sequential release of myo-inositol and inorganic phosphate along with several myo-inositol phosphate intermediates from phytic acid. Although, phytase was discovered by Suzuki and his coworkers in 1907, the catalytic sequence of the enzyme was established much later (Tomlinson and Ballou, 1962). Initially, two classes of phytases were classified by IUPAC-IUB in 1975, the 3-phytases (EC *3.1.3.8*) and 6-phytases (EC *3.1.3.26*), based on the position specificity of initial hydrolysis of phytates. The 3-phytases (myo-inositol hexakisphosphate 3-phosphohydrolase) are mainly of microbial origin and first attack the 3-position phosphate of the phytate (Johnson and Tate, 1969). On the other hand, 6-phytase (myo-inositol hexakisphosphate 6-phosphohydrolase) attacks the phosphate at 6-position of the phytate first (Cosgrove, 1969) and is typically observed in plants. Both, these groups belong to histidine acid phosphatases (HAP).

The number of enzymes described as phytases has increased over the years (Konietzny and Greiner, 2002). These enzymes exhibit variations in structure and catalytic mechanism. Consequently, the acid phytases have been categorized into histidine acid phytases (HAPhys), β-propeller phytases (BPP) and purple acid phosphatases (PAP) based on their active site motifs (Mullaney and Ullah, 2003). Among these HAPhys are the most widely studied phytases; they share a unique and conserved active site heptapeptide motif, RHGXRXP and the catalytically active dipeptide HD (Van Etten *et al.*, 1991). HAPhys have been isolated from filamentous fungi, bacteria, yeast as well as plants (Mullaney *et al.*, 2000). The recently discovered BPP class includes the phytases from *Bacillus subtilis* (Phy C) [Kerovuo *et al.*, 1998] and *B. amyloliquefaciens* (TS-Phy) [Kim *et al.*, 1998]. Their molecules display a basic structure similar to a β-propeller with 6 blades, and hence, the group was named so (Ha *et al.*, 2000). Another, recently isolated phytase, GmPhy (EC 3.1.3.2) from the cotyledons of germinating soybeans (Hegeman and Grabau, 2001) has the active site motif of a PAP. Apart from the acidic phytases, alkaline phytases (with optimal activity in alkaline pH range) are also widely distributed in nature (Liu *et al.*, 1998; Oh *et al.*, 2004). More focus, however, has been on acidic phytases due to their applicability in animal feeds and broader substrate specificity than those of alkaline phytases.

Sources

Phytases are widespread in nature, occurring in plants, micro-organisms, as well as in some animals.

(i) Plant Sources

Phytases have been reported from cereals, legumes and various kinds of seeds and pollen, where they are known to be induced during germination to provide the growing seedling with inorganic phosphorous (P_i) and the plant with concomitant free myo-inositol, an important growth factor (Reddy *et al.*, 1989). Suzuki *et al.* (1907), were the first to describe the enzymatic activity of rice bran phytase and to prepare an extract that retained its activity. It has since been reported in many plant species such as wheat, rye, barley, pea, bean, soybean, maize, rice, potato and other legumes or oil seeds. From seeds, both constitutive and germination-inducible phytases have been reported (Meyer *et al.*, 1971; Eastwood *et al.*, 1969). The enzyme is also associated with the root cell wall and mucilage in apical root zones. However, plant tissues contain very less amounts of phytases.

(ii) Animal Sources

In animal cells, the role of phytases is more obscure. Mc Collum and Hart (1908), first reported animal phytase from calf liver and blood. Since then, phytase has been detected in the blood of lower vertebrates like birds, reptiles, fishes and seaturtles (Rapaport *et al.*, 1941). A phytase like enzyme, multiple inositol polyphosphate phosphatase (MIPP) with the capacity to regulate cellular activities of phytic acid and IP_5 has been found in the erythrocytes and plasma of various species of vertebrates and in the mammalian small intestine (Craxton *et al.*, 1997; Chi *et al.*, 1999). The ruminant animals probably digest phytate through the action of phytase produced by microbial flora in their rumen, and the inorganic phosphates thus produced by the splitting of phytate are utilized by both the microbial flora and the ruminant host (Dvorakova, 1998, Yanke *et al.*, 1998).

(iii) Microbial Sources

Phytic acid is a very common compound in nature, hence various surveys have resulted in the discovery of many microbes with the ability to degrade it and to utilize the hydrolyzed phosphorous. A list of phytase-producing micro-organisms is presented in Table 1.

Table 1 : Phytase producing micro-organisms.

Micro-organisms	Enzyme Location	Reference
Bacteria		
Aerobacter aerogenes	IN	Greaves *et al.*, 1967
Bacillus amyloliquefaciens	EX	Ha *et al.*, 1999
B. subtilis	EX	Kerovou *et al.*, 1998
Enterobacter sp.4	EX	Yoon *et al.*, 1996

Contd.

Escherichia coli	IN	Greiner *et al.*, 1993
Klebsiella aerogenes	IN	Tambe *et al.*, 1994
Lactobacillus amylovorus	EX	Sreeramulu *et al.*, 1996
Mitsuokella multiacidus	IN	Yanke *et al.*, 1998
Pseudomonas sp.	IN	Irving and Cosgrove, 1971
Selenomonas ruminantium	IN	Yanke *et al.*, 1999
Filamentous Fungi		
A. niger syn A. ficuum	EX	Howson and Davis, 1983
A. niger	EX	Shieh and Ware, 1968
A. terreus	EX	Yamada *et al.*, 1968
Botrytis cinerea	EX	Howson and Davis, 1983
Emericella nidulans	EX	Pasamontes *et al.*, 1997
Geotrichum candidum	EX	Howson and Davis, 1983
Mucor piriformis	EX	Howson and Davis, 1983
Myceliophthora thermophila	EX	Mitchell *et al.*, 1997
Pencillium sp.	EX	Shieh and Ware, 1968
Rhizopus oligosporus	EX	Howson and Davis, 1983
Sporotrichum thermophile	EX	Ghosh, 1997
Talaromyces thermophilus	EX	Pasamontes *et al.*, 1997
Thermomyces lanuginosus	EX	Berka *et al.*, 1998
Yeasts		
Arxula adeninivorans	EX	Sano *et al.*, 1999
Candida intermedia	EX	Nakamura *et al.*, 2000
C. tropicalis	EX	Nakamura *et al.*, 2000
C. utilis	EX	Nakamura *et al.*, 2000
C. krusei	IN	Quan *et al.*, 2001
Clavispora lusitaniae	EX	Nakamura *et al.*, 2000

Contd.

Debaryomyces yamadae	EX	Nakamura *et al.*, 2000
Kluyveromyces lactis	EX	Nakamura *et al.*, 2000
Metchnikowia pulcherrima	EX	Nakamura *et al.*, 2000
Pichia anomala	EX	Nakamura *et al.*, 2000
P. anomala	IN	Vohra and Satyanarayana, 2001
P. fermentans	EX	Nakamura *et al.*, 2000
P. rhodanensis	EX	Nakamura *et al.*, 2000
Rhodotorula gracilis	IN	Bindu *et al.*, 1998
Saccharomyces cerevisiae	IN	Howson and Davis, 1983
S. cerevisiae	EX	Nakamura *et al.*, 2000
Schwanniomyces occidentalis	EX	Segueilha *et al.*, 1992

(*a*) **Bacteria:** Phytases have been reported from several bacteria, but not many have been used for their production due to low enzyme yields. Furthermore, their pH optimum in neutral to alkaline range precludes their use as feed additives (Wodzinski and Ullah, 1996). Bacterial phytases are mostly cell associated, with the exception of *Bacillus subtilis*, *B. amyloliquefaciens*, *Lactobacillus amylovorus*, and *Enterobacter* sp. 4, where they are extracellular (Konietzny and Greiner, 2004)

(*b*) **Fungi:** The incidence of phytase production is highest among Aspergilli, but species of *Mucor*, *Rhizopus* and *Penicillium* are also good producers (Wodzinski and Ullah, 1996). Fungal cultures are the most widely used for production of phytases due to high yields and acid tolerance, the desired prerequisites for animal feed supplementation (Pandey *et al.*, 2001; Liu *et al.*, 1998). Good fungal phytase producers have been mostly reported from ascomycetes, but recently phytases have been found in some basidiomycetous fungi: *Peniophora lycii, Agrocybe pediades, Ceriporia* sp. and *Trametes pubescens* (Lassen *et al.*, 2001). Phytases have also been reported from thermophilic fungi like *Thermomyces lanuginosus* (Berka *et al.*, 1998) and *Sporotrichum thermophile* (Ghosh, 1997) and from cultivated edible mushrooms (Callopy and Royse, 2004).

(c) Yeasts: Among yeasts, phytases have been reported in most of the cases like in *Schwanniomyces occidentalisi* (Segueilha *et al.*, 1992), *Saccharomyces cerevisiae* (Howson and Davis, 1983; Nayini and Markakis, 1984), *Arxula adeninivorans* (Sano *et al.*, 1999), *Pichia anomala* (Vohra and Satyanarayana, 2001), *Candida krusei* (Quan *et al.*, 2001), etc.

Production of Phytases

Commercially, both solid-state fermentations (SSF) and submerged fermentations (SmF) are employed for microbial phytase production (Pandey *et al.* 2001, Vohra and Satyanarayana, 2003, Vats and Banerjee 2004). The culture conditions, type of strain, nature of substrate and availability of nutrients are some of the critical factors that should be taken into consideration for selecting a particular production technique, as they affect the yield. The production of phytase from *Aspergillus ficuum* NRRL 3135 has been achieved by three different cultivation methods, namely, solid state (Bogar *et al.* 2003), semi-solid (Han *et al.* 1987) and submerged fermentations (Howson and Davis 1983; Ullah and Gibson 1987). A complete reduction of phytic acid content in canola meal by *A. niger* NRRL 3135 was reported using SSF (Nair and Duvnjak, 1990). Ebune and coworkers (1995) also studied phytase production by *A. ficuum* using canola meal and found that the age of inoculum had a profound affect on enzyme synthesis. Krishna and Nokes (2001), had studied the effect of culture conditions, particularly inoculum age, media composition and duration of SSF on phytase production by *A. niger*, while Bogar *et al.* (2003) had reported phytase production by *A. ficuum* NRRL 3135, *Mucor racemosus* NRRL 1994 and *Rhizopus oligosporus* NRRL 5905 on canola meal, cracked corn, soybean meal and wheat bran using SSF. The fermentation conditions of pH 5.3, 30 °C and 54.5 % moisture content for phytase production by *R. oligosporus* in SSF using canola oil cake with no additional nutrients were reported (Sabu *et al.,* 2002). Mayer *et al.,* (1999) developed a pilot scale process (2000 L) for the low cost production of phytase, using wild type phytase genes of *A. fumigatus* (Pasamontes *et al.* 1997) and *A. terreus* (Mitchell *et al.* 1997), transformed in *Hansula polymorpha*. Phytase production from *Aspergillus* sp. 5990 using SmF at 37 °C, pH 7.0 was studied by Kim *et al.* (1999a) and five-fold higher activity in liquid culture was obtained. Papagianni *et al.* (1999), investigated qualitative relationship between medium composition, morphology and phytase production by *A. niger*. *Mucor racemosus* NRRL 1994 secreted phytase on sesame oil cake but maximal production was achieved on coconut oil cake in solid-state fermentation (Bogar *et al.* 2003). Martin *et al.* (2003) had cloned and expressed phyA gene of *Aspergillus awamori* and *A. fumigatus* under the transcriptional control of glaA promoter of *A. awamori.* A Kex-2 protease cleavage site was inserted between native glucoamylase and heterologous protein for the efficient processing of chimeric proteins by endogenous Kex-2 protease. Maximum phytase expression (200 μml^{-1}) was achieved by SmF in 4 l batch fermentation.

The presence of high phosphate is known to repress the synthesis of acid phosphatases and phytases, while limiting phosphate conditions result in their expression (Vohra and

Satyanarayana 2003; Vats and Banerjee, 2004). *Aspergillus ficuum* produced highest amount of phytase, when the inorganic phosphorus content was in the range of 0.0001–0.005%, optimum being 0.4 mg/100 ml with 8% cornstarch (Shieh and Ware 1968). Han and Gallagher (1987) also confirmed that high phosphorus concentration inhibited phytase synthesis by *A. niger* NRRL 3135. Gibson (1987), further confirmed the effect of phosphorus level in the medium and compared the production from several sources, speculating that the phosphoester linkage in some starch sources may be more resistant to cleavage than others, resulting in low but steady supply of phosphorus. Vats and Banerjee (2002), also reported a sharp decline in phytase production by *A. niger* even at 0.05% phosphorus in the medium with absolute no production at 0.1% and above, indicating end product inhibition in phytase synthesis. Han *et al.* (1987) had observed a similar trend for phytase production by *A. ficuum* on semisolid substrate using soybean meal where 10 mg $P100g^{-1}$ substrate in the growth medium resulted in high phytase activity (82.5 μg^{-1} substrate) as compared to a control without added phosphate (8.0 μg^{-1} substrate) while higher phosphate levels inhibited phytase production. Kim *et al.* (1999a), showed that extracellular phytase production by *Aspergillus* sp. 5990 was maximum at lower phosphate concentration (50 mgl^{-1}), while at higher concentration (100 mgl^{-1}), enzyme production was greatly reduced.

Surfactants are known to increase cell membrane permeability, thus affecting enzyme secretion. Al-Asheh and Duvnjak (1994), studied the effect of surfactants such as Tween-80, Triton-X-100, Na-oleate on the phytase production and reduction of phytic acid content in canola meal by *Aspergillus carbonarius* in SSF. The phytase production increased in the presence of sodium oleate (1%) and Tween-80, suggesting alteration of the cell permeability, thus resulting in higher release of enzyme. Han and Gallagher (1987), tested the same surfactants for their affect on phytase production by *A. ficuum* in liquid medium and reported that besides dispersed growth of mycelium, there was also a resultant increase in phytase level of 1.3, 1.7 and 4.8 times, when 0.5% of Triton-X-100, Tween-80 and Na-oleate, respectively, were added to the medium. Similarly, Mandviwala and Khire (2000), reported 30% increase in phytase activity of *A. niger* NCIM 563 when 0.5% Triton-X-100 was added to the production medium.

For bacterial and yeast cultures, mostly SmF has been used. Among several lactic acid bacteria (*Lactobacillus* and *Streptococcus* sp.), *L. amylovorans* B4552 was found to be the best strain, producing 125-146 units phytase ml^{-1} in a glucose medium supplemented with inorganic phosphorus (Sreeramulu *et al.*, 1996). A genetically modified *B. subtilis* produced phytase ($2 \mu ml^{-1}$) and the yield was 100-fold higher than the wild type *B. amyloliquefaciens* DS11 (Kim *et al.*, 1999b). The *Bacillus* sp. strain KHU-10 produced extracellular phytase ($0.2 \mu ml^{-1}$) in a maltose, peptone and beef extract medium after 4 days of incubation (Choi *et al.*, 1999).

Several investigators have optimized the nutritional and physical parameters for maximizing the production of yeast phytases. In *Schwanniomyces castellii*, phytase production was carried out continuously in a fermenter aerated at 1 vvm and agitated at 600 rev min^{-1} (Segueilha *et al.*, 1992). Galactose (1%) was found to be the preferred carbon source and sodium phytate (0.06%) was required for phytase secretion. *Arxula adeninivorans* secreted high levels of phytase during its active growth phase at 44 °C. Galactose was found to be a better carbon source than glucose, while yeast extract (1%) and peptone (1%) served as good nitrogen sources. Phytate did not show an inducible effect on phytase production (Sano *et al.*, 1999).

Maximum phytase yield by *C. krusei* WZ-001 was attained in 48 h (late exponential phase) at 30 °C and pH 7.0. Glucose (5%) and polypeptone (0.7%) were suitable carbon and nitrogen sources, respectively; phytase synthesis was repressed by the presence of phosphate in the medium (Quan *et al.*, 2001). Phytase production from *Pichia anomala* has been extensively studied. A high phytase titre was attained in the synthetic medium that contained glucose (4%) and beef extract (1%), supplemented with Fe^{2+} (0.15 mM), at 20 °C in 24 h (Vohra & Satyanarayana, 2001). Further enhancement in the titres was achieved using the statistical approach, response surface methodology (RSM) [Vohra and Satyanarayana, 2002]. A medium consisting of cane molasses, a by-product of sugarcane industry, was also formulated that supported an improved phytase yield with reduced production cost as compared to that in the synthetic glucose-beef extract medium (Vohra and Satyanarayana, 2004). The economical cane-molasses medium was further optimized using statistical approaches, Plackett-Burman and RSM, for attaining a higher biomass yield and cell-bound phytase by *P. anomala* (Kaur and Satyanarayana, 2005). An overall 5- and 1.6-fold enhancement in phytase titres and biomass production were attained due to optimization, respectively.

Phytases in Combating Phosphorus Pollution

Feed and food industries, aquaculture and soil amendment are some of the areas where phytases can play significant roles to help overcome P pollution problems (Fig. 1).

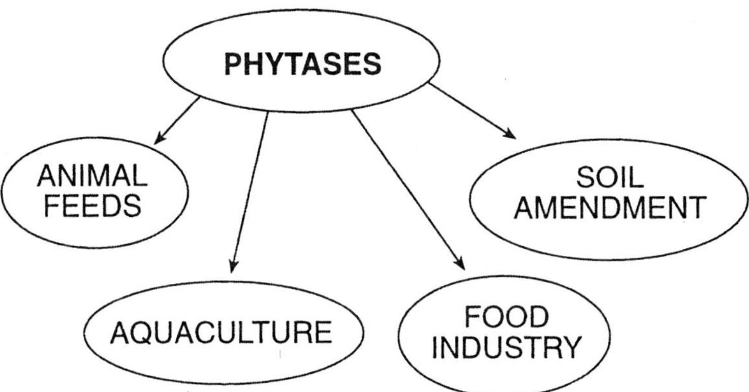

Fig. 1 : Multifarious applications of microbial phytases in combating phosphorus pollution

(i) Feed Application

Plant feedstuffs form a major constituent of animal feed, mainly swine and poultry diets and about two thirds of phosphorus of feedstuffs of plant origin is in the form of phytate P. Under most dietary conditions, phytate P is unavailable to these animals (Nelson, 1967), and the phytin-P is excreted in the manure, leading to additional P load. The phytic acid present in the manure of these animals is enzymatically cleaved by soil and water-borne micro-organisms and the phosphorus thus released is transported into the water bodies causing eutrophication problems as mentioned above. The phytate P also chelates several important minerals, and thereby, reduces their availability to the animals feeding on the diet. However, the ruminant animals sustain the microflora that enzymatically releases the inorganic phosphorus from phytic acid, thus avoiding the need for inorganic phosphorus supplementation. Phytases are incorporated in the feed to reduce the need for phosphorus supplementation and at the same time, degradation of myo-inositol phosphates yields myo-inositol, an important growth factor, and trace minerals also become available. This improves the digestibility, and therefore, the nutritive value of the feed, thus the growth rate of monogastric animals is enhanced; and it also lowers the level of phosphorus excretion, thus reducing chances of environmental pollution.

There are two ways of phytase incorporation in feeds. The first possibility is replacement of inorganic phosphorus supplementation with phytase. However, as the reaction conditions (pH, temperature, moisture, incubation time) in the animal stomach or intestine are not optimal, the second method of phytase use i.e. feed pretreatment, becomes more feasible (Simell *et al.*, 1989).

The effectiveness of phytase supplementation also depends on substrate specificity. Based on In vitro feed experiments, it has been found that phytases with broad substrate specificity are better than those with narrow substrate specificity for animal nutrition (Wyss *et al.*, 1999). Those with broad substrate specificity readily degrade phytate to myo-inositol monophosphate with minor accumulation of intermediates, while phytases with narrow specificity result in myo-inositol tris- and bisphosphate accumulation during phytate degradation coupled with a high rate of phosphate release. Only a few phytases have been, so far, reported to be highly specific for phytate. These include alkaline phytases from *Bacillus subtilis* (Powar and Jagannathan, 1982; Shimizu, 1992) and *B. amyloliquefaciens* (Kim *et al.*, 1998), and acid phytases from *E. coli* (Greiner *et al.*, 1993), *A. niger* and *A. terreus* (Wyss *et al.*, 1999). The problem with broad substrate specificity is that it is generally coupled with low specific activity (Konietzny and Greiner, 2004).

Several feed trial experiments with poultry as well as pigs have confirmed the possibility to replace inorganic phosphorus supplementation by the use of microbial phytase in a phytate-rich diet for monogastric animals. It has been shown that 500-1000 units of phytase can replace approximately 1 g Pi supplementation and reduce the total phosphorous excretion by 30-50 % (Kemme *et al.*, 1997; Liu *et al.*, 1997; Yi *et al.*, 1996). Besides increased phytate-P availability, it also enhanced digestibility of amino acids and minerals. However, the use of phytase as a feed additive is limited by cost, by inactivation at the feed pelleting temperatures (60-90^{0}C), and by the loss of activity during storage. These problems can be overcome by endogenous production of phytase by the monogastric animals, which would increase the bioavailibility of plant phytate and in turn lead to reduced phosphorus excretion. Another approach is to use thermostable phytases obtained by cloning of phytase from thermophilic fungi, or protein engineering; or supplementation of phytase with salts, polyols, starch etc. to increase enzyme thermostability (Vohra and Satyanarayana, 2003).

The availability of phosphorus can be improved by adding microbial phytase to the feed or by using phytase-rich cereal diet. The enzyme minimizes the need for supplementation with inorganic phosphorus due to improvement in the utilization of organic phosphorus in poultry, and thus markedly reducing the excretion of phosphorus in manure. The supplementation of feed of broiler chicks with cell-bound phytase of *Pichia anomala* resulted in improved growth (77.7 % gain in control over 90.2 % in biomass fed), better phosphorous retention in the body (29 % in control over 73.6 % in biomass fed) and reduced excretion of phosphorous in the faeces (Vohra *et al.,* 2005; Satyanarayana and Vohra, 2004). Thus, the FCR (feed conversion ratio defined as the ratio of feed consumed per unit gain in body weight) of biomass fed chicks was lower than the control chicks, proving the economic viability of the *P. anomala* phytase.

When microbial phytase was added to diets for growing pigs, it increased the apparent absorbability of P by 24 %. The amount of P in the faeces was 35 % lower (Simons *et al.*, 1990). In the future, transgenic poultry, hogs may produce phytase in their own digestive tract. Several attempts have already been made to transform and express a fungal phytase in an animal. Transgenic mouse models have been developed to determine whether endogenous expression of phytase transgenes in the digestive tract of monogastric animals can increase the bioavailability of dietary phytate. Transgenic pigs were generated with gene from *E. coli* incorporated to produce phytase in saliva (Forsberg *et al.*, 2003; Golovan, 2001). This provision of salivary phytase activity enabled almost the complete digestion of dietary phytate, thus, relieving the requirement for phosphate supplementation, and also reduced phosphate output by up to 75 %.

Canola meal, used as a feedstuff for livestock and fowl, was successfully dephytinized by *A. niger* NRRL 3135 in a solid state fermentation (Ebune *et al.*, 1995; Nair and Duvnjak, 1990). Segueilha *et al.* (1993) removed phytic acid in wheat bran and glandless cotton flour using phytase from the yeast *S. castellii.*

After the first commercialization attempts by Gist-Brocades Europe (1993-1994), several companies like Alko Co. (Finland), Altech (USA) and BASF (USA) started the industrial scale production of phytase and marketed under the names Finase, Allzyme and Natuphos, respectively, and successfully utilized it in feed applications. At the close of twentieth century, annual sales of phytase as an animal feed additive were estimated to be $500 million and still growing (Abelson, 1999).

(ii) Application in Foods

The presence of phytates in plant foodstuffs is well

known. A large proportion of global population tends to suffer from iron and zinc deficiencies due to the ingestion of phytate rich plant diet (Bentley *et al.*, 1997; Tatala *et al.*, 1998). The dietary phytase gets inactivated during cooking, and therefore, phytate digestion is very poor, and thus affects mineral absorption in the small intestines. Addition of *A. niger* phytase to the flour containing wheat bran has been shown to increase iron absorption in humans (Sandberg *et al.*, 1996). It has also been reported that microbial phytase could accelerate the process of steeping, required in the wet milling of corn, thereby improving the properties of corn steep liquor (Caransa *et al.*, 1988).

Moulds, commonly used in oriental food fermentation have been examined for their ability to produce phytase. Tempeh, a popular oriental fermented food made from soyabeans inoculated by moulds (*Rhizopus oligosporus*) in the koji process. The digestibility, vitamin content and flavour of soyabean improve by this mould fermentation (Fardiaz and Markakis, 1981). Since, phytate binds to proteins, protein isolates from soybeans are rich in phytate. Phytase has also been used in the production of phytate-free soybean milk due to the considerably high level of phytate (0.56 %) in soymilk. Anno *et al.* (1985), had used wheat phytase (Sigma) to eliminate phytase from soybean milk, while Khare *et al.* (1994), had successfully used immobilized wheat phytase.

Another application is in bread making, wherein the use of phytase is suggested for producing low phytin bread (Simell *et al.*, 1989). In commercial whole wheat bread, phytic acid is present at levels of 0.29 to 1.05 % (w/w). Addition of mould phytases, during bread making could almost completely eliminate the dough phytates (Knorr *et al.*, 1981). Degradation of phytate by lactic acid bacteria and yeasts (*S. cerevisiae*) during whole meal dough fermentation has been studied using NMR technique (Reale *et al.*, 2004).

Since, certain myo-inositol phosphates have been suggested to have beneficial health effects, such as reducing the risk of heart disease (Potter, 1995), renal stone formation (Modlin, 1980) and certain cancers (Graf and Eaton, 1993; Shamsuddin and Vucenik, 1999); phytases may find application in food processing to produce functional foods (Konietzny and Greiner, 2003).

Phytic acid, however, also has positive effects. It exerts an antineoplastic effect in animal models of breast carcinomas and the presence of undigested phytate in the colon may protect it against the development of colonic carcinoma (Igbal *et al.,* 1994).

(iii) Potential in Aquaculture

In aquaculture, feed costs may constitute upto 70% of total fish production costs (Rumsey, 1993). Several studies have been conducted on the use of soybean meal or other plant meals in aquaculture by substituting low cost plant protein for a more expensive protein source such as menhaden fish meal, a significant cost reduction could be achieved (Mullaney *et al.*, 2000). As in poultry and swine, fish lack an adequate digestive enzyme to effectively utilize the phytin-P in feed thereby excreting it in the water. Therefore, phytase has been evaluated as a means to both promote the use of low-cost plant meals in the aquaculture industry, and to maintain acceptable phosphorus levels in water. Several fish feeding trials have demonstrated the potential value of phytase in diets containing high levels of plant feed stuffs (Robinson *et al.*, 1996; Mwachireya *et al.*, 1999).

(iv) Soil Amendment in Promoting Plant Growth

Phosphorus deficiency in soil is a major constraint for agricultural production worldwide. P-based fertilizers are, therefore, applied to avoid this deficiency and promote high yields. Only 10-20% of fertilizer P is available to the plants, as a major portion becomes fixed into organic and inorganic fractions that are only poorly available to the plant roots. Of particular significance is the occurrence of soil organic P as phytate, and in certain locations, phytic acid and its derivatives may represent upto 50% of the total organic phosphorus in the soil (Dalal, 1978). Plants are known to produce phytases, but display only low activity in roots and other plant organs, and occurrence of plant-secreted phytase within the rhizosphere is not known (Hayes *et al.*, 2000). This suggests that plant roots may not possess an innate ability to acquire phosphorus directly from soil phytates. There are several reports where phytases have been used to improve the growth of the plants and thus to reduce phosphorus pollution. Yip *et al.* (2003), showed that the tobacco line transformed with a neutral *Bacillus* phytase exhibited phenotypic changes in flowering, seed development and response to phosphate deficiency. The transgenic line showed an increase in flower and fruit numbers, small seed syndrome, lower seed IP_6/IP_5 ratio, and enhanced growth under phosphate-starvation conditions compared with the wild type. These results suggested that the over-expression of *Bacillus* phytase in the cytoplasm of tobacco cells shifts the equilibrium of the inositol phosphate biosynthesis pathway, thereby making more phosphate available for primary metabolism.

The use of the promoter from the Arabidopsis Pht1;2 phosphate transporter to drive the expression of a secretable *Aspergillus niger* phytase gene only in the root epidermis of phosphate-deprived plants enabled the transformed Arabidopsis plants to grow on medium containing phytate as a sole P source. The growth rates and shoot P concentrations of these plants were similar when grown on phytate or phosphate as the P source, and were similar to transgenic lines in which the phytase was driven by the constitutive CaMV 35S promoter (Mudge *et al.,* 2003).

Phytase and phosphatase producing fungi were also used as seed inoculants, to help attain higher P nutrition of plants in the soils containing high phytate phosphorus. The extracellular phosphatases released by these fungi were less than their intracellular counterpart, but the trend was reversed in case of phytase production. The efficiency of hydrolysis of different organic P compounds by different fungi indicated that the identified fungi have enough potential to exploit native organic phosphorus to benefit plant nutrition (Yadav and Tarafdar, 2003). Transgenic Arabidopsis plant expressing MtPHY1, a full-length cDNA encoding an extracellular phytase from a legume, *Medicago truncatula* led to significant improvement in organic phosphorus utilization and plant growth. When phytate was supplied as the sole source of phosphorus, dry weight of the transgenic Arabidopsis lines were 3.1 to 4.0-fold higher than the control plants and total phosphorus contents were 4.1 to 5.5-fold higher than the control, suggesting the great potential of heterologous expression of phytase gene for improving plant phosphorus acquisition and for phytoremediation (Xiao *et al.*, 2005). A transgenic approach was used to alter soybean seed phytate content by expressing a soybean phytase gene (GmPhy) during seed development to degrade accumulating phytic acid (IP_6). An expression vector containing the soybean phytase cDNA controlled by the seed-specific beta-conglycinin promoter (alpha'-subunit) was used to transform embryogenic soybean cultures. Plants from four independent transgenic lines were analyzed for transgene integration and seed IP6 levels. The reduction in IP6 levels in transgenic seeds compared to control 'Jack' soybeans ranged from 12.6 to 24.8 as determined by HPLC. A low copy transformant was propagated to the T4 generation and examined in more detail for phytase expression and enzyme activity during seed development. Expression of phytase mRNA and phytase activity increased during seed development, consistent with the use of an embryo-specific promoter. Ectopic phytase expression during seed development offers potential as an effective strategy for reducing phytate content in soybean seed (Chiera *et al.,* 2005). *Arabidopsis thaliana* plants were able to obtain phosphorus from a range of organic phosphorus substrates that would be expected to occur in soil, but have only limited ability to obtain phosphorus directly from phytate. But the growth and phosphorus nutrition of Arabidopsis plants supplied with phytate was improved significantly after the introduction of phytase gene from *Aspergillus niger*. Growth and phosphorus nutrition of the transformed plants was improved and was equivalent to control plants supplied with inorganic phosphate suggesting the extracellular phytase activity of plant roots as a significant factor in the utilization of phosphorus from phytate and opportunity for using gene technology to improve the ability of plants to utilize accumulated forms of soil organic phosphorus (Richardson *et al.*, 2001). These approaches can be applied as a strategy for boosting productivity in agriculture and horticulture.

Recently, phytase from *Schwanniomyces occidentalis* was expressed in rice plants (Hamada *et al.*, 2005). The phytase activity of certain plant root-colonizing bacteria has also been shown to contribute towards its plant growth promoting activity (Idriss *et al.*, 2002). Phytase plays a dual role in plant nutrition, making the phytate phosphorous available to the plant roots and at the same time elimination of chelate-forming phytate.

Conclusions

Phytase research has progressed significantly in the last few decades. The enzyme is now being increasingly recognized for its beneficial environmental role in reducing the phosphorus levels in manure and minimizing the need to supplement phosphorus in animal diets. Their usage as an animal feed additive is growing since it is environment-friendly. They have an immense potential in the feed and food industry as they also improve the nutritional status by degrading phytic acid, which acts as an antinutritional factor. Other areas that offer tremendous opportunity are increasing the use of phytase in aquaculture so as to allow the use of low cost plant based fish feeds and the use of phytase for soil amendment and plant growth promotion.

Acknowledgements

We are grateful to DBT and ICAR for financial assistance while writing the article. Ms. Parvinder Kaur is grateful to CSIR for awarding JRF/ SRF.

References

Abelson, P. H. (1999) A potential phosphate crisis. Science, 283: 2015.

Al-Asheh, S. and Duvnjak, Z. (1994) The effect of surfactants on the phytase production and the reduction of the phytic acid content in canola meal by *Aspergillus carbonarius* during solid-state fermentation process. Biotech. Lett., 16(2): 183-188.

Anno, T., Nakanishi, K., Matsuno, R. and Kamikubo, T. (1985) Enzymatic elimination of phytate in soybean milk. J. Japan Soc. Food. Sci. Technol., 32: 174-180.

Bali, A. and Satyanarayana, T. (2001) Microbial phytases in nutrition and combating phosphorus pollution. Everyman's Science, 4: 207-209.

Bentley, M. E., Caulfield, L. E., Ram, M., Santizo, M. C., Hurtado, E., Rivera, J. A., Ruel, M. T. and Brown, K. H. (1997) Zinc supplementation affects the activity patterns of rural Guatemamlan infants. J. Nutr., 127: 1333-1338.

Berka, R. M., Rey, M. W., Brown, K. M., Byun, T. and Klotz, A. V. (1998) Molecular characterization and expression of a phytase gene from the thermophilic fungus *Thermomyces lanuginosus*. Appl. Environ. Microbiol., 64: 4423-4427.

Bindu, S., Somashekar, D. and Joseph, R. (1998) A comparative study of permeabilization treatments for in situ determination of phytase of *Rhodotorula gracilis*. Lett. Appl. Microbiol., 27: 336-340.

Bogar, B., Szakacs, G., Linden, J.C., Pandey, A. and Tengerdy, R.P. (2003) Optimization of phytase production by solid substrate fermentation. J. Ind. Microbiol. Biotechnol., 30 (3): 183 – 189.

Callopy, P. D. and Royse, D. J. (2004) Characterization of phytase activity from cultivated edible mushrooms and their production substrates. J. Agric. Food Chem., 52: 7518-7524.

Caransa, A., Simell, M., Lehmussari, M., Vaara, M. and Vaara, T. (1988) A novel enzyme application in corn wet milling. Starch, 40: 409-411.

Chi, H., Tiller, G. E., Dasouki, M. J., Romano, P. R., Wang, J., O'Keefe, R. J., Puzas, J. E., Rosier, R. N. and Reynolds, P. R. (1999) Multiple inositol polyphosphate phosphatase: evolution as a distinct group within the histidine phosphatase family and chromosomal localization of the human and mouse genes to chromosomes 10q23 and 19. Genomics, 56: 324-336.

Chiera, J.M., Finer, J.J. and Grabau, E.A. (2004) Ectopic expression of a soybean phytase in developing seeds of Glycine max to improve phosphorus availability. Plant Mol. Biol., 56(6): 895-904.

Choi, Y. M., Suh, H. J., and Kim, J. M. (2001) Purification and properties of extracellular phytase from Bacillus sp. KHU-10. J. Protein Chem., 20(4): 287-292.

Cosgrove, D. J. (1969) Ion exchange chromatography of inositol polyphosphates. Ann. N. Y. Acad. Sci., 165: 677-686.

Craxton, A., Caffrey, J. J., Burkhart, W., Safrany, S. T. and Shears, S. B. (1997) Molecular cloning and expression of a rat hepatic multiple inositol polyphosphate phosphatase. Biochem. J., 328: 75-81.

Dalal, R. C. (1978) Soil organic phosphorous. Adv. Agron., 29: 83-117.

Deevey, E.S. (1970) Mineral cycles. Sci. Am., 223 (3): 148-158.

Dvorakova, J. (1998) Phytase: Sources, preparation and exploitation. Folia Microbiol., 43 (4): 323-338.

Eastwood, D., Tavener, R. J. A. and Laidman, D. L. (1969) Induction of lipase and phytase activities in the aleurone tissue of germinating wheat grains. Biochem. J., 113 (Proc. Biochem. Soc): 32.

Ebune, A., Al-Asheh, S. and Duvnjak, Z. (1995) Effect of phosphate, surfactants and glucose on phytase production and hydrolysis of phytic acid in canola meal by *Aspergillus ficuum* during solid state fermentation. Biores. Technol., 54: 241-247.

Fardiaz, D. and Markakis, P. (1981) Degradation of phytic acid in oncom (fermented peanut press cake). J. Food Sci., 46: 523-525.

Forsberg, C.W., Phillips, J.P, Golovan, S.P., Fan, M.Z., Meidinger, R.G., Ajakaiya, A., Hilborn, D. and Hacker, R.R. (2003) The Environpig physiology, performance and contribution to nutrient management advances in a regulated environment: The leading edge of change in the pork industry. J. Anim. Sci., 81(E. suppl. 2): E68-E77.

Frossard, E., Brossard, M.B., Hedley, M.J. and Metherell, A. (1998) Reactions controlling the cycling of P in soils, In *Phosphorus in Global Environment: Transfers, cycles and management*, H. Tiessen (ed.), Chichester, UK: Wiley, pp., 107-137.

Ghosh, S. (1997) Phytase of a thermophilic mould *Sporotrichum thermophile* Apinis. M.Sc dissertation, Department of Microbiology, University of Delhi, Delhi.

Gibson, D. M. (1987) Production of extracellular phytase from *Aspergillus ficuum* on starch media. Biotech. Lett., 5: 305-310.

Golovan, S. P., Hayes, M. A., Phillips, J. P. and Forsberg, C. W. (2001) Transgenic mice expressing bacterial phytase as a model for phosphorus pollution control. Nature Biotechnol., 19: 429-433.

Graf, E. and Eaton, J. W. (1993) Suppression of colonic cancer by dietary phytic acid. Nutr. Cancer, 19: 11-19.

Greaves, M. P., Anderson, G. and Webley, D. M. (1967) The

hydrolysis of inositol phosphates by *Aerobacter aerogenes.* Biochim. Biophys. Acta, 132: 412-418.

Greiner, R., Konitzny, U. and Jany, K. D. (1993) Purification and characterization of two phytases from *Escherchia coli.* Arch. Biochem. Biophys., 303: 107-113.

Ha, N. C., Kim, Y. O., Oh, T. K. and Oh, B. H. (1999) Preliminary X-ray crystallographic analysis of a novel phytase from a *Bacillus amyloliquefaciens* strain. Acta crystallogr. D. Biol. Crystallogr., 55: 691-693.

Ha, N. C., Oh, B. C., Shin, S., Kim, H. J., Oh, T. K., Kim, Y. O., Choi, K. Y. and Oh, B. H. (2000) Crystal structures of a novel, thermostable phytase in partially and fully calcium loaded states. Nat. Struct. Biol., 7: 147-153.

Hamada, A., Yamaguchi, K., Ohnishi, N, Harada, M., Nikumaru, S. and Honda, H. (2005) High-level production of yeast (*Schwanniomyces occidentalis*) phytase in transgenic rice plants by a combination of signal sequence and codon modification of the phytase gene. Plant Biotechnol. J., 3(1): 43-56.

Han, Y.W., Gallagher, D.J. and Wilfred, A.G. (1987) Phytase production by *Aspergillus ficuum* on semisolid substrate. J. Ind. Microbiol., 2 (4): 195-200.

Harland, B. F. and Morris, E. R. (1995) Phytate: A good or a bad food component. Nutr. Res., 15(5): 733-754.

Hayes, J. E., Simpson, R. J. and Richardson, A. E. (2000) The growth and phosphorous utilization of plants in sterile media when supplied with inositol hexaphosphate, glucose 1-phosphate or inorganic phosphate. Plant and Soil, 220: 165-174.

Hegeman, C. E. and Grabau, E. A. (2001) A novel phytase with sequence similarity to purple acid phosphatases is expressed in cotyledons of germinating soybean seedlings. Plant physiol., pp. 1598-1608.

Howson, S. J. and Davis, R. P. (1983) Production of phytate hydrolyzing enzymes by some fungi. Enz. Microb. Technol., 5: 377-389.

Idriss, E. E., Makarewicz, O., Farouk, A., Rosner, K., Greiner, R., Bochow, H., Richter, T. and Borriss, R. (2002) Extracellular phytase activity of bacillus amyloliquefaciens FZB45 contributes to its plant-growth-promoting effect. Microbiol., 148: 2097-2109.

Igbal, T. H., Lewis, K. O. and Cooper B. T. (1994) Phytase activity in the human and rat small intestine. Gut, 35: 1233-1236.

Irving, G. C. J. and Cosgrove, D. J. (1974) Inositol phosphate phosphatases of microbiological origin. Some properties of the partially purified phosphatases of *Aspergillus ficuum* NRRL 3135. Aust. J. Biol. Sci., 27: 361-368.

Johnson, L. F. and Tate, M. E. (1969) The structure of myo-inositol pentaphosphates. Ann. N. Y. Acad. Sci., 165: 526-532.

Kaur, P. and Satyanarayana, T. (2005) Production of cell-bound phytase by *Pichia anomala* in an economical cane molasses medium: optimization using statistical tools. Process Biochem., 40 (9): 3095-3102.

Kaur, P., Singh, B., Vohra, A. and Satyanarayana, T. (2003) Fabulous phytases: Diverse functions in the living world and commercial prospects. The Botanica, 53: 35-42.

Kemme, P. A., Jongbloed, A. W., Mroz, Z. and Beynen, A. C. (1997) The efficacy of *Aspergillus niger* phytase in rendering phytate phosphorous available for absorption in pigs in influenced by pig physiological status. J. Anim. Sci., 75: 2129-2138.

Kerovuo, J., Lauraeus, M., Nurminen, P., Kalkkinen, N. and Apajalahti, J. (1998) Isolation, characterization, molecular gene cloning and sequencing of a novel phytase from *Bacillus subtilis*. Appl. Environ. Microbiol., 64: 2079-2085.

Khare, S. K., Jha, K. and Gupta, M. N. (1994) Entrapmant of wheat phytase in polyacrylamide gel and its application in soy milk phytate hydrolysis. Biotechnol. Appl. Biochem., 19: 193-198.

Khasawneh, F.E., Sample, E.C. and Kamprath, E.J. (eds.) (1980) *The role of phosphorus in agriculture*, Am. Soc. Agron., Madison, WI.

Kim, D. H., Oh, B. C., Choi, W. C., Lee, J. K. and Oh, T. K. (1999b) Enzymatic evaluation of *Bacillus amyloliquefaciens* phytase as a feed additive. Biotech. Lett., 21: 925-927.

Kim, D.S., Godber, J.S. and Kim, H.R. (1999a) Culture conditions for a new phytase producing fungus. Biotech. Lett., 21: 1077-1081.

Kim, Y. O., Kim, H. K., Bae, K. S., Yu, J. H. and Oh, T. K. (1998) Purification and properties of a thermostable phytase from *Bacillus* sp. DS11. Enz. Microb. Technol., 22: 2-7.

Knorr, D., Watkins, T. R. and Carlson, B. L. (1981) Enzymatic reduction of phytate in whole wheat breads. J. Food Sci., 46:1866-1869.

Konietzny, U. and Greiner, R. (2002) Molecular and catalytic properties of phytate-degrading enzymes (phytases). Int. J. Food Sci. Technol., 37: 791-812.

Konietzny, U. and Greiner, R. (2003) Phytic acid (b) Nutritional impact. In *Encyclopedia of Food Science and Nutrition*, (Eds, B. Caballero, L. Trugo and P. Finglas), Elsevier, London, pp. 4555-4563.

Konietzny, U. and Greiner, R. (2004) Bacterial phytase: Potential applications, *in vivo* function and regulation of its synthesis. Brazilian. J. Microbio., 35: 11-18.

Krishna, C. and Nokes, S. E. (2001) Influence of inoculum size on phytase production and growth in solid-state fermentation by *Aspergillus niger*. Transactions of the ASAE, 44: 1031-1036.

Lassen, S. F., Breinholt, J., Ostergaard, P. R., Brugger, R., Bischoff, A., Wyss, M. and Fuglsang, C. (2001) Expression, gene cloning and characterization of five novel phytases from four basidiomycete fungi: *Peniophora lycii, Agrocybe pediades,* and a *Ceriporia* sp., *and Trametyes pubescens*. Appl. Environ. Microbiol., 67 (10): 4701-4707.

Liu, B. L., Rafig, A., Tzeng, Y. M. and Rob, A. (1998) The induction and characterization of phytase and beyond: A review. Enz. Microb. Technol., 22: 415-424.

Liu, J., Bollinger, D. W., Ledoux, D. R., Ellersieck, M. R. and Veum, T. L. (1997) Soaking increases the efficacy of supplemental microbial phytase in a low-phosphorous corn-soybean meal diet for growing pigs. J. Anim. Sci., 75: 1292-1298.

Lopez-Bucio, J., Martinez de la Vega, O., Guervara-Garcia, A. And Herrera-Estrella, L. (2000) Enhanced phosphorus uptake in transgenic tobacco plants that overproduce citrate. Nat. Biotechnol., 18: 450-453.

Maga, J. A. (1982) Phytate: Its chemistry, occurrence, food interactions, nutritional significance, and methods of analysis. J. Agric. Food Chem., 30: 1-9.

Mandviwala, T.N. and Khire, J.M. (2000) Production of high activity thermostable phytase from thermotolerant *Aspergillus niger* in solid state fermentation. J. Ind. Microbiol. Biotechnol., 24 (4): 237 – 243.

Marieb, E.N. (1998) *Human Anatomy and Physiology*, Benjamin/Cummings, Menlo Park, CA.

Marschner, H. (1995) Mineral *Nutrition of Higher Plants* (2nd ed.), Academic Press, Boston.

Martin, A. and Cooke, G.D. (1994) Health risks in eutrophic water supplies. Lake Line, 14:24-26.

Martin, J.A., Murphy, R.A. and Power, R.F.G. (2003) Cloning and expression of fungal phytases in genetically modified strains of *Aspergillus awamori*. J. Ind. Microbiol. Biotechnol., 30 (9): 568 – 576.

Mayer, A. F., Hellmuth, K., Schlieker, H., Lopez – Ulibarri, R., Oertel, S., Dahlems, U., Strasser, A. W. and van Loon, A. P. (1999) An expression system matures: a highly efficient and cost effective process for phytase production by recombinant strains of *Hansenula polymorpha*. Biotechnol. Bioeng., 63 (3): 373-381.

Mc Collum, E. V. and Hart, E. B. (1908) On the occurrence of a phytin splitting enzyme in animal tissue. J. Biol. Chem., 4: 497-500.

Meyer, H., Meyer, A. M. and Harel, E. (1971) Acid phosphatases in germinating lettuce-evidence for partial activation. Physiol. Plant., 24: 95-101.

Mitchell, D.B., Vogel, K., Weimann, B.J., Pasamontes, L., van Loon, A.P.B.M. (1997) The phytase subfamily of histidine acid phosphatases: isolation of genes for two novel phytases from the fungi *Aspergillus terreus* and *Myceliophthora thermophila*. Microbio, 143: 245-252.

Modlin, M. (1980) Urinary phosphorylated inositols and renal stone. Lancet., 2: 1113-1114.

Mudge, S.R., Smitha, F.W. and Richardson, A.E. (2003) Root-specific and phosphate-regulated expression of phytase under the control of a phosphate transporter promoter enables Arabidopsis to grow on phytate as a sole P source. Plant Science, 165 (4): 871-878.

Mullaney, E. J. and Ullah, A. H. J. (2003) The term phytase comprises several different classes of enzymes. Biochem. Biophys. Res. Comm., 312: 179-184.

Mullaney, E. J., Daly, C. B. and Ullah, A. H. J. (2000) Advances in phytase research. Adv. Appl. Microbiol., 47: 157-199.

Mwachireya, S. A., Beames, R. M., Higgs, D. A. and Dosanjh, B. S. (1999) Digestibility of canola protein products derived from the physical, enzymatic and chemical processing of commercial canola meal in rainbow trout *Oncorhynchus mykiss* (Walbaum) held in fresh water. Aquacult. Nutr., 5: 73-82.

Nair, V. C. and Duvnjak, Z. (1990) Reduction of phytic acid content in canola meal by *Aspergillus ficuum* in solid state fermentation process. Appl. Microbiol. Biotechnol., 34: 183-188.

Nakamura, Y., Fukuhara, H. and Sano, K. (2000) Secreted phytase activities of yeasts. Biosci. Biotechnol. Biochem., 64 (4): 841-844.

Nayini, N. R. and Markakis, P. (1984) The phytase of yeast. Lebensm. Wiss. Technol., 17: 24-26.

Nelson, T. S. (1967) The utilization of phytate phosphorus by poultry. Poult. Sci., 46: 862-871.

Oh, B. C., Choi, W. C., Park, S., Kim, Y. O. and Oh, T. K. (2004) Biochemical properties and substrate specificities of alkaline and histidine acid phytases. Appl. Microbiol. Biotechnol., 63: 362-372.

Pandey, A., Szakacs, G., Soccol, C. R., Jose, A., Rodriguez, L. and Soccol, V.T. (2001) Production, purification and properties of microbial phytase. Biores. Technol., 77: 203-214.

Papagianni, M., Nokes, S.E. and Filer K. (1999) Production of phytase by *Aspergillus niger* in submerged and solid-state fermentation. Proc. Biochem., 35: 397-402.

Pasamontes, L., Haiker, M., Wyss, M., Tessier, M. and van Loon, A. P. G. M. (1997) Gene cloning, purification and characterization of a heat stable phytase from the fungus *Aspergillus fumigatus.* Appl. Environ. Microbiol., 63 (5): 1696-1700.

Posternak (1903) Compt. Rend. 137, 202. Phytase, In: *Advances in Applied Microbiology*, 42:263-302.

Potter, S. M. (1995) Overview of proposed mechanisms for the hypercholasterolemic effect of soy. J. Nutr., 125: 606S-611S.

Powar, V. K., and Jagannathan, V. (1982) Purification and properties of phytate specific phosphatase from *Bacillus subtilis.* J. Bacteriol., 151: 1102-1108.

Quan, C. S., Zhang, L. H., Wang, Y. J., and Ohta, Y. Y. (2001) Production of phytase in a low phosphate medium by a novel *yeast Candida krusei.* J. Biosci.Bioeng., 92 (2): 154-160.

Raghothama, K.G. (2000) Phosphate transport and signaling. Curr. Opin. Plant Biol., 3: 182-187.

Rapoport, S., Leva, E. and Guest, G. M. (1941) Phytase in plasma and erythrocytes of vertebrates. J. Biol. Chem., 139: 621-632.

Reale, A., Mannina, L., Tremonte, P., Sobolev, A. P., Succi, M., Sorrentino, E. And Coppola, R. (2004) Phytate degradation by lactic acid bacteria and yeasts during the wholemeal dough fermentation: a ^{31}P NMR study. J. Agric. Food Chem., 52: 6300-6305.

Reddy, N. R. Pierson, M. D., Stevis Sathe, S. K. and Salunkhe, D. K. (1989) Phytates in cereals and legumes, Boca Raton, FL: CRC Press.

Richardson, A.E., Hadobas, P.A. and Hayes, J.E. (2001) Extracellular secretion of *Aspergillus* phytase from Arabidopsis roots enables plants to obtain phosphorus from phytate. Plant J., 25(6): 641-649.

Robinson, E. H., Jackson, S. and Li, M. H. (1996) Supplemental phytase in catfish diets. Aquacult. Mag., 22: 80-82.

Rumsey, G. L. (1993) Fish meal and alternate sourced of protein in fish feeds: Update 1993. Fisheries, 18: 14-19.

Sabu, A., Sarita, S., Pandey, A., Bogar, B., Szakacs, G. and Soccol, C.R. (2002) Solid-State Fermentation for Production of

Phytase by *Rhizopus oligosporus*. Appl. Biochem. Biotechnol., 102-103: 251-260.

Safrany, S. T., Caffrey, T. T., Yang, X. and Shears, S. B. (1999) Diphosphoinositol polyphosphates: the final frontier for inositide research. J. Biol. Chem., 380: 945-951.

Sandberg, A. S., Hulthen, L. R. and Turk, M. (1996) Dietary *Aspergillus niger* phytase increases iron absorption in humans. J. Nutr., 126: 476-480.

Sano, K., Fukuhara, H. and Nakamura, Y. (1999) Phytase of the yeast *Arxula adeninivorans*. Biotech. Lett., 21: 33-38.

Sasakawa, N., Sharif, M. and Hanley, M. R. (1995) Metabolism and biological activities of inositol pentakisphosphate and inositol hexakisphosphate. Biochem. Pharmacol., 50: 137-146.

Satyanarayana, T. and Vohra, A. (2003) A synergistic feed composition to enhance phosphorous availability, assimilation and retention in non-ruminants. Indian Patent Appl no. 976/DEL/2003.

Satyanarayana, T., Vohra, A. and Kaur, P. (2004) Phytases in animal productivity and environmental management. Productivity, 44(4): 542-548.

Segueilha, L., Lambrechts, C., Boze, H., Moulin, G. and Galzy, P. (1992) Purification and properties of the phytase from *Schwanniomyces castellii*. J. Ferment. Bioeng., 74(1): 7-11.

Segueilha, L., Moulin, G. and Galzy, P. (1993) Reduction of phytate content in wheat bran and glandless cotton flour by *Schwanniomyces castellii*. J. Agric. Food Chem., 41: 2451-2454

Shamsuddin, A. M. and Vucenik, I. (1999) Mammary tumor inhibition by IP6: a review. Anticancer Res., 19, 36-71.

Shieh, T. R. and Ware, J. H. (1968) Survey of microorganisms for the production of extracellular phytase. Appl. Microbiol., 169(9): 1348-1351.

Shimizu, M. (1992) Purification and characterization of phytase from *Bacillus subtilis* (natto) N-77. Biosci. Biotechnol. Biochem., 56(8): 1266-1269.

Simell, M., Turunen, M., Pironen, J. and Vaara, T. (1989) Feed and food applications of phytase. Lecture at 3rd Meet Industrial Applications of Enzymes, Barcelona (Spain).

Simons, P. C. M., Versteegh, H. A. J., Jongbloed, A. W., Kemme, P. A., Slump, P., Bos, K. D., Wolters, M. G. E., Beudeker, R. F. and Verschoor, G. J. (1990) Improvement of phosphorus availability by microbial phytase in broilers and pigs. Brit. J. Nutr., 64: 525-540.

Smil, V. (2000) Phosphorus in the environment: natural flows and human interferences. Annu. Rev. Energy Environ., 25: 53-88.

Sreeramulu, G., Srinivasa, D. S., Nand, K., and Joseph, R. (1996) *Lactobacillus amylovorus* as a phytase producer in submerged culture. Lett. Appl. Microbiol., 23: 385-388.

Suzuki, U., Yoshimura, K., and Takaishi, M. (1907). Ueber ein Enzym "Phytase" das "Anhydro-oxy-methylen diphosphorsaure" Spaltet. Tokyo Imper. Univ. Coll. Agric. Bull., 7: 503-512.

Tambe, S. M., Kakli, S. G., Kelkar, S. M. and Parekh, L. J. (1994) Two distinct molecular forms of phytase from *Klebsiella aerogenes*; Evidence for unusually small active enzyme peptide. J. Ferm. Bioeng., 77(1): 23-27.

Tatala, S., Svanberg, U. and Mduma, B. (1998) Low dietary iron availability is a major cause of anaemia: a nutrition survey in the Lindi district of Tanzania. Am. J. Clin. Nutr., 68: 171-178.

Tomlinson, R. V. and Ballou, C.E. (1962) Myo-inositol polyphosphate intermediates in the dephosphorylation of phytic acid by phytases. Biochemistry, 1: 166-177.

Tyagi, P. K., Tyagi, P. K., and Verma, S. V. S. (1998) Phytate phosphorus content of some common poultry feed stuffs. Indian J. Poult. Sci., 33(1): 86-88.

U.S. Environmantal Protection Agency (1986) Quality criteria for water 1986: Washington, DC., U.S. Environmental protection Agency Report 440/5-86-001, Office of Water.

Ullah, A. H. J. and Gibson, D. M. (1987) Extracellular phytase (EC 3.1.3.8) from *Aspergillus ficuum* NRRL 3135: purification and characterization. Prep. Biochem., 17: 63-91.

Urbano, G., Lopez-Jurado, M., Aranda, P., Vidal-Valverde, C., Tenorio, E. and Porres, J. (2000). The role of phytic acid in legumes: antinutrient or beneficial function? J. Physiol. Biochem., 56(3): 283-294.

Van Etten, R. L., Davidson, R., Stevis, P. E., MacArthur, H. and Moore, D. L. (1991) Covalent structure, disulfide bonding and identification of reactive surface and active site residues of human prostatic acid phosphatase. J. Biol. Chem., 266: 2313-2319.

Vance, C.P. (2001) Symbiotic nitrogen fixation and phosphorus acquisition-Plant nutrition in a world of declining renewable resources. Plant Physiol., 127: 390-397.

Vats, P. and Banerjee, U.C. (2002) Studies on the production of phytase by a newly isolated strain of *Aspergillus niger* var teigham obtained from rotten wood-logs. Process Biochem., 38 (2): 211-217.

Vats, P. and Banerjee, U.C. (2004) Production studies and catalytic properties of phytases (myo-inositolhexakisphosphate phosphohydrolases): an overview. Enz. Microb. Technol., 35 (1): 3-14.

Vohra, A. and Satyanarayana, T. (2001) Phytase production by the yeast *Pichia anomala*. Biotechnol. Lett., 23: 551-554.

Vohra, A. and Satyanarayana, T. (2002). Statistical optimization of the medium components by response surface methodology to enhance phytase production by *Pichia anomala*. Process Biochem., 37: 999-1004.

Vohra, A. and Satyanarayana, T. (2003) Phytases: Microbial sources, production, purification, and potential biotechnological applications. Crit. Rev. Biotechnol., 23(1):29-60.

Vohra, A. and Satyanarayana, T. (2004) A cost-effective cane molasses medium for enhanced cell-bound phytase production by *Pichia anomala*. J. Appl. Microbiol., 97: 471-476.

Vohra, A., Rastogi, S. K. and Satyanarayana, T. (2005) Amelioration in growth and phosphate assimilation of poultry birds using cell-bound phytase of *Pichia anomala*. World J. Micobiol. Biotechnol. (In press).

Walker, T.W. and Syers, J.K. (1976) The fate of phosphorus during pedogenesis. Geoderma, 15: 1-19.

Wodzinski, R. J. and Ullah, A. H. J. (1996) Phytase. Adv. Appl. Microbiol., 42: 263-302.

Wyss, M. R., Brugger, R., Kronenberger, A., Remy, R., Fimbel, R., Oesterhelt, G., Lehmann, M., and van Loon, A. P. G. M. (1999) Biochemical characterization of fungal phytases (myo-inositol hexakisphosphate phosphohydrolases): catalytic properties. Appl. Environ. Microbiol., 65: 367-373.

Xiao, K., Harrison, M.J. and Wang, Z.Y. (2005) Transgenic expression of a novel *M. truncatula* phytase gene results in improved acquisition of organic phosphorus by Arabidopsis. Planta, 222 (1): 27 – 36.

Yadav, R.S. and Tarafdar, J.C. (2003) Phytase and phosphatase producing fungi in arid and semi-arid soils and their efficiency in hydrolyzing different organic P compounds. Soil Biol. Biochem., 35 (6): 745-751.

Yanke, L. J., Bae, H. D., Selinger, L. B. and Cheng, K. L. (1998) Phytase activity of anaerobic ruminal bacteria. Microbiol., UK., 144: 1565-1573.

Yanke, L. J., Selinger, L. B. and Cheng, K. J. (1999) Phytase activity of *Selenomonas ruminantium*: a preliminary characterization. Lett. Appl. Microbiol., 29: 20-25.

Yi, Z., Kornegay, E. T., Ravindran, V. and Denbow, D. M. (1996) Improving phytate phosphorous availability in corn and soybean meal for broilers using microbial phytase and calculations of phosphorous equivalency values for phytase. Poultry Sci., 75: 240-249.

Yip, W., Wanga, L., Wailan, C.C. Lung, W. and Lim, B.L. (2003) The introduction of a phytase gene from *Bacillus subtilis* improved the growth performance of transgenic tobacco. Biochem. Biophy. Res. Comm., 310 (4): 1148-1154.

Yoon, S. J., Choi, Y. J., Min, H. K., Cho, K. K., Kim, J. W., Zee, S. C. and Jung, Y. H. (1996) Isolation and identification of phytase producing bacterium, *Enterobacter* sp.4 and enzymatic properties of phytase enzyme. Enz. Microb. Technol., 18: 449-454.

CHAPTER 6

PHYTOPLANKTON AND ZOOPLANKTON DISTRIBUTIONS IN A STRESSED ENVIRONMENT : LANDFILL LEACHATE TREATMENT BASINS

Aleya Lotfi[1], Khattabi Hicham[1] and Mudry Jacques[2]

[1]Laboratoire de Biologie Environnementale, Université de Franche Comté, 1, Place Leclerc, 25030 Besançon cedex (France).

[2] Laboratoire de Géosciences, Université de Franche-Comté, 16, route de Gray, 25030 Besançon cedex (France).

ABSTRACT

The seasonal distribution of the phytoplankton community together with that of the zooplankton and several abiotic parameters were studied in the stabilisation ponds of Etueffont landfill leachate (Belfort, France) from May 1998 to May 1999. The results showed maximum phytoplankton abundance in the last lagooning basin during summer 1998, that coincided with an increase in temperature and better leachate quality. In addition, the phytoplankton was dominated by *Euglenophytes* sp., *Phacus* sp. and *Euglena* sp. known to resist constraints induced by the highly polluted aquatic environments. An improvement in water quality of the last basins translated into a shift in species composition with the substitution of the Bacillariophyceae (*Stephanodiscus dubius*) by the Chlorophyceae (*Coelastrum* sp.).

Key Words: Leachates, lagooning, phytoplankton, zooplankton.

Introduction

The domestic waste that accumulates wordwide pose a potential hazard. In France, the whole annual average of these wastes reached 20 millions tonnes (400 kg per capita) (ADEME, 1997). In this respect, landfilling which is still the most popular way for solid wastes treatment in the world, is of major concern since it may pollute the surrounding environment. The leachate produced from landfill contains large quantities of organic and inorganic matters and heavy metals (Kjeldsen *et al.*, 2002, Schwarzbauer *et al.*, 2002, Baun *et al.*, 2004). Moreover, Vrijheid *et al.* (2002), reported a 33% increase in the risk of congenital anomalies among residents near hazardous waste landfill sites in a European collaborative study (EUROHAZCON). Also, several studies have reported excesses of bladder, lung, and stomach cancer and leukaemia in populations living near waste landfill sites (Vrijheid, 2000). To reach European standards (ISO 14000) of the domestic waste treatments, the SICTOM (domestic waste treatment agency) constructed four stabilisation ponds in the landfill of Etuffont city (Belfort, France). Nevertheless, landfill leachate generated by the biodegradation of solid wastes have been shown to migrate away from a landfill and may pollute groundwaters as well as surface waters (Baun *et al.*, 2004; Christensen *et al.*, 2000; Silva *et al.*, 2004). As a result, contaminated water is injected into tributaries that are otherwise most often loaded with high amounts of nitrogen and phosphorus. These inputs enter lakes and reservoirs to induce intense spectacular phytoplankton proliferations (Aleya *et al.*, 1994; Nayar *et al.*, 2004; Arhonditsis *et al.*, 2004). From both ecological and economical points of view, this eutrophication is of much concern with respect to bodies of water that are used for recreational activities and/or for sources of drinking water in temperate and semi arid regions (Aleya and Devaux, 1989; Alaoui *et al.*, 1993; Pinel-Alloul *et al.*, 2004).

The waste stabilisation ponds are widely used for the treatment of domestic and agro-industrial wastes (Saqqar and Pescod, 1991; Shelef and Azov, 1996; Cauchie *et al.*, 2002), and the performance of the landfill leachate treatment depends on the efficiency of bacteria to degrade the organic matter. Furthermore, while an extensive literature dealing with the methods of lanfill treatments is now available (Kettunen, 1997; Welander *et al.,* 1998; Hoilijoki *et al.*, 2000), little is known on the dynamics of the phytoplankton communities that develop in these ecosystems and the role of algal species in the basin functioning.

This work aimed at studying the annual distribution of the phytoplankton abundance and biomass, the biochemical composition of the particulate matter together with the zooplankton dynamics and several physical chemical parametres in the four basins of the Etueffont landfill.

Materials and Methods

(i) Study site

The domestic landfill treatment station studied is located in Etueffont (Belfort, France). It covers a total surface area of 2.2 hectares and from 1974 to 2000 AD, has been operating in open air by crushing the waste before disposal. In 1999, the landfill was filled with 200 000 tonnes of refuse. The leachates were treated by four natural lagooning basins (see Aleya *et al* in this book).

(ii) Samplings and analysis procedures

Water samples for chemistry and phytoplankton were taken in the deepest part of each basin (1m) monthly using a Van-Dorn bottle between May 1998 and May 1999. The temperature (T), pH and dissolved oxygen (O_2), were measured *in situ* with a WTW multiparameter probe (Multiline P3 PH/LF-SET). Biological oxygen demand (BOD) was determined photometrically using a WTW spectrophotometer (Photolab Spektral). The phytoplankton species were collected monthly (May 1998 to May 1999). Identification of species was made on live cells to prevent cell destruction. Phytoplankton countings were achieved with an inverted microscope by Uthermol's method (1958) modified by Legendre and Whatt (1971-1972), after fixation with a Lugol's (4%) iodine solution (Bourrelly, 1985). The phytoplankton abundance was calculated using the following formula:

$$N = X/n * Rs * 1/v$$

Where, N: is the number of cells per ml of sample, X: is the total number of cells counted, n: is the number of optical fields, Rs: represents the ratio of the surface area of the sediment chamber to the surface area of the optical field, and v: represents the volume of sedimented water. Biovolumes were estimated from cell dimensions according to Lohman (1908) and converted to carbon biomass with the conversion factor 1 $\mu m^3 = 0.12\ 10^{-6}$ µgC. The biochemical composition of particulates was estimated after a gentle filtration (vacuum pressure <100 mm Hg) of samples on precombusted (550°C, over 6 hours) Whatman GF/C filters. The mixture of carbohydrates present which are mainly structural components of the cell wall, were hydrolyzed with concentrated sulphuric acid (97 wt.%). The phenol-sulphuric acid method of Dubois *et al.* (1956), modified by Moal *et al.* (1985) was used to determine the carbohydrate concentration. D-Glucose was used as the standard. Protein concentrations were determined by the method of Lowry (1951) with a bovine serum albumin (BSA) standard. Zooplankton was sampled in the four basins by a 75 µm pore size net.

Results

(i) Temperature

The temperature values of the leachate observed in the 4 Etueffont basins varied from 3.7 to 26.2 °C ($m \pm \sigma = 14.5 \pm 7.15$ °C) in B1, 1.7 to 26.2 °C ($m \pm \sigma = 13.4 \pm 8$ °C) in B2, 0.9 to 23 °C ($m \pm \sigma = 12.5 \pm 8$ °C) in B3 and 0 to 23.7 °C ($m \pm \sigma$ = 12,8 ± 8,3 °C) in B4 (Fig. 1a). These results provide evidence of similar seasonal evolutions of temperature in the 4 basins with warmer leachates observed in summer than in winter.

(ii) Dissolved oxygen

The dissolved oxygen concentrations measured in the 4 basins ranged between 0.17 and 12.5 mg. l^{-1} ($m \pm \sigma = 3.56 \pm 3.8$ mg. l^{-1}) in B1, 0.25 and 13.6 mg. l^{-1} ($m \pm \sigma = 5.4 \pm 3.6$ mg. l^{-1}) in B2, 1.5 and 17.1 mg. l^{-1} ($m \pm \sigma = 6.1 \pm 4.3$ mg. l^{-1}) in B3 and 1.5 to 16.1 mg. l^{-1} ($m \pm \sigma = 7.9 \pm 4.5$ mg. l^{-1}) in B4 (Fig. 1b). The distribution of dissolved oxygen concentrations pointed out two peaks, in summer and later in winter. The lowest values of dissolved oxygen concentrations were recorded in the first basin.

(iii) pH

pH values recorded in the 4 basins varied between 4.02 to 8.08 ($m \pm \sigma = 6.91 \pm 1.24$) in B1, 4.62 to 8.21 ($m \pm \sigma = 6.88 \pm 1.27$) in B2, 4.74 to 8.39 ($m \pm \sigma = 7.23 \pm 1.47$) in B3 and 4.55 to 8.86 ($m \pm \sigma = 7.23 \pm 1.47$) in B4 (Fig. 1c). The distribution of pH value showed a clear seasonal variability with alkaline pH in summer and more acidic values in winter and spring.

(iv) BOD

BOD values varied from 14 to 100 mg. l^{-1} O_2 ($m \pm \sigma = 26 \pm 46$ mg. l^{-1} O_2) in B1, 5 to 90 mg. l^{-1} O_2 ($m \pm \sigma = 24 \pm 23$ mg. l^{-1} O_2) in B2, 2 to 34 mg. l^{-1} O_2 ($m \pm \sigma = 17 \pm 8$ mg. l^{-1} O_2) in B3 and 2 to 50 mg. l^{-1} O_2 ($m \pm \sigma = 20 \pm 13$ mg. l^{-1} O_2) in B4 (Fig. 1d). These results pointed out both spatial and temporal decreases in organic content respectively from B1 to B2 and from summer to winter.

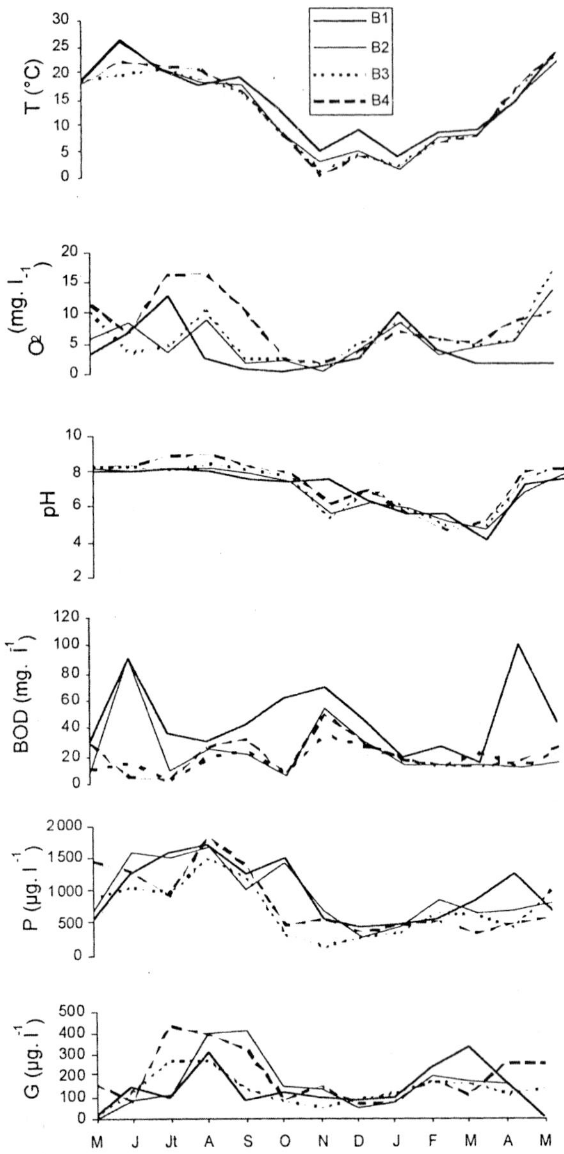

Fig. 1 : Spatio-temporal evolution of pH, temperature, dissolved oxygen (mgl^{-1}), biochemical composition of particulate matter (μgl^{-1}), BOD (mgl^{-1}) in the 4 basins

(v) Distribution of phytoplankton abundance and biomass

Basin 1: Phytoplankton density fluctuated between 0.016 x 10^6 and 2.9 x 10^6 cells l^{-1}, ($m \pm \sigma = 0.5 \times 10^6 \pm 0.8 \times 10^6$ cells l^{-1}) (Fig. 2) that corresponded to biomasses ranging between 2 and 1308 µg C. l^{-1} ($m \pm \sigma = 172 \pm 386$ µgC. l^{-1}). The calculated annual phytoplankton biomass was up to 4.6 mgC. l^{-1}, with maximum values registered in the summer of 1998 (i.e. May to August). The peak algal biomass (1.3 mgC. l^{-1}) recorded in August 1998 was chiefly associated with the development of *Chlamydomonas* sp..

Basin 2 : The Phytoplankton abundance measured in B2 ranged between 0.031 x 10^6 and 4.5 x 10^6 cells l^{-1} ($m \pm \sigma = 0.8 \times 10^6 \pm 1.3 \times 10^6$ cells. l^{-1}) (fig. 2), with an annual biomass of 5.9 mgC. l^{-1}. The phytoplankton biomass varied from 15 to 3769 µgC. l^{-1} ($m \pm \sigma = 456 \pm 1052$ µg C l^{-1}), with a maximal value of 3.76 mg C. l^{-1} recorded in August 1998; that coincided with the development of *Phacus* sp.

Basin 3 : The phytoplankton numbers estimated in B3 varied between 0.032 x 10^6 and 14.5 x 10^6 cells. l^{-1}, ($m \pm \sigma = 1.6 \times 10^6 \pm 4 \times 10^6$ cells. l^{-1}) (fig. 2) and biomass ranged between 3.47 to 5558 µgC. l^{-1} ($m \pm \sigma = 791.8 \pm 1777$ µgC. l^{-1}) with an annual calculated phytoplankton biomass reaching 10.29 mg C l^{-1}. The maximum biomass of 5.56 mgC. l^{-1} (May 1999) was attributed to the *Coelastrum* sp. development (49 % of the total biomass).

Basin 4 : The phytoplankton density ranged between 0.048 x 10^6 to 29 x 10^6 cells. l^{-1}, ($m \pm \sigma = 5.1 \times 10^6 \pm 10.2 \times 10^6$ cells. l^{-1}) (Fig. 2). This translated into phytoplankton biomasses ranging between 9 to 20685 µgC. l^{-1} ($m \pm \sigma = 3244 \pm 6936$ µg C. l^{-1}). The calculated annual phytoplankton biomass was up to 42 mg C. l^{-1}. The maximal algal development was registered in May 1998 and correlated with the blooms of *Coelastrum* sp. and *Euglena* sp.

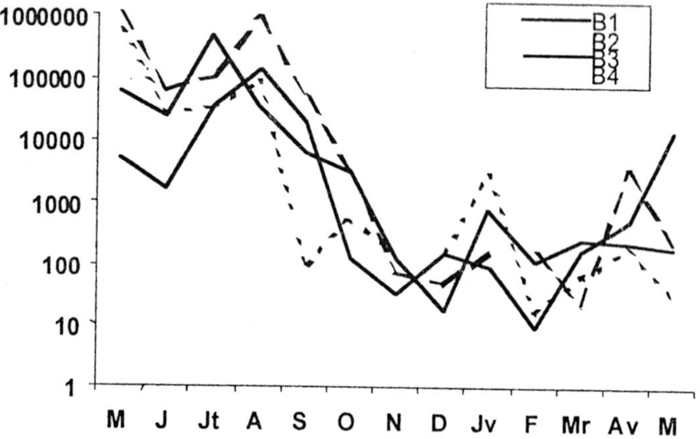

Fig. 2 : Spatio-temporal evolution of the algal abundance in the 4 basins (cells l^{-1})

(vi) Biochemical composition of the particulate matter

The particulate protein content of the leachate varied from 391 to 1680 µg. l^{-1} (m ± σ = 946 ± 467 µg. l^{-1}) in B1, 284 to 1669 µg. l^{-1} (m ± σ = 935 ± 452 µg. l^{-1}) in B2, 109 to 1468 µg. l^{-1} (m ± σ = 701 ± 413 µg. l^{-1}) in B3 and 330 to 1804 µg. l^{-1} (m ± σ = 797 ± 493 µg. l^{-1}) in B4 (Fig. 1e). The temporal distribution in protein contents showed high levels particularly in summer, that coincided with increased phytoplankton density. The particulate carbohydrate content of the leachate ranged between 8 to 324 µg. l^{-1} (m ± σ = 133 ± 100 µg. l^{-1}) in B1, 50 to 412 µg. l^{-1} (m ± σ = 160 ± 126 µg. l^{-1}) in B2, 37 to 265 µg. l^{-1} (m ± σ = 125 ± 37 µg. l^{-1}) in B3 and 60 to 425 µg. l^{-1} (m ± σ = 190 ± 125 µg. l^{-1}) in B4 (Fig. 1f). The distribution pattern of carbohydrate concentrations showed a clear decrease in winter concomitantly to that of proteins.

(vii) Spatio-temporal distribution of the Cladoceran community

The Cladocera population decreased from 30.000 individuals l^{-1} in the first basin to 800 individuals l^{-1} in the last basin. These metazoan communities were present only in summer and dominated by *Moina* sp. which is reputed to develop in rich organic matter leachate (Loedolf, 1965; Angeli, 1979). The decrease of individual numbers from the first basin to the last correlated with the increase in Rotifera and phytoplankton (*Stephanodiscus* sp. and colonial *Coelastrum* sp.) numbers. All these species have been shown to be poorly edible preys for *Moina* sp. (Angeli, 1979; Benider *et al.,* 1998).

Discussion

(i) Physico-chemical environment

The water temperature is an important and integral parameter in the functioning of aquatic ecosystems, and depends on the period of sunshine and exchanges with the atmosphere. Temperatures in the 4 basins were similar and varied between 18 to 25 °C in summer and 0 to 8 °C in winter (Fig. 1a) with the basins freezing in November 1998. The temperature of the leachate in basin B1 was the highest as this basin was immediately influenced by the inputs from the raw leachate and also shallower than basins B2, B3 and B4. We did not observe a clear thermal water stratification since the highest difference in temperature between the bottom and superfial layers did not exceed 6 °C.

The dissolved oxygen concentrations points out a spatial (between basins and from the bottom to the surface layers) and temporal (seasonal variation). The annual cycle appears to show two sequence of events. Firstly, elevated values varying from 3 to 12 mg l^{-1} are observed in summer in the euphotic zone. Secondly, in winter lower values ranging between 0 and 4 mg l^{-1} were closely related to cold temperatures, plant respiration, animals, micro-organisms and oxidation of dead organisms and their subsequent decomposition by heteroptrophic bacteria. However, during January 1999, we observed high levels of oxygen in the middle of the basins, most likely due to the winter algal bloom and wind-inducing oxygen water enrichment. The oxygen concentrations. In summer, oxygen concentrations were higher at the surface than in the bottom due to spring primary production.

PH is highly dependent on biological and chemical mechanisms. Among the factors which may influence pH, we will discuss temperature, photosynthetic activity and salinity. In summer, we observed an elevation in pH of (up to 8), with values decreasing in winter to reach 4. These values resulted in part from the collapse of the algal photosynthetic activity in the basins (consumption of H^+) and the supply of acidic leachates. The vertical evolution of pH did not appear to be influenced by water depth. However, the annual changes in the pH did not exceed 1 between the surface and the bottom of all sampling points. BOD values recorded in this work showed a progressive decrease from B1 to B4. This is most likely due to both sedimentation and degradation (oxidation) of organic matter by micro-organisms that colonized the leachate.

The distribution of protein and carbohydrate contents of the leachate showed increasing concentrations from B1 to B4, and from winter to summer that were associated to patterns of phytoplankton seasonal succession. Indeed, both proteins and carbohydrate concentrations peaked in summer when phytoplankton proliferated. The same results have already been reported by others but, to our knowledge, only from lacustrine environments (Ganf *et al.*, 1986; Bourdier,1998; Aleya, 1991; Michard *et al.*, 1996). In basin1, the increase in carbohydrate content resulted from supply via the protein and carbohydrate rich discharge originating from outside the basin. The protein to carbohydrate (P/C) ratios ranged between 2.34 and 123.72 in B1, 2.4 and 309.23 in B2, 2.92 and 522.12 in B3, and 1.84 and 17.29 in B4. In summer, the coupling of high supplies from very active leachate discharge and light levels had both favoured accumulation of carbohydrates whose production greatly exceeded protein synthesis. The same observations have been made by others from lab- experiments and aquatic freshwater and marine ecosystems (Morris and Skea, 1978; Ganf *et al.,* 1986; Aleya, 1992; Myklestad, 2000; Nagata, 2000).

(ii) Biological environment

Study of phytoplankton populations is highly informative and contribute to approch the community structures and allows to determine how communities are organized and which strategy they adopt, i.e. pioneer or mature development (Frontier, 1977; Reynolds, 1988; Aleya 1991). The presence of *Stephanodiscus* sp. and *Coelastrum* sp. in the basins, has also been reported from hypereutrophic lakes and reservoirs (Reynolds, 1984; Aleya *et al.*, 1994). In Etueffont landfill, the Euchlorophyceae represented approximately 10% of the algal population in B1, 13% in B2, 39% in B3 and 19% in B4. Euglenophyceae were more abundant representing 60 % of the total algal population in B1, 77% in B2, 58% in B3, and 76% in B4. The Bacillariophyceae accounted for 30 % of the total algal population in B1, 10% in B2, 3% in B3, and 5% in B4.

In basin1, the phytoplankton biomass showed a fluctuating trend all the sampling year round, most likely due to the interaction of a number of factors; (*i*) variations in temperature and day length; (*ii*) the leachate composition and input into the basins, that may supply the basin with organic and mineral nutrients able to induce phytoplankton proliferation; (*iii*) the grazing pressure exerted by zooplankton on edible phytoplanton preys yielding the waning of algal biomass in surface layers (*iv*) different structural parameters of the 4 basins.

The ecosystem found in the Etueffont basins is very particular and entailed an unpredictably low production of phytoplankton biomass and is dominated by populations of pollutant-resistant species such as *Stephanodiscus dubius* and *Euglena* sp. Despite high nutrient supplies, the water transparency period observed in summer (May to July 1998), seemed to be an important feature in the basin1 functionnig. While this behavioural pattern of prey-predator couples had been widely reported and modelled from lacustrine environments (Sommers *et al.*, 1986; Sterner, 1988; Aleya, 1991; Pinell-Alloul *et al.*, 2004), our study showed for the first time, to our knowledge this trend might occur in lagooning basins. The increase of phytoplankton biomass observed in winter 1999 (January 1999; 87.68 µgC. l^{-1}) is due to a decrease in mineral and organic contents (BOD decreased from 45 to 17 mg. l^{-1}) which originated from the rain-induced water dilution and the absence of zooplankton predators (Moinidae). Also, the phytoplankton community was monospecific (low diversity), and according to the theories of Margalef (1958, 1961), Odum (1960), Frontier (1977) and Sevrin-Ryessac (1998) who established a relationship between the specific diversity and degree of stability of a community, this trend correponds to a pionner strategy in species development. This leads to the break of system homeostasy and enhanced instability in the phytoplankton sequences of development yielding frequent algal invasions of surface layers .

The seasonal succession of phytoplankton in the other basins is characterised by two growth phases in summer and spring. In the summer of 1998, the increase in temperature, photoperiod, light intensity, and the presence of available nutrients, provided favourable conditions for the diverse algal species present to develop. However, this growth is downregulated by the prolific development of zooplankters (Rotifera and Moinidae) which actively exerted a significant grazing pressure of phytoplankton species. The collapse of zooplankton individuals linked to the drastic prey decline observed in August 1998 had induced new favourable conditions to phytoplankton species that underwent a valuable growth. In autumn, the fall in temperature, light intensity and the accumulation of both allochtonic and autochtonic organic matters, together with water overturn (which created homogenous temperature conditions, i.e. no stratification) induced the proliferation of the diatom *Stephanodiscus dubius.* This development went along with several reports pointing out a close relationship between *Stephanodiscus dubius* growth and the aformentioned conditions in lab experiments and field studies (Reynolds, 1990, Boumnich, 1992). During winter, an overall collapse of phytoplankton communities was observed except a short sequence of growth of primary producers in February 1999 correlating with an increase in both light intensity and water temperature and the decline in rotifer predators as reported by Sterner (1988), from limnic ecosystems. However, this episodic increase in phytoplankton biomass was not seen in basin4 due to rotifer *Keratella quadrata* grazing on algal species (Sommers *et al.*, 1986). In spring, the abiotic conditions improved and induced a shift in phytoplankton structure with the Chlorophyceae and Euglenophyceae, replacing the Bacillariophyceae. The decrease in algal density in May 1999 in the last basin was here again associated to the rotiferan grazing pressure.

(iii) Dynamics of the most abundant species

(a) Phacus orbicularis

The density of *Phacus orbicularis* decreased from the first to the last basin. This evolution correlated with an improve in leachate physico-chemical quality.

(b) Euglena sp.

This species that have been shown (Devars *et al.,* 1998) to efficiently tolerating highly polluted leachates in particular those containing metals (e.g. Hg, Cd and Pb), was the most dominant Euglenophyte in the 4 basins. In Basin1, *Euglena* sp. showed a clear pioneer-like strategy with short but intense phases of proliferation in May 1998, November and March and April. In the second basin, and from summer to autumn, *Euglena* sp. showed two short growth peaks; the first in August 1998 and the second in November. Thereafter, *Euglena* sp. disappeared to reappear in March 1999 but with a lower cell density than in summer. In the third basin, we observed the same dynamics as seen in B2 with relatively constant numbers from August to October, with a peak in August 1998. Finally, in the last basin the development of *Euglena* was constant during the year (1998) with a brief absence of growth in autumn. Maximum growth was observed in August.

(c) Stephanodiscus dubius

Stephanodiscus dubius is the most abundant algal species in the 4 basins and has been shown to exhibit a high tolerance to highly polluted waters (Germain, 1981). *Stephanodiscus dubius* was present throughout the year, and absent only in July 1998 in B1. The abundance decreased in B2 and a total absence was observed over three months during the summer of 1999 (May, June and August). The maximum total number of this species was observed in January. In the third basin, *Stephanodiscus dubius* was present throughout the year but with lower numbers than in the first two basins (B1 and B2). The maximum density of *Stephanodiscus dubius* in basin 3 was observed in August 1998. In basin 4, *Stephanodiscus dubius* numbers decreased to be absent even in 1998. Two peak growths had been observed, in August and in April.

(d) Chlamydomonas sp.

Chlamydomonas sp. is the only Euchlorophyceae specie that was commonly found in the 4 basins. This finding seemed obvious since *Chlamydomonas* sp. have been reported to develop in domestic treatment waters (Prat *et al.,* 1999). Nevertheless, observations of summer and spring growths in B1 showed a maximal growth in May 1998. In the other basins (B2, B3 and B4), *Chlamydomonas* sp. showed a slower rate of development compared to that observed in B1. In these last 3 basins, the dynamics of *Chlamydomonas* sp. were characterised by two growth phases, the first in May and June 1998 in B2, in May August and September 1998 in B3 and between June and August 1998 in B4. The second was observed in February and March.

(e) Chaetoptilis sp.

This species was absent in B1 likely due to its commonly

reported intolerance to highly polluted waters (Bourrelly, 1985). In the other basins, it developed sporadically.

(f) Coelastrum sp.

Also, this species was absent in B1 but present in B2 only in July. It developed preferentially in least polluted waters of B3 and B4.

(g) Kirchneriella sp.

This species was not present in the last basin, going along with its preference to poor organic matter waters. The other phytoplankton populations were consistently present in low density.

Conclusions

The inventory of taxa present in the basins (no inventory has been made before our work) showed a weak species richness. These results went along with the phytoplankton population inventories reported in the literature from domestic water treatment basins. Obviously, these findings underlined the strong environmental constraints in which algal species evolved.

The present study showed that the phytoplankton population in the Etueffont basins were dominated by pollutant-resistant species (*Stephanodiscus* sp. and *Euglena* sp.) However, a sharp qualitative improve in the phytoplankton population was noted from the first to the last basin, characterised by the substitution of diatoms (abundant in the first basin) by the Chlorophyceae (*Coelastrum* sp.). This qualitative evolution provides evidence for the decrease in leachate treatment. The leachate quality and the presence of predatory are cues to the dynamic of phytoplankton populations in the Etueffont basins.

Acknowledgements

The authors wish to thank the SICTOM (Syndicat Intercomunal de Traitement des Ordures Ménagères) of Etueffont (Territoire de Belfort, France) for financial support.

References

ADEME, *(Agence de l'environnement et de la maîtrise de l'énergie)* (1997) *Le traitement des déchets ménagers et assimilés en centres collectifs en 1995.*

Alaoui, M.M., Aleya, L. and Devaux, J. (1993) Phosphorus exchanges between sediment and water in trophically different reservoirs. Water. Res., 28 : 1971-1980.

Aleya, L. and Devaux, J. (1989) *Intérêts et signification écophysiologique de l'estimation de la biomasse et de l'activité photosynthétique de diverses fractions de taille phytoplanctoniques en milieu lacustre eutrophe,* Rev. Sci. Eau., 2: 353-272.

Aleya, L. (1991) The concept of ecological succession applied to an eutrophic lake trough the seasonal coupling of diversity index and several parameters. Arch. Hydrobiol., 3: 327-343.

Aleya, L. (1992) The seasonal succession of phytoplankton in an eutrophic lake through the coupling of biochemical composition of particulates, metabolic indicators and environmental conditions. Arch. Hydrobiol., 124 : 69-88.

Aleya, L., Desmolles, F., Bonnet, M.P. and Devaux, J. (1994) The deterministic factors of *the Microcystis aeruginosa* blooms over a biyearly survey in hypereutrophic reservoir of Villerest (Roanne, France), Arch. Hydrobiol. Suppl., 99 : 1-26.

Angeli, N. (1979) Relations entre le plancton et la qualité de l'eau', Ph.D. Thesis, *Université des Sciences et Techniques de Lille.*

Arhonditsis, G.B., Winder, M., Brett, M.T. and Schindler, D.E. (2004) Patterns and mechanisms of phytoplankton variability in Lake Washington (USA). Water. Res., 38 : 4013-4027.

Baun, A., Ledin, A., Reitzel, L.A., Bjerg, P.L. and Christensen, T.H. (2004) Xenobiotic organic compounds in leachates from ten

Danish MSW landfills—chemical analysis and toxicity tests, Water. Res. 38 : 3845-3858.

Benider, A., Tifnouti, A., Pourriot, R. (1998) 'Reproduction parthenogenitique de Moina macropa (Straus 1820) (Crustacea: Cladocera). *Influence des conditions trophiques, de la densité de la population, du groupement et de la température*', Annals Limnol., 34 : 387-399.

Boumnich, H. (1992) *Etude expérimentale des paramètres écophysiologiques des principales espèces phytoplanctoniques du lac d'Aydat (Puy-de-Dôme, France). Essai de modélisation des cultures algales.* Ph.D. Thesis, Univ. Blaise Pascale, pp. 148.

Bourrelly, P. (1985) *Les algues d'eau douce': les algues bleues et rouges,* Paris, France. Boubée et Cie, pp. 606.

Cauchie, H.M., Jaspar-Versali, M.F., Hoffmann, L. and Thomé, J.P. (2002) Potential of using *Daphnia magna* (crustacea) developing in an aerated waste stabilisation pond as a commercial source of chitin, Aquaculture., 205 : 103-117.

Christensen, T.H., Kjeldsen, P., Bjerg, P.L., Jensen, D.L., Christensen, J.B., Baun, A., Jensen, S.D., Bjerg, P.L., Christensen, T.H. and Nyholm, N. (2000) Toxicity of organic chemical pollution in groundwater downgradient of a landfill (Grindsted, Denmark). Environ. Sci. Technol., 34 : 1647-1652.

Devars, S., Hernandez, R. and Moreno-Sanchez, R. (1998) Enhanced heavy metal tolerance in two strains of photosynthetic *Euglena gracilis* by preexposure to mercury or cadmium, Arch. Environ. Contam. Toxicol., 34 : 128-135.

Dral-ides, C., Gervais, M. (1987) *Potentialités désinfectantes du lagunage par microphytes en climat chaud*, Premières observations. Inter-University Seminar on Wastewater in Waste Stabilization Ponds and Aerated Lagoons.

Dubois, M., Gilles, K.A., Rebers, P.A. and Smith, F. 1956, *Colorimetric method for determination of sugars and related substances*, Annal. Chem., 28 : 350--356.

Frontier, S. (1977) *Reflexions pour une théorie des écosystèmes*, Bull. Ecol., 8 : 445-464.

Ganf, G.G., Stone, S.J.L., and Oliver, R.L. (1986) Use of protein to carbohydrate ratios to analyse for nutrient deficiency in phytoplankton, Aust. J. Mar. Freshwat. Res., 37 : 183-197.

Germain, M. (1981) *Flore des Diatomées, eaux douces et saumâtres*, Paris, France, Boubée., pp 444.

Hoilijoki, T.H., Kettunen, R.H., Rintala, J.A. (2000) Nitrification of anaerobically pretreated municipal landfill leachate at low temperature, Water. Res., 34 : 1435-46.

Loedolf, G.J. (1965) The function of Cladocera in oxydation ponds, *2nd Int. Water. Poll. Res. Conf.* Tokyo, pp., 307-325.

Kettunen, R.K. (1997) Treatment of landfill leachates by low temperature anaerobic, sequential anaerobic_aerobic processes, *Ph.D. Thesis*, Tampere University of Technology, Finland.

Kjeldsen, P., Barlaz, M.A., Rooker, A.P., Baun, A., Ledin A. and Christensen, T.H. (2002) Present and long term composition of MSW landfill leachate, Crit. Rev. Environ. Sci. Technol., 32 : 297-336.

Legendre, L and Watt, W.D., (1971-1972) On rapid technic for plankton enumeration. Ann. Inst. Oceanogr. Paris, WLVIII, pp. 173-177.

Lohman (1908) *Untersuchungen zur festetellung des vollstandigen gehaltes des meeres an plankton*, Wiss. Meeresunters, Abt. Kiel N. F. 10 : 132-170.

Lowry, O.H., Rosebrough, N.G., Far, A.L. and Randal,l R.G. (1951) Protein measurement with the Folin phenol reagent J. Biol. Chem., 193, 265-275.

Margalef, R. (1958) Temporary succession and spacial heterogeneity in phytoplankton. *In : Perspectives in Marine Biology* (Ed. A.A. Buzzati Traverso) Univ. California press, Berkeley, pp., 323-347.

Margalef, R. (1961) *Algunas applicaciones de la informacion en el campo de biologia y concretamenta a la ecologia y al studio de la evolucion.* Scientia, Ser., 55 : 1-7.

Michard,. M., Aleya, L. and Verneaux, J. (1996) The mass occurrence of the Cyanobacteria *Microcystis aeruginosa* in the hypereutrophic Villerest Reservoir (Roanne, France):

Usefulness of the biyearly examination of N/P (Nitrogen/Phosphorus) and P/C (Protein/Carbohydrate) couplings, Arch. Hydrobiol., 135 : 337-359.

Morris, I. and Skea, W. (1978) 'Products of photosynthesis in natural populations of marine phytoplankton from the Gulf of Maine. Mar. Biol., 47 : 303-312.

Myklestad, S.M. (2000) Dissolved organic carbon from phytoplankton. *In: The Handbook of Environmental Chemistry. Marine Chemistry* (Ed. P. Wangerrky), pp. 111-148.

Nagata, T. (2000) Production mechanisms of dissolved organic matter. *In: Microbial Ecology of the Oceans* (Ed. D. Kirchman), pp. 121-152.

Nayar, S.L., Goh B.P. and Chou, L.M. (2004) Environmental impact of heavy metals from dredged and resuspended sediments on phytoplankton and bacteria assessed *in situ* mesocosms. Ecotox. Environ. Safety., 34 : 349-369.

Odum, E.P., Cantlon, J.E. and Kornicker (1960) 'An organizational hierarchy postulate for the interpretation on species individual distribution, species entropy, ecosystem evolution and the meaning of species variety index. Ecology, 41 : 395-399.

Pinell-Alloul, B., Méthot G., Malinsky-Rushansky, N.Z.: (2004) A short-term study of vertical and horizotal distribution of zooplankton during thermal stratification in Lake Kinnerest, Israel., 526: 85-98.

Prat, N., Toja, J., Solà, C., Burgos, M.D., Plans, M., Rieradevall, M. (1999) Effect of dumping and cleaning activities on the aquatic ecosystems of the Guadiamar River following a toxic flood. Sci. Tot. Environ., 242 : 132-248.

Reynolds, C.S. (1984) The Ecology of Freshwater Phytoplankton, Cambridge, Cambrige University Press.

Reynolds, C.S. (1988) The concept of ecological succession applied to seasonal periodicity of freshwater phytoplankton. Verh. Internat. Verein. Limnol., 23 : 683-691.

Reynolds, C.S. (1990) Temporal scales of variability in pelagic environments and the response of phytoplankton. Freshwat. Biol., 23 : 25-53.

Saqqar, M. M. and Pescod, M. B. (1991) Microbiological performance of multi-stage stabilization ponds for effluent use in agriculture (Kyoto). Water. Sci. Technol., 23 : 1517-1524.

Schwarzbauer, J. Heim, S. Brinker, S. and Littke, R. (2002) 'Occurrence and alteration of organic contaminants in seepage and leakage water from a waste deposit landfill. Water Res., 36 : 2275-2287.

Sevrin-Reyssac, J. (1998) Biotreatment of swine manure by production of aquatic valuable biomasses. Agr. Ecosyst. Environ., 68 : 177-186.

Shelef, G. and Azov, Y. (1996) The coming era of intensive wastewater reuse in the Mediterranean region. Water. Sci. Technol., 33 : 115-125.

Silva, A.C. Dezotti M.and Sant'Anna G.L.: (2004) Treatment and detoxification of a sanitary landfill leachate. Chemosphere., 55 : 207-214

Sterner, R.W. (1988) The role of grazers in phytoplankton succession. *In: Plankton Ecology.*, 107-170. Springer Verlag.

Sommer, U., Gliwicz, M., Lampert, W., and Duncan A. 1986, The PEG-model of seasonal succession of planktonic events in freshwaters. Arch. Hydrobiol., 106 : 432-471.

Utermöhl, H (1958) *Zur Vervollkommung der quantitative Phytoplankton-Methodik.* Mitt. Intern. Ver. Limnol., 9 : 1-38.

Vrijheid, M. (2000) Health effects of residence near hazardous waste landfill sites: a review of epidemiologic literature. Environ Health Perspect., 108 : 101-112.

Vrijheid, M., Dolk, H. and Armstrong, B. (2002) Hazard potential ranking of hazardous waste landfill sites and risk of congenital anomalies. Occup. Environ. Med., 59 : 768-776.

Welander, U., Henrysson, T., Welander ,T. (1998) Biological nitrogen removal from municipal landfill leachate in a pilot scale suspended carrier biofilm process. Water. Res., 32 : 1564-1570.

CHAPTER 7

MITIGATING WATER POLLUTION THROUGH FLORA AND FAUNA

V.S. Saxena

Ex-Additional Secretary; Environment: Rajasthan

A-2, Van Vihar; Tonk Road; Jaipur-302 018 (Raj.).

ABSTRACT

Increasing industrialization, urbanization and myriad forms of developmental activities including application of insecticides, pesticides and chemical fertilizers are polluting most of our water bodies. Mini-mata (mercury poisoning) of Japan is a glaring instance of sea water pollution.

Water is the elixir of life. In our country over 20 lacs of persons die annually due to water-borne diseases like typhoid, dysentery etc. Oil slick in waters of Gulf countries due to bombing devastated the marine life.

The chemical, mechanical and physical treatment of contaminated water through primary, secondary and tertiary treatments are highly costly. The paper highlights an alternative in Land Sewage disposal which is viable, symbiotic, replenishing and progressively productive. The entire bio-mass acts as a 'Living Filter'. Sewage lagoons or sewage filter beds, made on outskirts of towns provide excellent nitrogenous and phosphatic fertilizers. Water hyacinth - a pernicious water weed is harnessed to remove many injurious chemicals from water. The Duck-weed method employs tiny floating plants like big duckweed, water meal and water velvet which derive nutrients from the waste water and since they are extremely fast growing, they purify the water sooner. The polluted water when passed through the emergent aquatic plants like bulrush, spikerush, cattail and reed, is clear and neutral. Marshes too, are effective in treating waste water. Water chestnut, water spinach, sawan, kumudini, wild celery are desirable marsh plants.

In recent years, studies have proved that flora and fauna do serve as bio-indicators. Sago pond-weed tolerates high amount of TDS of 4200 to 7000 ppm. Dense growth of smart weed speaks of acidity in water. Water lettuce grows on potable water. Similarly, birds like small ring plovers, sand pipers in numbers suggest unpotable waters. Avocet and coots indicate increasing salinity in water. Pintails, cotton teal ducks occupy fresh water which is drinkable. Reptiles like crocodiles, gavials and turtles are reared to clean the Ganges waters. Mullee fish devours filth from water. Mirror carps are harnessed to control mosquitoes. A few decades back when frog legs were allowed to be exported, the menace of mosquitoes spread.

The bio-treatment of polluted water is thus both a cheap investment and heavy insurance to get sustained potable water.

Key Words : Bio-cide, mini-mata, sullage, sylvan, sacrosanct, eutrophication, aquifer, anoxic, pollutants.

Introduction

Water pollution is defined as "the adding to water of any substance or the changing of water's physical and chemical characteristics in any way which interferes with its legitimate use (Agarwal, 1987)". Polluted waters are turbid, not tasty in drinking, often smelling bad and are not suitable for bathing, washing and other human activities. They often serve as carriers of water borne diseases.

Most of our water bodies, such as, seas, ponds, tanks, dams, lakes, rivers, streams and even springs are getting polluted due to increasing industrialization, urbanization and other developmental activities like biocide application and fertilization in agriculture etc. Great Lakes of U.S.A., Rhine river of western Europe have been highly polluted. The minimata (mercury poisoning) of Japan is also a glaring example of marine water pollution. In India, all the 14 major rivers including Cooum, Ganga, Gomati, Cauvery, Damodar and mini-Mahi are polluted. The Damodar, nicknamed as "Sorrow of Bihar" in many sections, does not have any dissolved oxygen and so is almost dead for aquatic flora and fauna. Mini-Mahi river in Baroda is heavily loaded with industrial and petro-chemical wastes. The river Cooum, flowing through Chennai, is rendered so polluted with sewage etc. that even zoo-planktons can't sustain themselves. One litre of Cooum water contains 900 mg iron, 2765 mg lead, 1313 mg nickel and 32 mg zinc besides very high levels of phosphates, silicates, nitrate and sulphate levels being the highest among Indian rivers. The 2480 km long Ganges traversing particularly between Haridwar and Kolkata (with 27 major towns) is unfortunately the most convenient media to carry urban liquid wastes, half-burnt dead bodies, carrion, pesticides, insecticides etc. These 27 cities dump 902 million litres of waste water to the river every day. (Kanpur alone contributing 270 million litres of untreated sullage affecting 2.50 crores people in the northern India (Agarwal, 1987). Tests have revealed that the "pious" Ganges water at many places contain 8000 coliform bacteria /100 cc. of sample, more than 2000 chemical substances have been identified in water bodies, of which 700 have been found in drinking water all received from agricultural and industrial activities. About 50% of these are carcinogen (Chand, 1986). It is tragic that 20 lac persons die annually in India due to water borne diseases like typhoid, dysentery, cholera etc. Oil slick in Gulf countries, due to bombing in the water, killed marine life over a very large water expanse. These days physical pollutants are also significant. The chemical industries, fossil fuel and nuclear power plants use lot of water for cooling purposes and return the hot water to the stream. This thermal pollution affects aquatic life adversely. It has less oxygen.

Green Security Blanket

We are well aware that vegetation forms a 'green security blanket' protecting the fertile yet fragile soil, maintaining balance in atmospheric conditions, safeguarding supplies of fresh water and moderating their flow to prevent flash flood and destructive droughts. Human ingenuity will never be able to evolve better, cheaper and more efficient method of converting obnoxious carbon dioxide into life-giving oxygen than the subtle laboratory of nature in green chlorophyll of plants. Green leaf is the largest factory to provide oxygen. Greenary is thus, the most potential poison consumer. Plants are the 'lungs' for city dwellers. While designing human settlements, care should be taken to retain the existing plants on watersheds or else sylvan surrounds should be created simultaneously with house construction. This obviously also implies that trees along streams, lakes or other water bodies should be kept sacrosanct from felling to give the benefits of a green belt. Besides this, the hydrological regime of urban area can be improved by planting trees and shrubberies, perforating compacted lawns and using conservation practices like terracing, mulching, constructing sodded or turfed water ways for roof runoff.

Land Sewage Disposal

Sewage is defined as the water-borne waste derived from home (domestic waste) and animal or food processing plants and includes human excreta, soaps, detergents, paper and cloth (Agarwal, 1987). Most of the municipalities usually discharge untreated or partially treated sewage in water bodies. The organic matter is decomposed by aerobic bacteria resulting in depletion of oxygen (BOD). When dissolved oxygen is reduced below 4 to 5 ppm of water, fish becomes scarce. The sewage rich in phosphates and other nutrients encourages algal growth and also in the development of blue-green algae, leading to production of obnoxious blooms, floating scums or blankets of algae, giving rise to eutrophication as in river Chambal (Kota), Pichhola Lake (Udaipur), Jalmahal (Jaipur) etc. The aquatic plants grow profusely, die and decompose resulting in the increase in BOD value of water. Moreover, water bodies stink.

The chemical and mechanical treatment of the polluted water through primary, secondary and tertiary treatment are quite costly. There is an alternative in land sewage disposal which is viable and stable, organic and symbiotic, recycling and replenishing non-polluting yet progressively productive.

The waste water from residential areas, food processing plants and pulp mills are usually well suited for land disposal but in respect of industrial waste water, some treatment may be needed to remove the toxic substances which may be inimical to biological processes. The waste water is released on the land. The soil and vegetation the entire bio-system, acts as a "living filter". The mineral nutrients are degraded by micro-organisms particularly aerobic bacteria. The spongy floor covered with herbaceous vegetation and humus allow the water to percolate and extensive root system of trees, shrubs and grasses utilizes considerable amount of water. In fact, each root acts as a storage dam and helps in renovating the water bodies. The water is recycled and effluent is made use of for the ground water recharge. The utilization of higher plants, as an integral part of the system to complement the microbiological and physico- chemical processes in the soil is an essential component of the living filter concept and provides appreciable renovating capacity and durability to the system (Grey and Deneki, 1978). To maintain and improve water quality, studies were conducted by William Sopper in 1971 (Grey and Senki, 1978) in Masschusetts U.S.A. It was found that the living filter concept is feasible when following site conditions are available:

1. The soil must have higher infiltration rate than the recommended rate of applying waste water. Soil permeability must be high enough to permit drainage of renovated effluent and to maintain aerobic soil conditions. Forest soils, being porous, possess good percolation capacity.
2. Soil should be sufficiently deep upto ground water-table to retain dissolved minerals for utilization by plants and micro-organisms so that ground water is not contaminated.
3. Soil should not be compacted, otherwise chemical absorption and water retention quality will be negatively affected.
4. Land should have only gentle slope and relief so that accelerated water movement is impeded. Highly undulating and rocky hills are to be discarded.
5. Land must have adequate tree cover including ground vegetation, leaf litter and decomposed humus to abate surface run off.
6. An underground aquifer with a fairly deep water table, preferably with a horizontal permeability is preferable so that the renovated waste water could spread laterally.
7. There should be enough open land, close to the waste water disposal point so that bio-treatment is economic and effective.

It has been found that 4.5 million litres of waste water per day can be received well by a patch of plantation of 52 ha if the application rate of waste water is 5.08 cm per week. Thus, a city with a population of 1,00,000 people discharging 45 million litres of waste water can be accommodated in 520 ha. for a living filter system (Grey and Deneki, 1978). It is advantageous to dispose off the effluent on extensive blocks of forest land or agricultural fields. In cities and towns, the waste water could be discharged in parks, gardens, green belts, forest preserves, roadside avenues, median strips in highway and even golf courses.

The land sewage disposal has been in use for decades in many countries. Paris and Berlin had started using this system in 1850. The sewage of Tel Aviv (Israel) is put to use to grow fruits and vegetables in Negev Desert rather than contaminating the beautiful beaches of Mediterranean. In Seabrook Farms in Bridgeton, New Jersey (USA), 45 million litres of water used, every day for washing vegetables are spread on forest land. The Desert Inn Hotel and country club in Las Vegas, Nevada, uses purified sewage effluent to irrigate its 52 ha. golf course. In Rajasthan itself, sewage is used to irrigate lawns in municipal gardens, forest plantations (World Forestry Arboretum). Many industries are also coming forward to raise woodlots to recycle waste water. The water from *rasgulla* manufacturing units in Bikaner can be usefully employed for trees on small mounds where water-loving plants like *jamun, arjun, karanj, safeda, subabool, kalam, jarul, babool, palash* would do well.

Sewage Lagoons

Sewage lagoons or sewage filter beds are oxidation ponds and look like a pot-hole area in appearance. These provide effective and economical means for towns to handle sewage disposal. They are made on the outskirts of towns about 2 kms. away from the habitation. These are built on more or less level land in series and divided by dikes. These may extend to one hectare and may cover 10-15 ha. depending upon the extent of sewage (Linduska, 1964). The highly fertile effluent from sewage ponds often can be diverted into natural or man-made basins where it stimulates a vigorous growth of aquatic plants which serve as food for ducks and buffaloes and for wildlife (*sambhars*), if in or near the protected forests. The observer can walk along the dikes and enjoy the nature's gorgeous wildlife. Waste water whether in borrow pits, highway ditches, low lands, abandoned mines, swamps, marshes, basins near sewage lagoon are all useful. Fortunately, wildlife watchers are growing in number than wildlife users. They provide opportunities to scientist also for systematic studies and research.

In addition, aquatic weeds partially strip trees of harmful or odorous agents from drinking water including cadmium, nickel, mercury, phenol and potential carcinogens (NAS, 1976).

Sewage lagoons provide excellent nitrogenous and phosphatic fertilizers. Fertilizers manufacturing is energy intensive and thus increasingly expensive. For many rural farmers, the price of fertilizers is prohibitive. Aquatic plants to provide an indigenous source of cheap fertilizer and soil conditioners, which are readily available in rural areas. However, all aquatic plants are not equally adapted to grow on waste water. Some of the plants which grow best include water hyacinth (*Eichhomia crassipes)*, bulrush (*Scirpus spp.),* reed (*Phragmites spp.)* hydrilla (*Hydrilla verticiallata*), horn wort (*Ceratophyllum demersum)*, Duck weeds (*Spirodela, Lemna, Wolffia spp.),* (NAS, 1976). Fertilizer recovery is simple. The waste water effluent is allowed to settle in shallow ponds supporting aquatic vegetation. This crop is harvested regularly, each time leaving some plants to re-grow as a new crop to ensure a continuous water purification process. Alternatively, the water plants are allowed to grow for an entire season and then harvested; even after draining the pond. Waste from households and food processing (sugar, '*rasgulla*', potatoes, fruits) units can be purified by this process. In a sense, these aquatic plants are an agricultural crop utilizing free solar energy and growing on nutrients in the waste water. The techniques usually adopted in some cases are briefly given below:

Water Hyacinth Method

In warm countries, water hyacinth can increase at a phenomenal rate of 15% surface area per day. Under ideal conditions, water hyacinth has recovered the following elements:

Table 1 : Recovery of elements by water hyalinth

Element	Amount recovered (kg ha day^{-1})
Nitrogen	22 - 44
Phosphorus	8 - 17
Potassium	22 - 44
Magnesium	2 - 4
Calcium	11 - 22
Sodium	18 - 34

It has been reported that in Florida (USA) when sewage was passed through a pond at a rate of 22 lacs litres ha^{-1} day^{-1} water hyacinth removed 80% and 40% of nitrogenous and phosphorous compounds respectively in just 2 days. Water hyacinth culture reduces algae and faecal bacteria, suspended matter and odour causing compounds and therefore, the resultant affluent is clear, odourless and contains less nitrogen. Some phosphorus remains for it is removed rather slowly. Floating water hyacinth also encourages growth of zooplanktons like *Daphnia* that feeds on bacteria, it shades the lagoon and reduces wind and wave action, thus helping suspended matter to settle out.

It may be interesting to note that each kilogram of water hyacinth (dry weight) yields about 370 litres of biogas with an average methane content of 69% and calorific (heating) value (when used as a fuel) of about 22000 K J m^{-3}. Pure methane as we know, has the calorific value of 33000 KJ m^{-3}. Another advantage is the satisfactory digestibility of fresh water hyacinth as a roughage to the ruminants (whole plant 55.7%, leaf 50.8%, petiole 58.7% and submerged parts 51.2%). In South-east Asia, it is fed to pigs (1.5 to 2 kg fresh plants per day) while in China, chopped water hyacinth is mixed with other vegetable washes, salt etc. to make it a suitable feed for pigs. In Malaysia it is fed to ducks and pond fish also (NAS, 1976).

Duck Weed Method

The duck weeds (*Wolffia*, *Spirodela* and *Azolla* spp.) are fragile tiny free floating plants deriving the nutrients from water. Their vegetative reproduction is fast. They are easily skimmed or floated off with a rake or net as they cluster in colonies forming a scum on surface. Since, they are less fibrous, they are preferred by geese, fish, poultry, ruminants and pigs. These absorb nutrients through roots and lower surface of plant. The *Spirodela* or big duck weeds are as rich in proteins (37%) as soyabeans and make a good ration for swine. It grows well on wastes from swine and dairy cattle. It has high nitrogen value of 6-7% rivalling 8% inorganic fertilizers. *Wolffia arrhiza* or water meal is the smallest duck weed and indeed, it is the smallest flowering plant on earth (the size of a pin head). It has 20% protein, 44% carbohydrate and 5% fat on dry weight basis (NAS, 1976). The prolific plants can be harvested every 3-4 days during which time the unharvested few plants multiply into a thick yellow green mass of plants. Longer interval yield a brown, dead plant which is less valuable. In Thailand, the yield is 265 tons (fresh) or 10.5 tons (dry) ha^{-1} yr^{-1} better than even vegetable crops (NAS, 1976). *Azolla pinnata* (a small floating fern or water velvet) has been reported to double its weight in less than 7 days in Varanasi. Its special advantage is as a green manure especially for rice (NAS, 1976) where the yield increases upto 50%. A blue green microscopic alga *Anabaena azolla* lives in the cavities of the *Azolla* leaves. Interestingly, the *Anabaena azolla* algae uses light energy not only to fix nitrogen from the air but also to release hydrogen from water. It is considered to be the first known photosynthetic systems for producing hydrogen from water that is stable in air and that requires only water (H_2O) as a hydrogen source. In nature, the fixed nitrogen combines with hydrogen and forms ammonia that fertilizes the host *Azolla*. One may hopefully wish that one day *Azolla-Anabaena* symbiosis may be harnessed as a source of hydrogen for fuel.

Similar treatment to waste-waters can be given through emergent plants like bulrush (*Scirpus*), Spikerush (*Elaeocharis*), reed (*Phragmites*), cattail (*Typha*), etc. The water leaving these units is clear, neutral (pH 7.0) and will not exert an oxygen demand on the water. The submerged plants like horn-wort (*Ceratophyllum*) and *Hydrilla* (these plants do well only in oxygenated water and can not be relied to treat waste waters where microbial decomposition creates anoxic/anaerobic conditions) are also utilized similarly.

Lagooning waste waters is not regarded safe for public health, for if, mismanaged, the lagoons often become odorous and mosquito ridden, the water can seep and pollute groundwater and thus rendered ineffective to kill pathogenic bacteria. Modern research has however, established that when well-managed, the sweage lagoons are safe and possibly more efficient than conventional waste water treatment for removing pathogenic bacteria, parasitic worms (eggs), protozoa cysts and eggs and heavy metals. The role of aquatic plants is to remove inorganic nutrients from waste waters and they should not be used after harvesting, if they have had a direct contact with raw sewage (particularly that which contained pesticides, heavy metals or the industrial waste). Floating weedmats of duckweeds etc. that completely cover the water surface, reduce natural aeration of water and sunlight for photosynthesis by algae and submerged plants that also oxygenate the water, must be harvested systematically and regularly to maintain free water surface.

Marshes

The waste water that flows through marshes comes out cleaner and less enriched with nutrients than when it entered. This cleansing principle has been used widely to get rid of contaminants from the water. The emergents cattail (*Typha aungustata*) or *aira/patera* are useful for settling basins and nutrient traps. The run-off from agricultural areas contains significant amounts of pollutants such as fertilizers which induce eutrophication; herbicide which influence plant spp. composition and insecticides which modify invertebrate populations (Weller, 1981). It is obvious that the marsh is a forgiving and adaptable system but it should not be considered as a dump for excess nutrients. Water plants do remove nutrients from waste water with subsequent conversion to plant bio-mass, that can be used for livestock feed or for fuel. *Hydrilla* and duckweed produced 15.3 and 13.5 m tons of biomass ha^{-1} yr^{-1} respectively in Florida. Water hyacinth (*Jalkumbhi*) produced 88.3 tons ha^{-1} yr^{-1}. It is estimated that a 400 ha water hyacinth farm in southern

U.S.A. could generate 10^{12} PTU of energy as methane gas and remove nitrogen and other nutrients from waste water for a population of 7 lacs people (Weller, 1981). A few other useful marsh plants include water chestnut (*Trapa natans*), waterspinach (*Ipomoea aquatica*), *kaseru* (*Carex* spp.), *aincha* (*Pseudoraphis spinescens*), knot grass (*Paspalum* spp.), wild millet or *sawan* (*Echinochloa* spp.), wild celery (*Vallisneria* spp.), spikerush (*Elaeocharis* spp.), *kumudini* (*Nymphoides* spp.), chufa (*Cyperus* spp.) etc. The marsh as a productive system rivals the most productive natural or even intensively managed agro-ecosystem besides purifying water.

Bio-Indicators of Water Quality

The water is normally not pure in a chemical sense. It contains impurities which may be dissolved (gases like hydrogen sulphide, carbon dioxide, ammonia, nitrogen etc. and minerals like salts of calcium, sodium, magnesium etc.) or suspended particles (as clay, salt, sand, mud and microscopic organisms). These are natural impurities derived from atmosphere, catchment area and the soil but they are in such low concentration that they do not pollute the waters; rather their presence is often essential for maintaining the potable and other desirable properties of water (Agarwal, 1987).

Many plants serve as indicators of water quality. In fact, the composition of aquatic plants mirrors the chemical composition of its water body. If mining industrial activity extends to the natural rock formation add toxic materials or mineral to the water, the plants downstream can be toxic even though, the same plants upstream may not be toxic. These plants remove the concentrated harmful elements, which may become 4000 to 20000 times more concentrated in the plants than in the water (NAS,1976).

Sago pondweed (*Potamogeton pectinatus*) tolerates high amount of dissolved salts, the optimum growth is noticed when the total dissolved salts (TDS) concentration is 4200 to 7000 ppm, although it can be goown even upto 20000 ppm. Muskgrass (*Chara* sp.) and naiads (*Najas minor)* are also salt tolerant plants. The grass *Sporobolus* and the tree *farash* (*Tamarix aphylla*), the shrub *jhau* (*T. dioca*) are also suggestive of high salinity. Yellow lily (*Nuphar advena*) indicates a small amount of dissolved minerals in the water and that is why the adage "lilies and ducks do not go together' (Linduska, 1964). White waterlily (*Nymphaea nauchali*) or spatterdock is suggestive of turbidity in water which is not good for the development of submerged plants and aquatic animals. Smartweed (*Polygonum*), muskgrass and *Hydrilla* reduce turbidity. Dense growth of arrowhead (*Sagittaria sagittifolia*), spatterdock and smartweed etc. speak of acidity in water. Heavy cattail and bulrush lead to botulism in water. Green scum (certain blue-green algae- some of them poison producing) appear abundantly where sewage and other organic wastes have been dumped. The blue-green *alga-Spirulina plantensis* has, however, been harnessed to produce rich proteinous food even for human beings. Pure stands of water spinach or *nadi* often point to the occurrence of soft drinking water; the floating tender shoots and leaves of it make a delicious green vegetable. Water lettuce (*Pistia stratiodis*) also grows on potable water. Lotus or *kamal* (*Nelumbium nucifera*) develops well in muddy waters.

Among animals, the birds small ring plover, blackwinged stilts, sandpipers in numbers suggest dirty and unpotable water. The presence of avocets and coots in flocks point to an increasing salinity in the water. The flamingoes, cormorants and crested grebes (migratory bird) prefer saline water but they inhabit soft waters also. On the other hand, the common river terns, pintails, comb duck, cotton teal, blue (small) kingfishers always come to fresh potable water. The reptiles-crocodile, gaviale and turtles feed on dung, carcass and carrion and thus keep the water clean (Saxena, 1989). The Ganges Cleaning Project is also encouraging their rearing for subsequent release in Ganga waters. The fish *'mullee'* *(Wallage attu)* devours filth from water; the seagulls pick up garbage from water and thus help in sanitation of water. Mirror carp and the frogs feed upon larvae of mosquitoes on stagnant waters. These are some of our useful water scavengers provided by the Nature.

Conclusion

It would thus be seen that the bio-treatment of water is economical, efficient and can be practically executed. In fact, it is both a cheap investment and heavy insurance for getting sustained supply of potable water for the living beings.

References

Agarwal, A.L., and Sharma, H.C. (1985) Air quality status and management. *In : Air Pollution and Plants.* A state of the art report, Ministry of Environment and Forest, Govt. of India, New Delhi , pp., 1-9.

Agarwal, Anil, Kashyap Neera, *et.al.* (1987) *The Wrath of Nature*, Cen. Science and Environment, Delhi.

Agarwal, K.C. (1987) *Environmental Biology,* Agro-Botanical Publisher (India), Bikaner.

Anonymous (1981) *Down with the Acid Rain Story.* Environment Canada, Cat. No. In. 56-56/1981. E. ISBN-0-662 1182-3.

Arnold Henry, F. (1980) *Trees in Urban Design.* Van Nostrand Reinhold Co., New York.

Bakhre, Prakash, (1980) *Pollution threats to avifrauna of wetlands.* Wetland Conservation Env. Comm. Centre, Udaipur.

Brady, Jone, E., (1985) *Achchhe Swastha Ke Liye pani*, Sarovottam (Readers Digest) Vol., 5. May, 1985, pp. 12, New Delhi.

Chand Attar (1985): *Environmental Challenges : A Global Survey.* WDH Publishers, Delhi.

Goyal, M.K. (1989) *Environment and its Preservation.* Environmental perception DOE, Jaipur.

Grey, Gene W. and Deneki, Frederick J. (1978) *Urban Forestry.* John Wiley and Sons, New York.

Gupta, R.K. (1980) "*Plants for Environmental Conservation,* (Eds. Bishan Singh and Mahendra Pal Singh) Dehra Dun.

Kumar, K (1972) *Environmental Pollution,* Civil Services Chronicle, Delhi.

Linduska, J.P. (1964) *Water fowl tomorrow;* Fish and WL. Service, U.S.A. Washington DC.

Nat. Aca. Sciences (1976) *Making acquatic weeds useful,* Washington DC.

Saxena V.S. (1975) A study of flora and fauna of Bharatpur Bird Sanctuary. Tourism Deptt. Rajasthan, Jaipur.

Saxena, V.S. (1981) Plants in the improvement of urban environment, *Proc. Workshop on "Modern Techniques of site identification for Afforestation and Pasture development.* I.P.I. Dehra Dun, pp. 170-176.

Saxena V.S. (1989) Wetland and their management as, waterfowl habitat. In : *Wetland Conservation,* Env. Comm. Centre, Udaipur.

Saxena, V.S. (2003) Plants in Pollution Control. *In Current Environmental Issue* (Eds. B.B.S. Kapoor, Ahmed Ali, K.K. Singh and Chandrakanta) Madhu Publication, Bikaner,

Weller, M.W. (1981) *Fresh Water Marshes.* Univ. of Minnesota Press, Minnesota, U.S.A.

CHAPTER 8

WATER POLLUTION AND ITS MANAGEMENT

Alka Tomar[1], Ashok K. Choudhary[2] and Gayatri Verma[3]

[1] CMS Environment, Centre for Media Studies, (Research House) Community Centre, Saket, New Delhi 110 017.

[2] Dept. of Soil Science and Agril. Chem., S.K.N. College of Agriculture, Jobner (Raj.).

[3] S.M. Degree College, Palidongra, Sonkh, Mathura (U.P)

ABSTRACT

The paper deals with various kinds of sources of water pollution. Various river systems like North and South Indian rivers with different pollution loads are described in detail. Water pollution due to pesticides and their residues in both abiotic and biotic components of the environment are dealt with. Heavy metal pollution in water and their effects on fresh water bodies and control of metal pollution are described.

Key Words : Indian Rivers, Water Pollution, Management

Introduction

Water pollution is one of the greatest concern now-a-days whose impact on agriculture is significant. Loss of nutrients is caused through different processes like leaching etc. Chemicals used in agriculture sometimes leave considerable amount of residues depending upon the persistence, directly affecting beneficial soil organisms adversely. In recent years, considerable attention has been paid to industrial wastes (distillery and paper industries etc.) discharged on land or into sources of water. Industrial effluents often contain various toxic metals, harmful gases such as SO_2, CO_2 etc., several organic and inorganic compounds. These may accumulate in soil in excessive quantities in long-term use, ultimately causing physiologically adverse effects on crop productivity (Sarkar and Mishra, 2004).

Water is polluted by four kinds of substances : traditional organic waste, waste generated from industrial processes, chemical agents of fertilizers and pesticides used for crop protection and silt from degraded catchments. While it is estimated that three-fourths volume from municipal sources, industrial wastes contribute over one-half of the total pollutant load, and major portion of this is coming from large and medium industries. There has been a steady increase in the amount of waste water produced from urban communities and industries. Generally, these water are discharged into lagoons or dumped on low lying areas without any pretreatment, thereby creating sewage pools, contaminating ground waters, salinizing good quality lands around cities, acting as source of foul smell/odour and breeding grounds from mosquitoes and other pathogens. At many places, this waste water is discharged into drains and rivers causing serious water pollution (Martin, 1998).

There are about 3200 major industries in India and a large number of small industries. The major industries polluting our rivers include pulp and paper, textile, tannery, sugar, distillers, vegetable oil, chloralkali, plastic, fertilizer, detergent, petrochemical, steel and several miscellaneous industries like paint, rubber, antibiotics, chemicals and dairies (Table 1). To control air and water pollution, the Union Ministry of Environment and Forests has identified 17 most polluting industries and asked them to install pollution control devices/equipment or face punitive action, including forcible closures. The 17 industries declared as most polluting are sugar, fertilizer, cement, fermentation and distillery, aluminium, petrochemicals, thermal power, caustic soda, oil refineries, tanneries, copper smelters, zinc smelters, iron and steel, pulp and paper, dye and dye intermediates, pesticides and pharmaceuticals (Table 1). The latest figure released by the Ministry of Environment and Forest on March 30, 1993 show a total of 1624 units in India which fall under these categories (Abel *et al.*, 1995).

Table 1 : Toxic chemical production in India (In '000 tonnes)

Industries	1960	1970	1980	1986-87
Pesticides	1.46	3.00	40.68	56.2
Dyes & pigments	1.15	13.55	30.85	-
Organic Chemicals Petrochemicals	580	17100	24100	42500
Fertilizers	153	1059	3005	7000
Steel (Ingots)	1500	3400	8000	9000
Non-ferrous metals	8.5	34.6	82.9	123.4
Caustic soda	101	304	457	764
Pharmaceuticals	1.23	1.79	5.07	-

Source : GOI Publication, India, 1988-89

Generally, the pollutants come from three sources (i) sewage discharged into the river, (ii) industrial effluents discharged into the river without any pretreatment, and (iii) surface run-off from agricultural land where chemical fertilizers, pesticides, insecticides and manures are used. This makes the river water unsafe for drinking and bathing. About 1500 substances have been listed as pollutants in fresh water ecosystems and a generalized list of pollutants includes acids and alkalies, anions (e.g. sulphide, sulphite, cyanide), detergents, domestic, sewage and farm manure, food processing water, gases (chlorine, ammonia), heat, metals (cadmium, zinc and lead), nutrients (phosphates and nitrates), oil and oil dispersants, organic toxic wastes (formaldehydes, phenols), pathogens, pesticides, polychlorinated biphenyls and radionuclides. In addition to oxidizable material, domestic sewage contains detergents, nutrients, metals, pathogens and a variety of other compounds.

River Pollution in India

Water pollution in India has now reached a crisis point. Almost, every system in India is now polluted to a considerable extent. As assessed by the scientists of the National Environment Engineering Research Institute (NEERI), Nagpur, nearly 70% of water in India is polluted. India has five major river systems, namely, the Ganga, the Brahmaputra, Indus river system in North and the Peninsular East Cost and the West Coast river systems in the South.

(a) North Indian Rivers

Many large rivers are closely associated with the Indian culture and heritage. The pollution situation in our country is worse than that of some of the industrialized countries of western Europe and America. The Ganges, the most sacred and important river in India, is regarded as the cradle of Indian civilization. The 2525 km long river starts from Gangotri in the Himalayas and joins the Bay of Bengal at Ganga Sagar. According to a report of the Central Pollution Control Board, despite river Ganges' considerable resilience as a self-purifying and fast-flowing river, its organic pollution load is significantly high. At Kanpur, 45 tanneries and 10 textile mills are the major sources of liquid wastes discharged into the river Ganges. The wastes contain heavy organic load and putrescible material. It is estimated that 1400 million litres of sewage and 200 million litres of industrial effluents are being discharged everyday into the river Ganges. The BOD (106 tonnes/day), total solids (2308 tonnes/day) and suspended solids (1.251 tonnes/day) are not only very high but also exceed the prescribed limits of Indian Standards Institution. Recently, discharges from the Barauni oil refinery caused gross pollution on a long stretch of the main Ganges. Preliminary observations were made on the pollution of the river *Kali* and a limnological survey was made of the river with reference to fish mortality. The main factories, which pollute the stream are sugar, distillery, tin, glycerin, paints, soap works, spinning, rayon, silk and yarn (Table 2).

Table 2 : Incidences of fish kill in Indian waters due to water quality deterioration

	Place	Year	Pollutant
1	Kankaria lake, Ahmedabad	1982	Domestic waste
2	Naini lake, Nainital	1980, 81	Domestic waste
3	R.Gomati, Lucknow	1983, 84, 86	Distillery waste
4	R.Chaliyar, Alivaye	1974	Pesticide
5	R.Tungabhadra, Harihar	1984	Rayon polyfibre
6	The Ganges, Allahabad	1981	Fertilizer effluent
7	R. The Ganges, Monghyr	1968	Oil refinery
8	R.Adyar, Chennai	1981, 82	Tannery
9	Rihand Reservoir	1970, 78, 80	Chemical & Thermal effluent

Source : Martin (1998)

A limnological survey was carried out in 1965 in 25 km stretch of the river Gomati in the vicinity of Lucknow receiving 19.84 million gallons of wastes per day from pulp and paper factory, distillery and sewage. Heavy fish mortality was reported in Rihand reservoir due to high free chlorine content (62 ppm) discharged from Kanoria Chemical Industries (Tandon, 1988). The organic wastes from a sugar factory and a distilleries plant cause year round pollution of the small river *Daha*. A case of heavy fish mortality was recorded in 1962 and 1966. Wastes from different factories such as those engaged in the manufacture of paper, chemicals, sugar cement etc. are the major sources discharging over 4 million gallons of wastes per day into the river *Sone*.

The river *Hooghly* at Kolkata receives wastes from various types of factories dealing with pulp and paper distillery, tannery, textile, heavy chemicals, paints and varnishes, shellac, hydro-generated soil, matches, cycle rim, petroleum oil, tarpigment, insecticides and fungicides. Of these, wastes from paper and pulp distillery, chemicals, textiles shellacs and a number of domestic outfalls contribute substantially to the pollution complex. River *Damodar*, which flows through the coal belt area in Bihar is also a seriously polluted area. The river experiences pollution due to the wastes released from large number of industries such as the Sindri unit of the Fertilizer Corporation of India, the Bihar Government's Superphosphates factory and the associated cement company. The entire Asansol-Durgapur industrial belt on lower Damodar valley suffers from severe pollution caused by the discharge of wastes containing high phenol, cyanide and ammonium nitrogen (Sinha, 1988).

The indiscriminate discharge of large volumes of highly putrescible liquid wastes of the Orient Paper Mills creates a serious pollution problem in the river *Ib* (Orissa) of the

Mahanadi river system. The river *Bhadra* (Krishna river system) receives effluents from pulp & paper and steel industries.

Industries generate a significant quantity of waste water which ultimately finds its way to a stream/river. Industrial discharges containing toxic and hazardous substances contribute to the severe kind of pollution in the aquatic systems. Industrial development is largely because of the production of chemicals resulting in the generation of toxic and hazardous substances which have been continuously on the increase during the last three decades.

Industrial effluents, though comparatively lesser in volume, cause serious menace to aquatic environment and the biotic communities including fish and ultimately affect man through food chain.

(b) South Indian Rivers

River *Godavari* at Rajahmundry (Andhra Pradesh) is polluted by the effluent of Andhra Paper Mill at Rajahmundry. The river *Kalu* in Mumbai receives highly acidic and untreated wastes from Amar Dye and Chemical Company, Indian Dyes, Century Rayon, National Rayon, Central Chemicals, etc. Effluents of the Gwalior Rayon factory at Mavoor, about 21 km from Beypore, have created a pollution hazard in the river Chaliyar at Calicut, Kerala. A large scale fish mortality in 1966 was attributed to highly putrescible organic matter creating almost anaerobic conditions in the river with very low or nil oxygen.

In Tamil Nadu, river *Cooum* at Chennai gets polluted by the washings from a large number of slums, cattle yards, overflow from sewage pumping station, wastes from automobile workshops and many factories. Nearly, 300 tanneries are spread along the banks of river Palar over a stretch of 120 km from Vaniambadi to Ranipet. The wastewater discharge from these tanneries affects the ground water quality because of sodium and chlorides present in the tannery waste. River Cauvery is polluted by Mettu Chemical and Industrial Corp. Ltd., Mettur Dam. River Vaigai receives effluents from many chemical and soap factories, and large quantities of municipal sewage.

The rate of pollution in South Indian rivers seems to be higher than those of the North Indian rivers. The main reason for this is the summer season during which the icebergs get melted and the melted water is drained into the major North Indian rivers like the Ganges, the Brahmputra etc. During the rainy season, rivers get a good current from the natural shower itself. The only possibility of pollution for such rivers is, by the catchment of pollutants when they pass through the urban and the industrial belts. Whereas the South Indian rivers do depend upon the North-East and the South-West monsoons. Deforestation also affects rainfall and ultimately changes the river flow in South Indian rivers. Already, these rivers are under stress due to lack of rainfall caused by deforestation and pollution is an additional/secondary stress.

Water Pollution Due to Pesticides

A large number of pesticides are being used for destroying, repelling or reducing a wide range of pests in agriculture, forestry and public health today. Soil serves as a major environmental sink for bulk of the pesticides used in agriculture. A portion of the applied pesticides irrespective of crop, applicator or the formulation used, ultimately finds its way into the soil (Edward, 1972). According to several estimates as much as 50% of the pesticides applied to the foliage falls on the soil depending on the crop canopy and the mode of application.

The use of chemical in plant protection is a profit induced poisoning of the environment. The concentration of pesticide residues in air, soil, water, flora and fauna is continuously increasing day by day and in the near future it may reach the level of poisoning (Singh and Verma, 2000).

The tendency of pesticides to leach from soils is closely related to their potential for adsorption. Strongly adsorbed molecules are not likely to move down the profile. Likewise, conditions that encourage such adsorption will discourage leaching. Leaching is apt to be favoured by water movement, taking place most readily in permeable sandy soils that are low in clay and organic matter. In general, herbicides seem to be more mobile than either fungicides or insecticides (Table 3).

Table 3 : Comparative ease with which pesticides move in the soil.

Mobility class 5 moves most rapidly, while class 1 is quite immobile. Note that herbicides generally are more mobile than the other (bold type) pesticides.

5	4	3	2	1
TCA	Picloram	Propachlor	Siduron	Parathion
Dalapon	Fenac	Fenuron	Prometryne	Disulfoton
2,3,6-TBA	MCPA	2,4,5-T	Propanil	Diquat
Tricamba	Amitrole	Propham	Diuron	Paraquat
Choramben	Dinoseb	Flueometuron	Linuron	Trifuralin
		Monuron	Purazon	Benefin
		Atrazine	Vernolate	Heptachlor
		Simazine	Chlorpropham	Aldrin
		Propazine	Azinphosmethyl	Chlordane
			Diazinon	Toxaphene
				DDT

Source : Helling *et al.* (1971)

The residues of pesticides also contribute significantly towards contamination of air, water, soil and food. Many western countries have established intensive monitoring programmes to estimate the levels of pesticide residues in both abiotic and biotic components of the environment. However, national programme to monitor pesticide residues and their biological effects are still lacking in India. The limited monitoring data collected by different workers on water are given in tables 4-5.

Table 4 : Pesticide residues in water from different regions in India

Sampling area	Pesticide	Residue level
Ponds in coffee plantations, Chikmanglur (Karnataka)	HCH	0.02-0.2 ppm
River Hooghly	Dimetheoate	0.2-1.0 ppm
Ludhiana and Muktsar (Punjab)	HCH	0.9 ppb
Yamuna, Delhi	DDT	2.9-21.8 ppb
Srinagar (J&K)	HCH	2.5-73.5 ppb
	DDT	2.9-21.8 ppb
Malwa Region, Jaipur (Raj.)	HCH	0.0025-0.340 ppb
Mahalan Lake	Heptachlor	0.09-3.32 ppm
	Aldrin	0.02-2.80 ppm
	Total DDT	0.027-24.65 ppm
Jalmahal lake	HCH	0.01-2.01 ppm
	Heptachlor	0.01-2.01 ppm
	Aldrin	0.01-1.55 ppm
	Total DDT	0.04-47.4 ppm

Contd.

River Khan (near Indore, MP)	Total HCH	0.049-0.391 ppm
River Kshipra (near Ujjain, MP)	Total HCH	N.D.-2.7720 ppm
	Total DDT	N.D.-0.219 ppm
	Aldrin	N.D.-5.00 ppm
River Chambal (near Kota, Rajasthan)	Total HCH	0.06-1.488 ppm
Drinking water	Total HCH	1.576-15.88 ppm
Sources around Bhopal	Total DDT	3.153-34.771 ppm

Source : Kulshrestha (1991)

Table 5 : Pesticide Residues in Water-Ganga Action Plan Project

Location	Year	Number of samples analysed	Insecticides detected	Residue (ppm)
UP (16 locations)	1986-87	125	Total HCH	8.9-971.5
	1987-88*			3.6-720.7*
	1988-89*			ND-327.10**
		192	Total DDT	ND-352.20
		192		ND-866.03
				ND-5808.20**
			Endosulfan	ND-25.20
				ND-671.70*
				ND-79.50**
			Malathion	ND-6902.1
				ND-4610.90*
				ND-144.90**

Contd.

			Methyl parathion	ND-546.00
				ND-169.70*
				ND-279.30**
			Dimethoate	ND-1508.00
				ND-8771.90*
				ND-193.60**
			Ethion	ND- ND
Bihar (7 locations)	1986-87	52	Total HCH	ND-68.90*
	1987-88*	84		1.2-5133.8*
	1988-89**	70		ND-231.80**
			Total DDT	9.4-117.3
				ND-469.01*
				ND-1605.55**
			Endosulfan	ND-83.40
				ND-52.90*
				ND-234.60**
			Malathion	ND-840.60
				ND-568.00*
				ND-120.00**
			Methylpara-thion	ND-120.00
				ND- ND*
				ND-40.30**
			Dimethoate	ND-545.0
				ND-2335.7*
				ND-1701.90**

Contd.

			Ethion	ND- ND
				ND-48.6*
				ND-1995.30**
West Bengal	1986-87	24	Total HCH	15.6-789.7
	1987-88*	45		4.9-6571.1*
	1988-89**	44		1.70-512.00**
			Total DDT	10.6-256.3
				ND-183.52*
			Endosulfan	ND-15.3
				ND-337.1*
				ND-12.10**
			Malathion	ND- ND
				ND-99.6*
				ND-155.20**
			Methylpara-thion	ND-120.00
				ND-203.10**
			Dimethoate	ND-762.0
				ND-531.90*
				ND-938.90**
			Ethion	ND- ND
				ND-58.1*

* One year data

** Two year data

ND = Non-detectable

Source : Handa (1996)

Heavy Metal Pollution in Water

In an exhaustive survey, six metals viz., zinc (Zn), copper (Cu), chromium (Cr), cadmium (Cd), lead (Pb) and mercury (Hg) have been analysed in water samples collected from the banks and midstream at nine locations near Rishikesh, Hardwar, Kanpur, Allahabad, Varanasi, Buxar, Patna, Barauni and Bhagalpur along the river Ganga and four locations near Delhi, Mathura, Agra and Allahabad along the river Yamuna (Joshi, 1991).

Metal levels in the river Ganga have been recorded upto Zn, 285 μg^{-1}, Cu, 178.9 μg^{-1}, Cr, 200 μg^{-1}, Cd, 13.7 μg^{-1}, Pb, 26.11 μg^{-1}, and Hg 1.34 μg^{-1} in filtered water (0.45μg^{-1}) which are appreciably higher than the background levels for natural fresh waters. The analysis of fish (whole body dry wt. basis) showed Zn upto 189.6 mg kg^{-1}; Cu, 31.2 mg kg^{-1}; Cr, 8.33 mg kg^{-1}; Pb, 25.2 mg kg^{-1}; Cd, 0.8 mg kg^{-1} and Hg, 0.53 mg kg^{-1}.

In the tidal stretch of the Ganga, the industrial zone around Kolkata, extending upto 92 km, shows appreciable metal concentration along the banks. In unfiltered water, Zn, Cu and Cr, are encountered upto the maximum level of 1060, 40 and 588 μgl^{-1}, respectively. Zn is highest in sediments (382 $\mu g\ g^{-1}$) around Rayon factory outfall followed by 160 μgl^{-1} near paint and varnish factory. Although, the magnitude of the metal bearing wastes discharged into this tidal stretch of the river Ganga is quite significant (0.11 million cubic meter per day) from industries, the average metal levels in the estuarine water are lower than those recorded near the upstream locations.

In the river Yamuna between Delhi and Allahabad, the rising levels of metals in the ambient waters are reflected in high levels of Zn, 284.5; Cu, 81.35; Cr, 59.45; Cd, 3.85; Pb, 105.12 and Hg, 1.052 mg kg^{-1} dry wt. in sediments, Zn, 36.3;

Cu, 3.47; Cr, 1.25; Cd, 0.188; Pb, 1.56 and Hg, 1.38 mg kg^{-1} wet wt. in fish and Zn, 193; Cu, 18.8; Cr, 6.72; Cd, 1.8; Pb, 38.6 and Hg, 0.62 mg kg^{-1} wet wt. in mollusks (Jhingran and Joshi, 1987) (Table 2). Surface water samples from 20 different locations in the Brahmputra river including various public ponds, municipal drains, natural lakes and rivers along Greater Guwahati have been analysed for trace metals such as Na, K, Ca, Mg, Fe, Cu, As, Cd, Cr, Hg, Pb and Zn. Their concentrations in water are given in Table 6. The appearance of the trace metals and their concentrations in various sources of water of the Greater Guwahati area in general do not show any regular pattern (Kakati and Bhattacharya, 1990).

Table 6 : Metal Levels in Different Water Bodies in Greater Guwahati

Metals	**Range (mg l^{-1})**
Na	1.2-89.5
K	0.724-8.66
Ca	1.07-18.49
Mg	0.09-0.45
Fe	0.11-12.8
Pb	ND*-0.14
Cd	ND-0.01
Cu	ND-0.243
Cr	ND-0.03
As	ND-0.56
Hg	ND-0.33
Zn	0.01-0.97

* ND = Non-detectable

Source : Joshi (1996)

In the Hussain Sagar lake receiving the sewage and industrial effluents of the Hyderabad city, the concentration of metal ions in water is reported to be Cu, 141; Cr, 68.0; Cd, 4.6; Pb, 361 and Hg 22.0 $\mu g\ L^{-1}$. Similarly, the high metal ion concentration in Byramangala reservoir receiving the municipal waste waters of Bangalore city have been found upto Zn, 123; Cu 23; Cr, 15; Pb, 22; and Hg, 1.2 $\mu g\ L^{-1}$. The subsequent contamination of sediments and biomagnification along the aquatic food chain poses threat to the over all productivity of these ecosystems (Joshi, 1990).

Measures to Prevent Pollution

We not only conserve water, but also protect it from pollution.

- The industrial waste waters should be treated to the maximum possible extent to prevent pollution.
- The sewage from the city drains, with the partially treated industrial effluents should be processed in a sewage treatment plant, which at present is not available in major cities.
- In order to avoid the release of night soil and urban wastes which eventually join the river, the unsewered water be sewered forthwith.
- Defecation by the road side and ablution in the raw water channels should be made punishable by law so that contamination of raw water by enteric viruses and bacteriological pathogens could be avoided.
- The already existing laws for the prevention and control of water pollution need to be implemented forcefully.

Control of Metal Pollution

The installation of electrostatic precipitators and scrubbers in stacks and other outlets of factories handling Cd has proven to be an effective means to reduce the emission of metals into the atmosphere (Cuffee and Gerstle, 1967). In one particular instance the combined installation of cyclones, bag filters and precipitators resulted in the daily collection of 15000 kg of dust, 500 kg of which was Cd (Robertson, 1960).

Controlling the chemistry of Cd in soils offers another possibility to diminish the entry of metal into the food cycle. Liming the soil may precipitate the metal not only as carbonate, but also as sulphate and phosphate, depending on the abundance of these anions. Furthermore, the competitive effect of Ca^{++} and the physiological and chemical consequences of a rise in soil pH may be helpful in reducing Cd uptake by plant roots. Again, limited tillage may benefit deep rooting plants and turning the top soil may favour shallow rooting ones (Lagerwerf, 1972). The delicate balance between Cd, Zn and Hg regarding their competition for Se and for -SH groups of proteins and enzymes in plants and animals is an aspect not to be neglected in managing the trace element status of soils. The absorption of metals by plants would also be useful for removing metals from the aquatic ecosystems.

Conclusions

The control of metal pollution is necessary to stop the accumulation of metals in aquatic and terrestrial food chain and possible transport to humans. Besides, the removal of metals by chemical precipitation, electrolysis, ion exchange or biological means, there is urgent need to minimize use of metals in manufacturing processes which act as potential source of discharge of hazardous and toxic metallic compounds into the environment.

Among the sources of toxic chemicals causing pollution, the chemical industry plays a dominant role. The industry produces significant quantities of inorganic and organic chemicals used in manufacturing various products including drugs and pharmaceuticals, fertilizers, pesticides, textiles, plastics and detergents.

In view of the widespread effect of environmental pollution, it may be that in the near future, alarming adverse effects could paralyze the production of crops in due course of time. However, it is also matter of hope that nature has provided alternatives to bypass the unusual circumstances of environmental pollution. Overall, the whole community needs an integrated approach to sustain and save our ecosystem. In conclusion, it may be pointed out that government can frame stringent laws and rules, and also sometimes it can be ruthless in the implementation of these regulations.

References

Abel, W., Faiberg, L.T. and Shival, H. (1995) Problems of Deterioration of the Environment, Chapter 1, *In : Environment & Ecology : The Global Challenge* (Ed. Deepender Basu), Printwell, Jaipur, pp. 1-35.

Edwards, C.A. (1972) Insecticides, *In : Organic Chemicals in the Soil Environment* (Eds. C.A.I.Goring and J.W.Hamakar). Marcel Dekkar Inc., New York, pp. 513-520.

Handa, S.K. (1996) Monitoring of Pesticide Residues in Indian Environment, Chapter 7, *In : Agrochemicals and Sustainable Agriculture* (Ed. N.K.Roy), pp., 97-108, APC Publications Pvt. Ltd., New Delhi.

Helling, C.S., Kearney, P.C. and Alexander, M. (1971) Behaviour of Pesticides in Soils. Adv. Agron., 23 : 147-240.

Jhingran, A.G. and Joshi, H.C. (1987) Heavy metals in water sediments and fish in the river Yamuna. J. Industrial Fish Soc., 19(1) : 13-23.

Joshi, H.C. (1990) Water Pollution Problems in Indian Reservoirs. Proceedings of the National Workshop on Reservoir Fisheries, 3-4 Jan., 1990. A special publication of Asian Fisheries Society, Mangalore, India.

Joshi, H.C. (1991) Monitoring of Toxic and Hazardous Substances in the River Ganga. Proc. Work Trg. Biomon. R. Ganga CICFRJ, Barrackpore, 3-7, June, 1991, pp. 62-68.

Joshi, H.C. (1996) Heavy metal pollution in soil and water and remedial measures for protection of the environment. chapter 14, *In : Agrochemicals and Sustainable Agriculture* (Ed. N.K. Roy), pp; 197-206, APC Publications Pvt. Ltd., New Delhi.

Kakati, G.N. and Bhattacharya, K.G. (1990) Trace metals in surface water of greater Guwahati. Indian J. Environ. Health, 32(3) : 276-279.

Kulshrestha, S.K. (1991) Environmental Pollution and Resources of Land and Water, pp. 43-53

Lagerwerf, J.V. (1972) Lead, Mercury and Cadmium as Environmental Contaminants. *In : Micronutrients in Agriculture* (Ed. R.C.Dinauer). Soil Science Society of America, Wisconsin.

Martin, P. (1998) River Pollution in India : An Overview. Employment News, 22(52) : 1-2.

Robertson, D.J. (1960) Filtration gases at Hudson Bay Mining and Smelting Company Ltd. Canad. Min. Met. Bull., 18 : 674.

Sarkar, N.C. and Mishra, B.N. (2004) Environmental Pollution and Agriculture : Its Management. Employment News, 24(10) pp. 1.

Singh, K.K. and Verma, Gayatri (2000) Agrochemicals : Virtue or Bane. Science and Culture, 66(9-10) : 296-298.

Sinha, M.P. (1988) Effect of Waste Disposal on Water Quality of River Damodar in Bihar : Physico-Chemical Characteristics, Chapter 9, *In : Ecology and Pollution of Indian Rivers,* I edn. (Ed. R.K.Trivedy) Ashish Publishing House, 8/81, Punjabi Bagh, New Delhi-110026, pp. 219-246.

Tandon, R.S. (1988) River Pollution and Fish - A Report on Pollution Calamity of Uttar Pradesh (India), Chapter 21, *In : Ecology and Pollution of Indian Rivers* I edn. (Ed. R.K.Trivedy) Ashish Publishing House, 8/81, Punjabi Bagh, New Delhi, New Delhi-110026, pp. 383-391.

CHAPTER 9

ROLE OF MICRO-ORGANISMS IN RELATION TO WATER POLLUTION AND MANAGEMENT

A.G. Devi Prasad and N.R. Rajendra Prasad

Post Graduate Department of Environmental Sciences, University of Mysore, Manasagangothri, Mysore – 570 006, Karnataka, India.

ABSTRACT

Water is the basic unit of life and has become an inseparable integral part of life activities on this biosphere. Without water security, it is impossible to ensure food and energy security which are essential for development and poverty alleviation. The scarcity and availability of fresh water to mankind has become a nightmare owing to all kinds of water pollution. The crux of this crisis can be tackled to a reasonable extent by the judicious utilization of microbes which play a significant role in providing potable and useful water for human sustenance. The present paper gives a fleeting glimpse of the role of microbes in water pollution and management.

Key Words : Micro-organism, water pollution, management.

Introduction

Water, an indestructible natural resource is a vital fluid beset with life. No living entity can exempt water for its day to day activity. It is considered as the elixir of life. It is essential for all metabolic activities of organisms.

About 70 percent of the earth is water and over 97 percent of the earth's water is in oceans. Practically, only 3 percent of the total water available on earth is freshwater. Out of the 3 percent, only one percent is accessible surface freshwater whereas the rest 2 percent is in the form of ice-caps and glaciers in the polar region. The one percent surface freshwater is regularly renewed by rainfall and other means. To quantify this 'usable' part would imply a total world renewable water resource of 43,750 cubic kilometers per year. But even this is not uniformly distributed.

While almost all liquid fresh water of the planet occurs underground as groundwater, its long-term suitability as a source of water is threatened by non-point source pollution from agriculture and other sources and by aquifer depletion due to groundwater withdrawals in excess of groundwater recharge (Bouwer, 2003). At the continental level, America has the largest share of the world's total freshwater resources (45 percent) followed by Asia (28 percent), Europe (15.5 percent) and Africa (9.0 percent). If one looks at water resources per inhabitant in these continents, the distribution changes – America still leads with 24,000 cubic meter/year/inhabitant. The second largest in terms of water resource per inhabitant is Europe with 9,300 cubic meter/year followed by Africa with 5,000 cubic meter/year and Asia 3,400.1 cubic meter/year. The variations swing further when one looks at country-level figures. Globally, on an annual basis, for human use 12.5 to 14 billion cubic meters water is considered available. As per estimation in 1989, there were 9,000 cubic meters of freshwater available for human use per person. By 2000, this amount reduced to 7,800 cubic meters per person due to rise of global population. If this population growth continues it is expected that by 2025, the global population will reach 8 billion and the per capita water use will come down to 5,100 cubic meters. This amount of water may not be adequate to meet the human needs, as it is not properly distributed. Moreover, the advent of urbanization, industrialization and modern materialistic culture of humans have made this resource a vulnerable one. The demand for unpolluted water is on the rise.

Inspite of the advancement in technosphere, the living entities of 'micro' nature play a significant role in this biosphere to provide clean and potable water. Chemically pure water in nature is unknown. Natural water may contain many impurities. A WHO report has estimated that 1.1 billion people in the world do not have access to clean water and that some countries are already overusing their ground water. An assessment of the environment, made by Tata Energy Research Institute (TERI), suggest that rivers in India are still dirty. Of the monitoring stations along India's rivers extending over a riverine length of about 45,000 km, 14 percent show high pollution and 19 percent are moderately polluted.

We know that the quality of water is of vital concern to mankind, since, it is directly linked with human welfare. There are various factors contributing to water pollution which are broadly categorized into physical, chemical and biological factors. Plants, animals and humans constitute the biotic or biological factors and are related to water pollution through disposal of sewage, domestic wastes, industrial wastes, agricultural wastes, garbages, oil spillage and radioactive wastes. All these wastes compound the toxic chemicals and pollutants in water.

The accumulation of these toxicants and pollutants in water bodies vary from region to region in different seasons of a year. Most of the polluted water bodies in India are occupied either by *Microcystis aeruginosa* or *Eichhornia crassipes*. The distribution of microbial flora in such water bodies is governed by physical and chemical characteristics of water such as temperature, pH, amount of carbonates, bicarbonates, calcium, magnesium, free and saline ammonia, total alkalinity, total hardness, nitrate nitrogen, dissolved oxygen, etc. Large numbers of micro-organisms in a water body generally indicate high nutrient levels in the water. Micro-organisms tend to grow on stationary surfaces and on particulate matter in water bodies with low nutrients. The occurrence and distribution of microbial population of a water body is mainly affected by the light and availability of oxygen. Sufficient oxygen will support the growth of *Pseudomonas* and species of *Cytophaga, Hyphomicrobium* and *Caulobacter*. In the deeper waters and sediments, a region poor in oxygen, supports the growth of purple and green sulphur bacteria, *Desulfovibrio* and *Clostridium* species.

Most of the eutrophicated water bodies, support abundant growth of algae in addition to bacteria, protozoans and viruses. The presence of Enterobacteriaceae members especially *Escherischia coli* or coliforms, *Staphylococcus aureus*, *Enterobacter aerogens*, *Proteus*, *Streptococcus faecalis* and *Clostridium perfringens* indicate the faecal pollution of water. Similarly, abundant occurrence of *Nitzschia* species, *Anabaena planktonica, Cymbella tumida, Oscillatoria boryana, Phacus species*, etc, indicate a high degree of water pollution. Thus, micro-organisms also serve as good indicators of pollution.

The microbes which are water-borne also cause various diseases of humans and a few examples are shown in Table 1.

Table 1 : Water borne diseases caused by micro-organisms

Micro-organisms	Diseases
Bacteria	
Salmonella typhimurium	Salmonellosis
S. typhi	Typhoid
S. paratyphi	Paratyphoid
Vibrio cholerae	Cholera
Mycobacteria sp.	Tuberculosis
Legionella pneumophila	Legionella Respiratory infection
Escherischia coli	Diarrhoea
Aeromonas hydrophila	Gastroenteritis
Yersinia entercolitica	Waterborne - Gastroentertis
Shigella sp.	Shigellosis (Bacillary dysentery)
Leptospira icterohaemorrhagiae	Leptospirosis (Weil's disease)
Legionella pneumophila	Legionnaires
Camphylobacter fetus	Camphylobacter diarrhoea
Viruses	
Poliovirus	Poliomyelitis
Enteroviruses	Paralysis, Aseptic Meningitis
Coxsackie virus-A	Herpangia, Aseptic Meningitis Paralysis
Coxsackie virus-B	Pleurodynia, Nephritis fever
Adeno virus	Pharyngoconjunctival fever
Rota virus	Diarrhoea
Norwalk virus	Gastrointestinal disease
Algae	
Anabaena frosaquae	Neural disease
Microcystis aerogenosa	Skin disease
Lyngbya majuscule	Skin rash
Aphanizomenon flosaquae	Neural disease
Chlorella	Chlorellosis
Prototheca wickerhamii and *P.zopfi*	Protothecosis
Fungi	
Pythium insidiosum	Pythiosis insidiosi
Protozoa	
Giardia Lamblia	Giardiasis
Entamoeba histolytica	Amoebic dysentery
Cryptosporidium parvum	Cryptosporidiosis
Naegleria gruberi	Amoebic meningocephalitis
Balantidium coli	Balantidiasis
Aquatic Protistan Parasite	
Rhinosporidium seeberi	Rhinosporidiosis

Though, pathogenic micro-organisms cause diseases, there are still other non-pathogenic organisms that can be exploited for purification of wastewater. The wastewater contains various types of chemical compounds, which if not degraded, may cause harm to organisms. The biodegradation of these harmful compounds can be achieved by using micro-organisms. These micro-organisms are having the ability to degrade various compounds by inducing the formation of concerned degradative enzymes. It is a well established fact that specific organisms attack specific substrates. The micro-organisms degrade the chemical compounds of wastewater by different mechanisms. It was found that a mixed culture of micro-organisms will effectively remove the difficult pollutants in industrial waste treatment processes. For example, the studies carried out by Sastry (1986) on the influence of cyanide, ammonia and thiocyanate on phenol degradation by *Candida tropicalis* indicated that this organism is capable of degrading phenol upto a concentration of 2,000 mg/l. As early as in 1898, the Royal Commission, UK on disposal of domestic sewage found that clean natural water in a water course is normally well-oxygenated and contains large number of varied forms of life such as bacteria, algae, protozoa, etc., which cleared pollution to a great extent. This paved the way for better understanding of stabilization of organic matter in natural environment such as soil and water for the subsequent development of biological treatment methods such as Trickling Filters, Waste Stabilization Ponds, Activated Sludge, etc. In the biological treatment of wastewater a mixture of microflora (bacteria, fungi, actinomycetes, algae, protozoa) are used for an effective biodegradation of a variety of organic compounds in waste waters. Heterogeneity of the microbial population is a characteristic which differentiates the open biological waste treatment system from other bioengineering systems such as fermentation. The microbial inoculum used in degradation of various compounds is often obtained by selective culture techniques.

The common methods employed in biological waste treatment are trickling filters, activated sludge, oxidation ponds and lagoons. The micro-organisms associated with trickling filters of sewage treatment plants include *Micrococcus, Pseudomonas, Nitrosomonas, Thiobacillus, Zoogloea, Flavobacterium, Vibrio, Nitrobacter* among bacterial group; *Chlorella, Oscillatoria, Ulothrix* and *Nitschia,* among algal group; *Fusarium, Arthrobotrys* among the fungi, and *Vorticella, Paramecium and Opercularia* among the protozoans.

The micro-organisms associated with oxidation of organic matter in activated sludge process include *Achromobacter, Azotobacter, Beggiatoa, Bdellowvibrio, Chromobacterium, Corynebacterium, Micrococcus, Alcaligenes, Aerobacter, Bacillus, Comamonas, Streptococcus, Zoogloea, Nocardia, Leucothrix, Flavobacterium, Mycobacterium, Nitrobacter, Nitrosomonas, Pseudomonas* (among bacterial group); *Arthrobotrys, Alternaria candida, Cladosporium, Penicillium, Trichosporium, Geotrichum* (among fungi); *Amoebae, Actinopods, Vorticella, Arcella, Epistylis* and *Paramecium* (among protozoans); *Chlorella, Scenedesmus* and *Oscillatoria* (among algae) and *Bdelloidea*, a rotifer. In the sludge digestion process anaerobic micro-organisms like *Methanococcus, Methanosarcina, Methanospirillum and Methanobacterium* produce methane. In aerobic algal oxidation ponds, the oxidation of organic matter is carried out by algae such as *Chlorella, Spirulina, Scenedesmus, Oscillatoria, Anabaena, Phormidium* and *Euglena.* The bacteria present in oxidation ponds include Brevibacterium, *Sarcina, Pseudomonas, Corynebacterium, Flavobacterium, Micrococcus, Streptococcus, Zoogloea, Vibrio* and *Bacillus.*

Some examples of the micro-organisms known to degrade or metabolise the wastes and thus helping in pollution control are briefly summarized as below.

Oil spillage by super tankers has resulted in pollution of marine water by oil, which has become a major threat to the environment. Now, it is established that *Pseudomonas putida*, if inoculated in oil spilled areas, it can metabolise four major hydrocarbons of petroleum namely; camphor, octane, xylene and naphthalene. *P. putida* has plasmids carrying the genes coding for such enzymes, which can bring about degradation. Four such plasmids are; i) OCT – which can degrade octane, hexane and decane, ii) XYL – which can degrade xylene and toluene, iii) CAM – which can degrade camphor and iv) NAH – which can degrade naphthalene.

Parathion, an insecticide, is decomposed by the co-metabolism of *Pseudomonas aeruginosa* and *Pseudomonas stutzeri*.

A variety of micro-organisms like *Bacillus, Flavobacterium, Corynebacterium, Pseudomonas, Saccharomyces, Candida* and *Protheca* have been found to metabolise hydrocarbons. *Bacillus* species can degrade phenols, celluloses, pyridine, pesticides, ammonia and cyanide. *Flavobacterium* species are known to degrade phenols, celluloses and pesticides. Celluloses are degraded by *Streptomyces, Pseudomonas, Nocardia, Bacillus, Flavobacterium*, etc. *Rhizopus, Aspergillus* and *Penicillium* are also known to degrade celluloses. Polyvinyls are found to be degraded by *Aspergillus* and *Pseudomonas*. *Pseudomonas* and *Penicillium* are having the potential of degrading tannins. Cyanide is known to be metabolized by a number of micro-organisms like *Bacillus pumilus, Bacillus subtilis, Pseudomonas* species, *Nocardia* species, *Rhizopus nigricans, Fusarium solani* and *Aspergillus niger*. *Nitrosomonas* and

Aspergillus are known to degrade ammonia of the wastewater from industries. Micro-organisms which can biodegrade the surfactants of industrial wastewaters and sewage have been identified in recent years. For example, *Salmonella enteritidis, Proteus vulgaris, E. coli,* etc., degrade linear alkyl sulphates; and *Cladosporium resinae, Alcaligenes faecalis, Pseudomonas flourescens,* degrade linear alkyl benzene sulphonates.

Various types of pesticides are also degraded by micro-organisms like *Achromobacter, Pseudomonas sp., Aspergillus flavus, Trichoderma* sp., *Chlorella pyrenoidosa,* etc.,.

Thus, from the above discussion, we have seen some of the possibilities of water pollution management through micro-organisms. Knowing the potentialities of these micro-organisms, judicious selection of the microbial innoculum with suitable creation of environment for their activity or biodegradation should be employed in any water or wastewater treatment processes. The water, thus purified can be used for purposes with higher, social, ecological or economic returns or saved for the future. This will help significantly in solving the problem of 'water crisis' also.

Conclusions

Experts today believe that water will be the next natural source to become the cause of wars around the world. This is because, unlike other precious sources like oil, water consumption remains million times more and it is rising with industrialization and urbanization. In view of this, sustainable utilization and development of water resources, their conservation and management is the need of the hour. Micro-organisms can be exploited for achieving the light of success in such programmes.

References

Bouwer (2003) Integrated water management for the 21st century: Problems and Solutions. J. Food, Agril and Environment.

Chakraborthy, A.M. (1980) Genetic Engineering – Applied aspects. Ind. J. Microbiol. 20 : 103-108.

Chakraborthy, A.M. (1985) Microbial degradation of toxic environmental pollutants. *Intl. Workshop on Molecular Biosci. and Biotech*. SPIC, Madras, pp. 21-23.

FAO (2003) Review of World Water Resources by Country.

Giri Rao, J.S and Pattnaik, S. (2003) Water – The elixir of life, Employment News, Nov. 1-7.

Grey, N.F. (2000) Water Technology – An Introduction for Environmental Scientist and Engineers. Pub. of Viva Book Pvt. Ltd.

Kirk, T.K. (1984) Microbial degradation of organic compounds (Ed. D.T. Gibbson) E.D. Dekkar, New York.

Lal B. (2005) Oil eating bacteria. Deccan Herald, March, 28, 2005.

Modi, V.V. (1981) Microbiology and Management of Environment'. *Proc. Natl. Workshop on Microbial degradation of Industrial Wastes*. NEERI, Nagpur, Feb. 23-27.

Park, K. (2001) Preventive and Social Medicine, 16th Edn., Pub. of Banarsidas Bharat, Jabalpur, India.

Pfaller, M.A and Diekema D.J. (2005) Unusual fungal and pseudofungal infections of Humans. J. of Clinical Microbiol., 43.4; 1495-1504.

Sapna S. Hiremath (2004) It's do or die time. Deccan Herald, September, 7, 2004.

Sastry, C.A. (1986) Industrial waste biodegradation. Encology. 1 (6) : 29-33.

Suess, M.J. (1982) Examination of water pollution control. Vol.3. Biological, Bacteriological and Virological Examination. Pergamon Press.

Sullia, S.B and Shantharam S. (2000) *General Microbiology*. Pub. of Mohan Primlani for Oxford and IBH Pub. Co. Pvt. Ltd., New Delhi.

CHAPTER 10

CONTROL TECHNIQUES FOR ORGANIC VAPOUR EMISSIONS FROM POINT AND AREA SOURCES

B. Padma S. Rao, P. R. Thawale, A. Kumar and Asha A. Juwarkar

Environmental Biotechnology Division

National Environmental Engineering Research Institute (NEERI)

Nehru Marg, Nagpur - 440020, India.

ABSTRACT

Toxic air pollutants of organic and inorganic compounds represent 95% and 5% respectively, of the toxic air releases reported in the USEPA's Toxic Release Inventory. The inventory and control studies of organic vapour emissions from both process and periodic accidental releases in India are limited. A systemic study of the control options has been delineated in this chapter.

Key Words: Organic emissions, adsorptions, biofilters.

Introduction

The organic vapour emissions come from both process and periodic (Bounicore and Wayne, 1992) accidental releases such as: materials storage & handling, process sources, equipment leaks, solvent evaporation, combustion sources, waste treatment etc. In India, the studies on organic emissions and its control are limited. Toxic air (Commission of the European communities, 1992; World Bank 1996; Chen *et al.*, 1996) pollutants of organic and inorganic compounds represent 95% and 5% respectively of the toxic air releases reported in the USEPA's Toxic Release Inventory. This includes carcinogens, mutagens or reproductive toxins. Some organic vapours are air toxics while other are not. Of the 50 billion pounds per year of organic vapours released to the atmosphere, only one billion pounds are attributable to compounds listed as toxic air pollutants by the 1990 Clean Air Act (CAA) Amendments. A wide range of residential, commercial and industrial discharges contributes organic vapour and toxic pollutants (Garg *et al.*, 2003; Hakamii *et al.*, 2004; Jeffery, 1998; World Health Organisation, 1993). An even wider range of pollutants is discharged to industrial wastewater treatment plants, depending on the specific type of industrial activity generating the wastewater. The organic emissions emitted from various point as well as fugitive sources can be controlled by Incineration, Adsorption, Combustion, Condensation, Biofiltration and proper house keeping maintenance. The requirements of emission stream (Jeffery, 1998; World Health Organization, 1993; Petroleum refinery fugitive emission Hand book, 2003; Richard, 2003) for organic vapour control from point and fugitive sources are given in Table 1 and 2.

Table 1 : Emission stream requirements and control strategies

S. No.	**Control**	**Organic content (ppm)**	**Heat content Btu/Scf**	**Flow rate (Scfm)**	**Temp. Limits ^{o}C**	**Moisture Content**
Combustion						
1.	Thermal Incinerator	> 20 or <25% LEL	—	<100,000	—	—
2.	Catalytic incinerator	50-10,000 PPM or <25% LEL	—	<100,000	—	—

Contd.

3.	Flare	—	> 300	<2,000,000	—	—
4.	Boiler / process heater	—	> 150	Steady flow	—	—
5.	Condenser	< 5000	—	< 2000	—	—
Adsorption						
6.	Carbon Adsorber*	1000-10000 or <25% LEL	—	300-100,000	100-200	—
Absorber						
7.	Absorber	250-10,000	—	1000-100,000	—	50%
Bio Filters						
8.	Bio Filters	20 - 1500mg/m^3	—	—	<50	—

Mol wt. Range limited to 40-130, LEL: Lower Explosive limit

Table 2: Emission control techniques for fugitive organic emissions

S. No.	Emission Source	Control Technique	Control Effectiveness (%)
1.	Pumps	Monthly leak detection and repair	50-60
		Seal less pumps	90-100
		Dual Mechanical Seals	90-100
		Closed vent systems	90-100
2.	Valves Gas Light Liquid	Monthly leak detection and repair	50-75
		Diaphragm valves	90-100
3.	Pressure relief valves	Rupture Disk	90-100
		Closed vent System	90-100

Contd.

4.	Open ended lines	Caps, plugs, blinds	90-100
5.	Compressors	Mechanical seals with vents followed by bio filters	60-80
6.	Storage tanks of petroleum products	Floating roof	50-70
7.	Filling of petroleum products in gantry	Submerged filling	70-90
8.	Waste water treatment plant	Covering of API/TPI separators	70-80

Combustion Systems

The point source organic emissions can be controlled (Ritter *et al.*, 2000) through effective combustion systems. This includes Flares, Thermal Oxidizers, Catalytic Oxidation, Process Boiler, and Energy recovery system. Combustion is a chemical process occurring from the rapid combination of oxygen with various elements or chemical compounds, resulting in the release of heat. The process of combustion is also referred to as oxidation. This is widely used to control the emissions of organic emissions from process industries. At a sufficient high temperature and adequate residence time, these emissions oxidises to CO_2 and water vapour. These devices are capable of achieving very high removal efficiencies. They consist of burners, which ignite the fuel and organic vapors and a chamber, which provides appropriate residence time for the oxidation process. Equipment used to control waste gases by combustion can be divided into three categories, direct combustion of flaring, thermal oxidation and catalytic oxidation (Table 3).

Table 3 : Combustion constants and approximate limits of flammability of gases and vapors in air

Substance	Lb/ft^3	Ft^3/lb	Heat of Combustion				For 100% total air (mol/mol of combustible) (ft^3/ft^3 of combustible)						For 100% total air (lb/lb of combustible)						Flammability	
			(Btu/ft^3)		(Btu/ft^3)		Required for combustion			Flue products			Required for combustion			Flue products			(% by volume)	
			Gross (High)	Net (low)	Gross (high)	Net (low)	O_2	N_2	Air	CO_2	H_2O	N_2	O_2	N_2	Air	CO_2	H_2O	N_2	Lower	upper
Paraffin series																				
Methane, CH_4	0.0424	23.565	1013	914	24.879	21.520	2.0	7.53	9.53	1.0	2.0	7.53	3.99	13.28	17.27	2.74	2.25	13.28	5.00	15.00
Ethane, C_2H_6	0.0803	12.455	1792	1611	11.420	20.432	3.2	13.18	16.68	2.0	3.0	13.18	3.73	12.39	16.12	2.93	1.80	12.39	3.00	12.50
Propane, C_3H_8	0.1196	8.365	2590	2382	.061	19.944	5.0	18.82	23.82	3.0	4.0	18.82	3.63	12.07	15.70	2.99	1.68	12.07	2.12	9.35
n-Butane, C_4H_{10}	0.1582	6.321	3370	3113	.308	19.680	6.5	24.47	30.97	4.0	5.0	24.47	3.58	11.91	15.49	3.03	1.55	11.91	1.86	8.41
Olefin series																				
Ethylene, C_2H_4	0.0746	13.412	1614	1613	.614	20.295	3.0	11.29	14.29	2.0	2.0	11.29	3.42	11.39	14.81	3.14	1.29	11.39	2.75	28.60
Propylene, C_4H_6	0.1110	9.007	2336	2186	24.011	19.691	4.5	16.94	21.44	3.0	3.0	16.94	3.42	11.39	14.81	3.14	1.29	11.39	2.00	11.10

Contd.

n-Butene, C_4H_8	0.1480	6.756	3084	2883	20.810	19.496	6.0	22.59	28.59	4.0	4.0	22.59	3.42	11.39	14.81	3.14	1.29	11.39	1.75	9.70
Aromatic series																				
Benzene, C_6H_6	0.2060	4.852	3751	3601	18.210	17.480	7.5	28.23	35.73	6.0	3.0	28.23	3.07	10.22	13.30	3.38	0.69	10.22	1.40	7.10
Toluene, C_7H_8	0.2431	4.113	4484	1281	18.140	17.620	9.0	33.88	42.88	7.0	4.0	33.88	3.13	10.40	13.53	3.34	0.78	10.40	1.27	6.75
Xylene, C_8H_{10}	0.2803	3.567	5230	4980	18.650	17.760	10.5	39.52	50.02	8.0	5.0	39.52	3.17	10.53	13.70	3.32	0.85	10.53	1.00	6.00
Misc gases																				
Napthalene, $C_{10}H_8$	0.3384	2.955	5854	5654	17.298	16.708	12.0	45.17	57.17	10.0	4.0	45.17	3.00	9.97	12.96	3.43	0.56	9.97	--	--
Methyl alcohol, CH_3OH	0.0846	11.820	868	768	10.259	9.078	1.5	5.65	7.15	1.0	2.0	5.65	1.50	4.98	6.48	1.37	1.13	4.98	6.72	36.50
Ethyl alcohol, C_2H_5OH	0.1216	8.221	1600	1451	13.161	11.929	3.0	11.29	14.29	2.0	3.0	11.29	2.08	6.93	9.02	1.92	1.17	6.93	3.28	18.95
Xylene, C_8H_{10}	0.2803	3.567	5230	4980	18.650	17.760	10.5	39.52	50.02	8.0	5.0	39.52	3.17	10.53	13.70	3.32	0.85	10.53	1.00	6.00

Flares

Flares are simple burners that are designed to handle varying rates of Organic emissions while burning smokelessly. In general, flares can be classified as either elevated or ground level. One reason for elevating a flare is to eliminate any potential fire hazard at ground level. Ground level flares must be completely enclosed to conceal the flame. Either type of flare must be capable of operation over a wide range of waste flow rates in order to handle all plant emergencies. The range of waste gas flow, within which a flare can operate and still burn efficiently, is referred to as the turndown ratio. Flares normally handle turndown ratios of 1000:1. Most industrial boilers seldom handle more than a 10:1 turndown ratio. A flare should be capable of maintaining complete combustion for waste gas flow rates ranging from 700 to 700,000 ft^3hr^{-1}.

Thermal Oxidizers

Thermal oxidizers or Incinerators refer to any device that uses a flame (temperature) combined with a chamber (time and turbulence) to convert combustible material to carbon dioxide and water. It consists of a refractory lined chamber that is equipped with one or more sets of burners. The contaminant leaden stream is passed through the burners where it is heated above its ignition temperature. The hot gases then pass through one or more residence chambers where they are held for a certain length of time to ensure complete combustion. Depending on the particular needs of the system, additional fuel and / or excess air can be added through the burners. Also, since the fuel gases are discharged at elevated temperature a system to recover the heat may be included. Incinerators on industrial processes are most often used to control gas streams with a low concentration of organic vapors and operate at temperature between 1300 and

1500°F with a residence time of 0.1 to 0.5 second. The residence time is determined by the size of the combustion chamber and is measured after the required temperature has been reached.

Catalytic Oxidation

A catalyst is a substance, which causes or speeds a chemical reaction without itself undergoing a change. In catalytic incineration, a waste gas is passed through a layer of catalyst known as the catalyst bed. The catalyst causes the oxidation reaction to proceed at a faster rate and at a lower temperature than is capable in thermal oxidation. Catalytic incinerators operating in a 700 to 900°F range can achieve the same efficiency as a thermal operating between 1300 and 1500°F. This can result in a 40 to 60% fuel savings. Catalytic reactions can be classified as either homogeneous or heterogeneous. In air pollution control applications, all reactions are heterogeneous or at the surface of the catalyst. The most effective and commonly used catalysts for oxidation reactions come from the noble metals and Palladium.

Adsorption Systems

These are catagorised as regenerable and non-regenerable (Venkatesh and Moores, 1998 and William, 1994) systems.

Regenerable Adsorption Systems

A large regenerable adsorption system can be categorized as a fixed, moving, or fluidized bed. The most common adsorption system for controlling air pollutants is the fixed carbon bed. These systems are used to control a variety of organic vapors and are usually regenerated by direct steaming of the bed. Condensing the exhaust from the regeneration step and separating out the water and solvent may recover the organic compounds.

Fixed Bed Adsorbers

Fixed bed adsorption systems generally involve multiple beds. The solvent-laden-air then usually passes down through the fixed carbon bed. Upward flow through the bed is usually avoided (unless flow rates are low (<500 cfm) to eliminate entraining carbon particles in the exhaust stream).

Other Adsorber systems

Adsorbers where the bed moves from the polluted fluid to the regeneration fluid to the drying bed and cooling fluid are called moving bed adsorbers. In a fluidized bed adsorption system, the solvent-laden air stream is introduced at the middle of the tower, then it passes up through the tower, fluidizing the activated carbon in a series of trays.

The adsorption forces are physical and chemical in nature and the adsorbent material are activated carbon, silica gel, molecular sieves, aluminum oxide (Activated alumina). Three key variables that need to be considered in the design of an absorber are (1) the amount and type of adsorbent required, (2) the pressure drop, and (3) regeneration requirements. A routine maintenance program must accompany effective air pollution control utilizing carbon adsorption. The characteristics of chemisorptions and physical adsorption are in Table 4.

Table 4: Characteristics of adsorption

Chemisorptions	**Physical adsorption**
Release high heat 10,000 cal mol^{-1}	Releases low energy, 100 cal mol^{-1}
Forms a chemical compound	Dipolar interaction
Desorption is difficult	Desorption is easy
Impossible adsorbate recovery	Easy adsorbate recovery

Activated Carbon

Activated carbon can be produced from a variety of feedstocks such as wood, coal, coconu, nutshells and petroleum-based products. Because of its nonpolar surface, activated carbon is used to control emission of organic solvents, odors, toxic gases, and gasoline vapors.

Silica Gel

Silica gels are made from sodium silicate. Sodium silicate is mixed with sulfuric acid, resulting in a jellylike precipitate from which the "gel" name comes. Silica gels are used primarily to remove moisture from exhaust streams, but are ineffective at temperatures above 500 F (260°C).

Molecular Sieves

Unlike the other adsorbents, which are amorphous (not crystalline) in nature, molecular sieves have a crystalline structure. Molecular sieves can be used to capture or separate gases on the basis of molecular size and shape. An example of this is refining processes, which sometimes use molecular sieves to separate straight-chained paraffins from branched, and cyclic compounds. However, the main use of molecular sieves is in the removal of mixture from exhaust streams.

Aluminum Oxide (Activated Alumina)

Aluminium oxides are manufactured by thermally activated alumina or bauxite. These are not commonly used in air pollution applications. Micropores are openings whose radii are 200 nm (20°A) or less. Pores larger than 2000 nm (200A) are macropores. Transitional pores are those with radii between 200 ml and 2000 nm. Most gaseous air pollutant molecules are in the 40 to 90 nm size range. If a large portion of an adsorbent's surface area is in pores smaller than 40 nm. Many contaminant molecules will be unable to reach these active sites. Air pollution control involves contaminant vapors at low partial pressure. Therefore, the micropore structure of an adsorbent plays an important role in determining the overall efficiency. Another reason for the wide use of activated carbon is that 90 to 95% of its surface areas is in the micropore size range.

Condensation

Condensation is the process of reducing a gas or vapor to a liquid and achieved by increasing pressure or reducing temperature, or both. In air pollution control, removal of heat from the vapor to cause condensation is mostly practised. As a hot vapor stream contacts a cooler surface, the temperature of the gas stream lowers to a point where a pollutant's vapor pressure is at or below its entering partial pressure in the gas stream.

Quantitative condensation of many substances normally requires very low temperatures. Vapor-liquid equilibrium, and the corresponding energy needed to produce very low temperatures or high pressures, restricts the application of condensers as a primary control or final purification device. More typically, condensation is used in processing streams from reactors, dryers, distillation columns, absorbers etc. In these applications, the condenser is not really viewed as an emission control device. The characteristics of contaminants that affect their potential recovery by condensation are volatility, concentration, miscibility, stability and value. Some of these are presented in (Table 5).

Table 5: Characteristics of organic emissions for its control through Condensation

Organic emissions	Condensing temp, °F	LEL (%)	Miscibility in water[b]
Toluene	-38	1.3	i
Formaldehyde	-167	7.0	m
Methylene chloride	-64	15.0	p

Contd.

Ethylene	-271	2.70	i
m-Xylene	-6	1.1	i
Benzene	-71	1.4	i
o-Xylene	-3	1.0	i
p-Xylene	-32	1.1	i
Chlorobenzene	-14	1.3	i
Trichloroethylene	-36	12.5	p
Methychloride	-177	8.1	p
Methanol	-40	6.0	m
P-Dichlorobenzene	-92	2.2	I
Vinyl chloride	-184	4.0	p

Contact Condensers

Contact condensers require liquid coolants; usually water, to come in direct contact with the condensing vapors. These are relatively uncomplicated and are configured as spray towers, jet ejectors, or barometric units. They are configured such that the vapor entering the bottom of the tower is counter currently contacted by the coolant spray from above. Condensate from contact units usually cannot be reused and may constitute a waste disposal problem. These normally afford a greater degree of air pollution control than surface condensers do because of condensate dilution. With direct contact units, about 15 lb of 60°F water is required to condense 1 lb of steam at 212°F and cool the condensate to 140°F. The resultant 15:1 dilution greatly reduces the concentration and vapor pressure of volatile materials that are miscible or soluble in water.

Surface Condensers

In surface condensers, the coolant is separated from the vapors by a heat transfer surface. There are two distinct mechanism through which condensation occurs dropwise and filmwise condensation. In dropwise condensation, the vapor condenses and forms liquid droplets onto some sufficiently cold surface with which it is brought into contact. A film occurs and coats the condensing surface. Additional vapors must then condense on this film rather than the base metal surface. This is called filmwise condensation. Dropwise condensation has been found to take place various times when a mixture of vapors and gases is present. Using certain promoters may possibly attain some degree of dropwise condensation. Promoters such as oleic acid on nickel or chrome plate, and benzyl mercaptan on copper or brass become absorbed on the surface as a very thin layer to prevent the metal surface from being wetted by any condensate. The control efficiency achievable by a condenser is a function of the outlet gas temperature. A typical exhaust gas leaving a process will contain significant amount of noncondensable material (sometimes called inerts) such as air or nitrogen as well as a lesser fraction of contaminant material.

The percentage of contaminant condensed can be calculated from:

$$PC = \frac{MFS_1 - 100[1-(MFS_1)\,(MFS_2)]/(1-MFS_2)}{MFS_1}$$

Where : PC = Percent of organic emissions condensed

MFS_1 = mole fraction of organic emissions into condenser

MFS_2 = mole fraction of organic emissions out of condenser

The mole fractions of organic emissions into and out of the condenser are obtained by determining the partial pressure of the contaminants at the temperatures involved and dividing by the total pressure of the condenser, in consistent units.

Biofiltration

In a biofilter, an off-gas containing biodegradable volatile organic compounds (VOCs) is passed through a bed packed (William, 1994; World Bank Group Hand book, 1998; Yang and Yinnping, 2004) with damp, porous organic particles. These compounds are sorbed by the biologically active filter bed. Micro-organisms attached to the wetted filter material aerobically degrade the sorbed chemical compounds. This process is similar to conventional activated sludge treatment for wastewater purification since in both instances micro-organisms oxidize the organic compounds to carbon dioxide and water in a moist, oxygen-rich environment.

The principal difference is that in a biofilter, the micro-organisms are immobilized on the solid filter material, while in wastewater treatment they are dispersed as a suspension in the liquid phase. Biofiltration is a highly efficient and low-cost alternative to other, more conventional, air pollution control (APC) technologies such as thermal oxidation, catalytic incineration, refrigerated condensation, carbon adsorption and absorption by chemicals and water scrubbers. These traditional techniques can effectively reduce odors, but have serious capital and operating cost drawbacks including large fuel, chemical, or water requirements. About 500 biofilters are currently operating in Europe vs. less than 50 in the U.S.

The biofilters have been successfully employed in a wide range of applications for removal of VOCs and other air toxics with high destruction efficiency (>90%) for many common air pollutants including organic compounds such as alcohols, aldehydes, amines, and inorganic compounds such as hydrogen sulfide and ammonia. Since, biofiltration utilizes the same natural biological process occurring in soils and water, it is generally considered a safe, environmentally friendly technology have been energy requirements and do not generate additional environmental problems since the pollutant is not transferred to another medium thereby creating a secondary discharge. This process involves :

1. The collection of the raw waste gas from the emission sources with transport via a ductwork and blower system through the pretreatment equipment and biofilter reactor.
2. Pretreatment of the raw gas is typically required to remove particulates, adjust the temperature, and increase relative humidity to saturation.
3. Following pretreatment, the influent gas is uniformly dispersed throughout the biofilter reactor via an air distribution system.

In a biofilter the contaminated off-gas stream typically flows upward though one or more packed layers of organic filter material. Soil or compost are the most common filter materials. The filter material performs three functions:

1. It provides a substrate for microbial attachment.
2. It is a source of elemental nutrients required by the micro-organisms for growth.
3. It provides a porous structural matrix through which the influent gas can readily pass.

Biofilters can be constructed in an open bed design with the filter material covering the air distribution system or an enclosed design with the filter contained within a structure, protected from weather conditions. The oldest and simplest biofilter design is a soil bed. The raw gas must contain adequate oxygen content for aerobic degradation. The raw gas pollutants, both individually and as a mixture, must not be present at concentrations, which are toxic to the micro-organisms (Table 6). Some application for adsorber and the biodegradability of individual raw gas components and classes of compounds are listed in Tables 7, 8, 9 and 10.

Table 6: Some application for nonregenerative absorbers

Air conditioning systems	Kitchen range hoods
Allergy patients (air purif)	Laboratories
Amine odors[a]	Laundries
Archives	Mercaptans
Automobile exhaust fumes (organic)	Monethalomine (MEA)

Table 7: Some applications for regenerative adsorbers

Acetone	Isopropyl alcohol
Adehsive solvents	Isotrons (some)
Amyl acetate	Ketones
Benzene	Methyl alcohol
Benzol	Methyl chloroform
Brom-chlor methane (BCM)	Methyl ethyl ketone (MEK)
Butyl acetate	Methylene chloride
Butyl alcohol	Mineral spirits

Table 8: Biodegradability of individual and classes of volatile compounds

Inorganic Rapid	**Organic**			
	Rapid	**Good**	**Slow**	**Very Slow**
Hydrogen sulfide	Alcohols	Esters	Aliphatic	Many halogenated
Ammonia	Methanol	Ethylacetate	Hydrocarbons	Hydrocarbons
Sulfur dioxide	Butanol	Ketones	Methane	1.1.1. Trichloroethane
	Aldehydes	Acetone	Pentane	Polyaromatic

Contd.

	Formaldehyde	Phenols	Cyclohexane	Hydrocarbons
	Acetaldehyde	Benzene		
	Amines	Styrene		
	Organic Acids	Mercaptans		
	Butyric Acid	Methyl mercaptan		

Table 9: Currently operating full-scale biofilters in the international scenario and micro-organisms frequently identified in biofilters

Industry (Ref. #)	Location	Inlet gas (Flow m^3hr)	Inlet gas (Conc. gm^{-1})	Compounds	Efficiency (VOC removal)
Yeast (22) production	East Brunswick NJ	60,000	1.0	Ethanol Aldehydes	85%
Casting (23) foundry	Northridge CA	17,000	1.9	Mainly ethanol	85%
Polymer (24) production (2) biofilters efficiency-equal)	Trenton, MI and Springfield MA	35,00	04 – 0.7	Alcohol Aldehydes Easters	90 – 95%
Plastics (22) production	Bergen op Zoom The Netherlands	1,000	?	Toluene Phenol Acetone	80 – 95%

Table 10 : The most active microorganisms in the biofilter

Bacteria	Fungi
Actinomycetes	*Penicillium*
Micrococcus albus	*Cephalosporium* sp.
Micromonospore vulgaris	*Mucor* sp.
Proteus vulgarus	*Circinella* sp.
Bacillus cereus	*Cephalotecium* sp.
Streptomyces sp.	*Oxularia* sp.
	Stemphilium sp.

Biofilters typically treat low-concentration air emissions. Following are general conclusions based on pilot-scale trials regarding the capability of biofiltration for the treatment of different classes of VOCs and the effect of inlet concentration.

1. Alphatic compounds with less than seven carbon atoms, such as ethanol, acetone, isopropyl alcohol, methyl formate, and methyl ethyl ketone, are very degradable. These compounds can be treated at high destruction efficiency in concentrations greater than 1500 mg m^{-3}. Control-effieciency of greater than 95% is possible with less than 1 min. retention time.
2. Aliphatic compounds with more than six carbon atoms an aromatic compounds such as toluene, xylene, phthalates, and mixtures of aromatic paint solvents are moderately degradable. A control efficiency of 95% is possible at an inlet concentration of 500 mg m^{-3} with moderate retention time. Utilizing biofiltration to treat a higher inlet concentration of to achieve higher destruction efficiency is possible. A longer retention time, however, is required.
3. Some compounds such as benzene, degrade poorly, and treatment by biofiltration is normally limited to an inter concentration of 20 mg m^{-3}. In some cases, where there is a mixture of organic compounds, biodegradation can be improved by co-metabolism.
4. Chlorinated hydrocarbon compounds with one or two chlorine atoms, such as methyl chloride and 1,2-dichloroethane, can be treated by biofiltration. Inlet concentration is normally limited to 20 mg m^{-3} and the filter material must contain a buffering agent to neutralize the hydrochloric acid formed by the biodegradation reactions. Currently, operating full-scale biofilters in the international scenario and micro-organisms frequently identified in biofilters are:

The micro-organisms, which are the most active agents in a biofilter, are the same bacteria and fungi that degrade waste compounds in nature, activated sludge wastewater treatment, and landfills. Biofilter conditions, such as moisture, pH, temperature, and nutrients are controlled to maintain a favorable environment for microbial growth and activity. The diversity of the active microbial population in a biofilter depends on the specific components being degraded. Waste gases from industrial sources may contain a small number of chemical constituents and only a few microbial species in the biofilter may be actively involved in the degradation. Suitable strains include: Nocardia, which degrades aromatics like xylene and styrene, a Hyphomicrobium sp., which degrades dichloromethane, Xanthobacter for 1,2-di-chloethane, and a Mycobacterium for vinyl chloride. Continued research is expected to result in development of improved microbial strains and filter materials to make the application of biofiltration more cost effective for treating recalcitrant chemicals.

The main components and design (Ying and Yinking, 2004; Hicham *et al.*, 2004), considerations of a biofiltration system typically include: raw gas collection and transportation, preconditioning, humidification, influent gas distribution, and filter material. A wide variety of biofilter materials have been utilized, with the most common being soil or compost produced from leaves, bark, wood chips, activated sludge, paper, or other materials of organic origin. Peat and heather have been used in some applications, as well as inert materials. A strong adsorbent such as activated carbon is added in some situations to increase biofiltration efficiency. In order to maintain a porous structure and avoid compaction, large particles such as wood and bark chips, plastic spheres, ceramics, or lava are added to the filter medium mixture to provide strength and create voids for low-pressure drop. The height of the compost filter bed is typically 1.0 to 1.5 m. The maximum height is 2.0 m for an optimized by P filter material. The minimum height is limited by the need for a pressure differential across the filter for a uniform gas distribution, and at least 0.5 m is recommended.

The optimum condition for microbial growth is a neural pH range. Below a pH of about 3, most micro-organisms are inhibited. Acidic products are often formed by oxidation of some pollutants, particularly volatile inorganics such as H_2S, SO_2 and NO_X, and halogenated organics. A wide range of biofiltration system capital costs have been published, from a low of $5 per cubic foot per minute ($5/CFM) to a high of about $100/CFM.

Absorption

Absorption is transfer of a gaseous component from the gas phase to a liquid phase. In air pollution control, it involves the removal of objectionable gaseous contaminants from a process stream by dissolving them in a liquid. Some common terms used when discussing the absorption process follow:

1. Absorbent : the liquid, usually water, into which the contaminant is absorbed.
2. Absorbate or solute : the gaseous contaminant being absorbed, such as SO_2, H_2S, etc.
3. Carrier gas : the inert portion of the gas stream usually air, from which the contaminant is to be removed.
4. Interface : the area where the gas phase and the absorbent contact each other.
5. Solubility : the capability of a gas to be dissolved in a liquid.

In absorption mass is transferred as a result of a concentration difference between the absorbent and the gas from which the contaminant is being removed. Absorption equipment used to remove gaseous contaminants are referred to as absorbers or wet scrubbers. Wet scrubbers are also used to remove particulate matter from gas streams. In designing absorbers from gaseous emissions, optimum mass transfer can be accomplished by :

1. Providing a large interfacial contact area,
2. Providing good mixing between gas and liquid phases,
3. Allowing sufficient residence or contact time between the phases,
4. Ensuring a high degree of solubility of the contaminant in the absorbent.

To remove a gaseous contaminant by absorption, the contaminant laden exhaust stream must be passed through (contacted with a liquid. In the first step of the absorption process the pollutant (or solute) diffuses from the bulk area of the gas phase to the gas-liquid interface. In the second step gaseous pollutants transfer across the interface to the liquid phase. In the third step, the pollutants diffuse into the bulk area of the liquid, making room for additional gas molecules to be absorbed.

The purpose of analyzing these three steps is to determine which variables control the process. The most efficient system can be designed by knowing these variables. It is assumed that once the solute arrives at the interface area, transfer across it occurs simultaneously. This second step in the absorption mechanism is extremely rapid. Therefore, it does not need to be considered when deriving absorption efficiency equations. The rate of mass transfer (absorption) is dependent upon the diffusion rate in either the gas phase or the liquid phase. Two terms are used to describe mass transfer rates: gas phase controlled absorption and liquid phase controlled absorption. Each mechanism depends on the rate of diffusion of both phases and upon the solubility of the pollutant in the liquid phase. The most common method of analyzing solubility data is to use an equilibrium diagram. An equilibrium diagram is a plot of the mole fraction of solute in the liquid phase denoted x, vs, the mole fraction of solute in the gas phase, denoted y. Under certain conditions, Henry's law may also be used to express equilibrium solubility of gas-liquid systems. Henry's law is expressed as:

$$y^* = Mx$$

Where y^* = mole fraction in gas phase in equilibrium with liquid, M = Henry's law constant, mole fraction in vapour phase/mole fraction in a liquid.

The absorption equipment is designed to maximize the mass transfer rate. In absorption, the rate of mass transferred depends largely on the surface areas of the air and liquid stream exposed to each other. Absorption proceeds at a finite rate. Increasing the time the two streams are in contact will increase the potential for absorption to occur. The following properties must also be kept in mind when selecting a liquid:

1. Gas solubility : high solubility increases the absorption rate and minimizes the quantity of liquid needed.
2. Volatility : low volatility of the liquid will reduce the amount of vapour that is lost in the existing gas stream.
3. Viscosity : low viscosity promotes rapid absorption rates, improves flooding characteristics, and lowers the pressure drop.
4. Chemical stability : the absorbent should not degrade but remain effective throughout its useful lifetime.
5. Flammability : if at all possible, the liquid should be nonflammable, noncorrosive, non-toxic, and inexpensive.

The principal types of gas absorption equipment may be classified as follows :

1. Packed columns (continuous operation)
2. Plate columns (stage operation)
3. Miscellaneous

Of the three categories, the packed column is by far the one most commonly used for the absorption of gaseous pollutants.

Conclusions

The organic vapour control option is very specific to the pollutants and process parameter. A thorough study of the emission along with process parameter with application of suitable control would help reduce such emission. The information from this inventory and control studies of organic vapour emission from this process will help in the delineating the control option. Biofilter is the best option to reduce or control the organic vapour emission from point and area sources.

Acknowledgements

Authors are thankful to the Director, NEERI, Nagpur for providing permission to publish this work. The cooperation and support provided by the refinery staff during the course of this study is also gratefully acknowledged.

References

Bounicore, Anthony J., and Wayne T. Davis, (eds.). (1992) *Air Pollution Engineering Manual*. New York: Van Nostrand Reinhold, pp., 33-44.

Commission of the European Communities. DG XI A3. (1991) "Technical Note on the Best Available Technologies to Reduce Emissions of Pollutants into the Air from the Refining Industry." Brussels, pp 85-96.

World Bank. (1996) Pollution Prevention and Abatement: Petroleum Refining. Draft Technical Background Document. Environment Department, Washington, D.C.

Chen, H., Rogers, T.N., Bruce, A. and Shonnard, D. R. (2003) Automating Hierarchical Environmentally conscious design using integrated software VOC Recovery case study Environ Prog., 22: 134-175.

Gary, W., Watson, Edwar, Staples, J. and Shekar, (2003) Performance Evaluation of a surface acoustic wave analyser to measure VOC in air and water. Environ Prog., 22: 78-106.

Hakami, A., Harley, R. A., Milford, J. B., Odman, M.T. and Russell, A. G. (2004) Regional, three- dimensional assessment of the ozone formation potential of organic compounds. Atmos Environ., 38: 121-134.

Jeffrey SieGell, H. (1998) Monitor your fugitive emissions correctly. Chem Engg. Prog., 33:125-171.

Model for air emission inventories and controls (1993) A guide to rapid source inventory techniques and their use in formulating environmental control strategies-World Health Organization, Geneva.

Petroleum refinery fugitive emissions (2003) http://www.baaqmd.gov/permit/handbook/petroleu.htm. pp., 1-7.

Richard, Dobbins, A. (2003) Environmental guidelines for oil and gas-petroleum refineries pp. 187-298.

Ritter, K., Nordrum, S. and Shires, T. (2000) Application of the API compendium of Greenhouse gas emissions estimation methodologies for the oil and gas industry to examine potential emissions reduction. Chem. Eng. http://www.che.com/ceextra, pp., 215-226.

USEPA (2000) Petroleum refinery equipment leaks. SIP-Ecology, 173-490:

Venkatesh, M. and Moores, C.W. (1998) Control air toxins from difficult process sources, Chem, Eng. Prog. , 33: 26-30.

William PL Carter (1994) Development of ozone reactivity scales for volatile organic compounds air Waste Manage Assoc., 44: 881-899.

World Bank Group (1998) Pollution prevention and abatement handbook, pp., 135-145.

Ying Xu and Yinping Zhang (2004) A general model for analyzing single surface VOC emission characteristics from building materials and its application. Atm. Environ. 38 : 113-119.